# FRAMING A LEGEND

# FRAMING

*A*

# LEGEND

*Exposing the Distorted History of*
*Thomas Jefferson and Sally Hemings*

M. ANDREW HOLOWCHAK

Ⓟ**Prometheus Books**
59 John Glenn Drive
Amherst, New York 14228–2119

Published 2013 by Prometheus Books

Cover design by Nicole Sommer-Lecht
Portrait of Thomas Jefferson by Rembrandt Peale

Inquiries should be addressed to
Prometheus Books
59 John Glenn Drive
Amherst, New York 14228–2119
VOICE: 716–691–0133 • FAX: 716–691–0137
WWW.PROMETHEUSBOOKS.COM

17 16 15 14 13    5 4 3 2 1

Library of Congress Cataloging-in-Publication Data

Holowchak, Mark, 1958-
    Framing a legend : exposing the distorted history of Thomas Jefferson and Sally Hemings / by M. Andrew Holowchak.
        p.  cm.
    Includes bibliographical references and index.
    ISBN 978-1-61614-729-7 (cloth : alk. paper)
    ISBN 978-1-61614-730-3 (ebook)
    1. Jefferson, Thomas, 1743–1826—Relations with women. 2. Jefferson, Thomas, 1743–1826—Relations with slaves. 3. Hemings, Sally. 4. Paternity testing—United States—Case studies. I. Title.

E332.2.H663 2013
9734'60922—dc23
                                                                                    2012048876

Printed in the United States of America on acid-free paper

To my friend JZ,
for her invaluable assistance and moral encouragement
in this undertaking.

# CONTENTS

**8**    CONTENTS

# FOREWORD

*I*n March 2000, I was asked to chair a panel of more than a dozen scholars from across the nation for the purpose of investigating every aspect of the allegation that Thomas Jefferson had engaged in a sexual relationship with an enslaved woman named Sally Hemings over a period of several decades that had produced one or more children. Most of those involved had written or edited books that have been sold in the Monticello gift shop, and have either served as a departmental chair or held a chaired professorship at universities from California to Maine to Alabama. The invitation came from a group of Jefferson admirers who felt he had not received a "fair trial" on this issue and had formed the Thomas Jefferson Heritage Society. They decided to seek an independent review by a panel of experts that came to be known as the Jefferson-Hemings Scholars Commission. We were promised (and received) complete independence, and our mission was simply to investigate the various facts and arguments thoroughly and to make a public report of our findings.

In all candor, I was surprised by the request. I had not carefully followed the issue, but I had read in the newspapers that DNA tests reported in the prestigious science journal *Nature* in late 1998 had confirmed that President Jefferson had fathered at least Sally's youngest child Eston; and even the Thomas Jefferson Memorial Foundation had conceded the point. As surprised as I was, I nevertheless assumed the issue was settled.

But, with some hesitation (primarily because I had recently become a single parent), I agreed to take part in the inquiry. A year later, in April 2001, we issued a lengthy report concluding with but a single, very mild, dissent, that the story is probably *false*. During our investigation we found that many of the alleged "facts" being proffered to support the story were simply not true (such as that Jefferson freed Sally Hemings and all of her children when they turned twenty-one or in his will, and that Sally and her children received "extraordinary privileges" at Monticello), and some of the documents being relied upon had been materially altered in transcription. These are discussed in the book version of our report, titled *The Jefferson-Hemings Controversy: Report of the Scholars Commission,* which was published in 2011 by Carolina Academic Press and contains in excess of 400 pages with more than 1,400 footnotes.

Despite *Nature*'s misleading heading, "Jefferson Fathered Slave's Last Child," we discovered that the DNA tests had not even involved a DNA sample from *Thomas* Jefferson, and the actual conclusion of the scientists was that one of the more than two dozen Jefferson men known to have been in Virginia at the time of Eston Hemings's conception was almost certainly Eston's father. Based on the scientific evidence alone, the probability that Eston's father was President Jefferson was about 4 percent. Limiting suspects to only those Jefferson males for whom there was strong reason to believe were present at Monticello at the time of Eston's conception, the odds that the president was his father rise to about 17 percent. But if we then factor in President Jefferson's advanced age (sixty-four, in an era where most men did not live to see forty), declining health, and character, the odds that he was Eston's father drop precipitously.

We were not asked to identify Eston's most likely father, but most of us felt the strongest case pointed to the president's much younger and less cerebral brother, Randolph—or perhaps one of Randolph's five sons, who ranged in ages from mid-teens to twenty-seven years and were also likely present at Monticello at the time of conception. There is one report that the widower Randolph fathered children by other slaves, we know he was invited to visit Monticello (to see the twin sister he dearly loved, who had just arrived for a visit) fifteen days before Eston's most likely conception date, and an oral history taken down from a Monticello blacksmith—published years later by the University of Virginia Press under the title *Memoirs of a Monticello Slave*—asserted that when brother Randolph visited Monticello, he would "come out among black people, play the fiddle, and dance half the night." There is no evidence that Thomas Jefferson ever socialized with his slaves.

When President Jefferson was in Washington, his daughter Martha was in charge at Monticello, and surviving family letters establish that Randolph was widely known at Monticello as "Uncle Randolph" at the time of Eston's birth. We found it noteworthy that the oral tradition passed down by generations of Eston Hemings's descendants was that he was *not* the child of President Jefferson, but rather of an "uncle." So Randolph is the only potential father who fits all of the evidence.

Those were just some of the findings of our commission.

Having studied Thomas Jefferson for four decades and spent more than a dozen years focused heavily on this specific controversy, when I was approached about writing the foreword to this volume, I did not expect to learn a great deal as I began reading the manuscript. To my delight, I was profoundly mistaken. There have been several volumes written about this issue since our initial report came out a dozen years ago and was posted on the Internet. The best of them, in my view, was self-published by a remarkably able genealogist who has been studying the Jefferson family in the Charlottesville area for decades, Cynthia Harris Burton. Her book is titled *Jefferson Vindicated: Fallacies, Omissions, and Contradictions in the Hemings Genealogical Search* (2005). I highly recommend it. It is filled with the product of considerable original research and thoughtful analysis, and it reaffirms the conclusion I reached when I worked with Ms. Burton, while preparing my own "Individual Views" for the Scholars Commission report, that she is among the finest "natural scholars" I have ever encountered. I was pleased to learn that Dr. Mark Holowchak shares that view.

Rather than largely recounting the facts and arguments set forth in the 2001 Scholars Commission report, as have some other recent volumes on this issue, Dr. Holowchak applies an impressive skill set to examine some of the specific arguments made by key scholars in what might be termed the pro-paternity camp. To do this, he brings to the table a remarkable array of scholarly expertise of great relevance to this debate. With five academic degrees in psychology, philosophy, and the history and philosophy of science, he has taught and/or authored books about logic, critical reasoning, ethics, ancient philosophy, psychoanalysis, Freud, and Thomas

Jefferson as well. As readers will quickly discover, he makes excellent use of his impressive background in examining and unraveling some of the popular "scholarship" that has driven much of the modern debate on the Jefferson-Hemings issue.

For a century and a half after Thomas Jefferson's death, serious scholars tended to dismiss the accusation that America's third president was sexually involved with a slave woman—if they bothered to take note of it at all. First of all, there was widespread agreement that it was totally out of character for Jefferson. But, more important, the charge was originated by a disreputable scandal-monger named James Thomson Callender, who declared that he was seeking "ten thousand fold vengeance" after his efforts to blackmail Jefferson into appointing him to public office had failed. According to an 1802 Federalist newspaper (published shortly before Callender got around to the Sally Hemings accusation, when he was still trying to portray Jefferson as a "French agent" and/or an atheist), after being turned away by a servant Callender stood on the sidewalk in front of the White House and shouted "My lies made you president," referring to a series of libels he had published against President John Adams during the election of 1800. He demanded appointment as postmaster of Richmond in compensation, but Jefferson ignored him. Both Jefferson's political enemy Alexander Hamilton and John Adams dismissed the liaison story as false—as they were both quite familiar with Jefferson's character and Callender's notorious lies.

Things began to change when Fawn Brodie published her "psychobiography," *Thomas Jefferson: An Intimate History*, in 1974. With but undergraduate and master's degrees in English, and no apparent formal training in psychology or psychoanalysis, Brodie nevertheless sought to exhume Jefferson's inner feelings by "psychoanalyzing" his writings. An editor at her publisher, W. W. Norton, reportedly wrote in assessing the manuscript: "Doesn't [Brodie] know about making the theory fit the facts instead of trying to explain the facts to fit the theory? . . . [S]he doesn't play fair."[1]

Ironically, this was the same reaction of Berkeley-educated playwright Karyn Traut (the spouse of Scholars Commission member and University of North Carolina Medical School professor Thomas Traut), who was so moved after reading Brodie's book that she began researching a play (*Saturday's Children*) about the son "Tom," whom both Callender and Brodie contended was conceived in Paris and born after Sally Hemings returned to Monticello with the Jeffersons at the end of 1789. But, after carefully researching the topic, she concluded that Brodie had "thrown out the pieces of the puzzle that didn't fit her model."[2] Ms. Traut ultimately concluded that the president's brother *Randolph* Jefferson was most likely the father of Brodie's "Tom."

Speaking of "Tom"—the focus of both Callender's and Brodie's accounts—for decades, the strongest bit of evidence supporting a possible Jefferson-Hemings sexual relationship was a collection of almost-identical oral traditions passed down by descendants of former slave Thomas Woodson, who had settled in different parts of the country. Woodson had surfaced after Jefferson's death and claimed to have been the "Tom" conceived by Jefferson and Hemings in Paris upon whom Callender had premised his allegations. He claimed that, after the story was published, President Jefferson sent him down the road to be raised by the Woodson family, and several credible witnesses left testimony that Tom Woodson was a highly intelligent, tall and lean man, with erect and dignified posture, who even had a tinge of Jefferson's red in his hair to support his claim.

However, in addition to comparing DNA from a descendant of Eston Hemings with that of descendants of Thomas Jefferson's cousins and those of his nephews Peter and Samuel Carr (sons of Jefferson's sister Martha and his childhood friend Dabney Carr, who had been identified by Jefferson grandchildren as having admitted to fathering children by Sally Hemings), the scientific study reported in *Nature* also tested the DNA of six descendants of three sons of Thomas Woodson. In so doing, it conclusively eliminated Woodson as a possible son of Thomas or any other member of the Jefferson family. We have no way of knowing whether Woodson was the son of Sally Hemings, but his father could not have been Thomas Jefferson.

Returning to Fawn Brodie, her Jefferson biography was a commercial success and earned her hundreds of thousands of dollars in royalties.[3] It became a Book-of-the-Month-Club selection, and lay reviewers showered it with praise. In contrast, reviews by serious scholars dismissed it as unserious. Perhaps no critical review was more devastating than the *New York Review of Books* appraisal by Johns Hopkins professor Garry Wills. Noting that Brodie's first bit of evidence in her "psychohistory" of Jefferson was that he had frequently written the word *mulatto* in his journal to describe soil color during a 1788 trip through Europe—which Brodie interpreted as clear evidence that he was longing for the arms of his alleged mulatto mistress (Sally Hemings) back in Paris—Wills observed that Brodie was apparently unaware of the fact that during the late eighteenth century *mulatto* was a term of art used by American geologists to identify a specific soil color. Continuing, Wills observed that during the same trip Jefferson used the words *red* or *reddish* nearly five times more frequently than *mulatto*, and wondered why Brodie missed this obvious subliminal expression of lust for his red-headed, nine-year-old daughter, Polly. Wills characterized Brodie's biography as "sub-freshman absurdity." He said: "Error on this scale, and in this detail, does not come easily. There is skill involved."[4] Cornell history professor Michael Kammen declared in the *Washington Post*: "Mrs. Brodie does not so much humanize Jefferson as trivialize him. She is a historical gossip, incapable of distinguishing between cause and effect."[5]

Relying heavily upon Brodie's scholarship, in 1997 Professor Annette Gordon-Reed published *Thomas Jefferson and Sally Hemings*, using her legal training to make a more compelling case that it was "possible" Thomas Jefferson and Sally Hemings began a sexual relationship while in Paris. Speculating that Jefferson "might" have felt this, and that Hemings "could" have done that, she argues that such a relationship might have occurred. Since virtually everything we know with any certainty about Sally Hemings of possible relevance to this issue could be written on a three-by-five-inch index card (which we demonstrated in the Scholars Commission report[6]), there is considerable opportunity for speculation and fantasy.

Although common sense and the limited information that has survived strongly suggest that, while in Paris, Sally Hemings resided in the Abbaye Royale de Panthemont (a Catholic boarding school across town from Jefferson's residence that was known to have had servants quarters) with Jefferson's daughters, Professor Gordon-Reed simply assumes that she must instead have lived in Jefferson's residence. A contrary assumption would obviously have greatly undermined her premise. Why let little things like Sally's duties as the ladies' maid to Jefferson's daughters (which she acknowledges), the absence of any surviving reference to Sally by the many Americans who visited and wrote about Jefferson's Paris residence, or the existence of letters from a Paris classmate—written years later to Jefferson's daughter Martha at Monticello and extending warm greetings to Sally—interfere with her speculation?

The Gordon-Reed volume appeared at a time when it was popular among some historians to try to topple the great "dead white males" of American history. As Mount Holyoke professor Joseph Ellis has observed, Thomas Jefferson is "the dead-white-male who matters most," and the "most valued trophy in the cultural wars."[7] Not surprisingly, Professor Gordon-Reed quickly became a favorite of the politically correct establishment.

When it was widely reported the following year that a scientific study published in *Nature* had confirmed that Thomas Jefferson fathered at least Sally's youngest child, many assumed the debate was over. After all, Thomas Jefferson was a man of science, and he would have wanted us to embrace scientific proof from the latest technological advances.

Building upon these erroneous news stories, Professor Gordon-Reed produced a new book—*The Hemingses of Monticello*—that simply assumed that the paternity of all of Sally's children had been scientifically proven by science and went on to tell the story of those children and their descendants. Despite the fact that the DNA tests compared only DNA from a single Hemings child, pro-paternity scholars declared that the tests had eliminated the possibility that either of the Carr brothers had fathered *any* of Sally's children and concluded that Jefferson's grandchildren who pointed suspicion at them were misrepresenting the truth.[8] In their view, the debate was over.

Professor Gordon-Reed and her new book received virtually every award for which they might have been eligible, including the Pulitzer Prize in History, the National Book Award, the National Humanities Medal from the president of the United States, a half-million-dollar "genius grant" from the MacArthur Foundation, and induction into the American Academy of Arts and Sciences. Harvard University appointed her to *three* professorships, including in law and history.

Now comes Dr. Holowchak to caution "not so fast." In the pages that follow, he examines claims by Professor Gordon-Reed and several other prominent scholars in the pro-paternity camp, and he painstakingly reveals error after error. He draws upon his knowledge of ancient and modern Greek, Latin, ancient history and philosophy, and logic to expose careless scholarship and—to put it kindly—shoddy reasoning.

Almost exactly four decades ago, when I was a fellow at Stanford University's Hoover Institution on War, Revolution and Peace, I had the great pleasure of getting to know Professor Sidney Hook, who had recently retired as chairman of the Department of Philosophy at New York University. We had several lengthy conversations, and during more than one of them he emphasized the importance of *courage* in the character of a good scholar. You must be prepared to pursue the truth wherever it leads, he told me, without regard to what others might believe or the possible costs their disagreement might impose. Without this vital element, you will never achieve your full potential as a scholar.

His comment reminded me very much of advice Thomas Jefferson had given to various young friends and relatives. Indeed, it was a core principle in his founding of the University of Virginia, where it has been my great pleasure to work and teach for more than twenty-five years. In a famous and oft-quoted letter to British historian William Roscoe, Jefferson said of his new university: "This institution will be based on the illimitable freedom of the human mind. For here we are not afraid to follow truth wherever it may lead, nor to tolerate any error so long as reason is left free to combat it."

I mention this because Jefferson's admonition frequently came to mind as I was reading this book. Perhaps above all else, this book is an exercise in *courage*. Even here at the University of Virginia, in the eyes of some, defending Thomas Jefferson is beyond the pale, and I have faced some negativity as a direct result of my participation in the Scholars Commission inquiry.

For the record, those who have reacted negatively to my role in this project are not bad people. I suspect that some believed (as I had when first approached) that science had conclusively resolved this issue, and thus anyone who continued to resist the truth was either a racist or a fool. Alternatively, some who have followed the issue more closely may have realized there was a compelling case to be made in Jefferson's defense but feared that anyone who spoke out publicly on the issue was likely to draw fire in the form of allegations of racism that might do collateral damage to the university's reputation. I, too, understood that risk, as I had observed several very able scholars who had in my presence expressed dismay that Jefferson was being treated very unfairly nevertheless decline an invitation to join in the inquiry.

On October 27, 2012, the Thomas Jefferson Heritage Society hosted a daylong program at the University of Virginia's Newcomb Hall on the Jefferson-Hemings issue. Believing that the audience would benefit from a good debate, the group's president on August 21 invited Peter Onuf, the Thomas Jefferson Memorial Foundation Professor of History at the University of Virginia, to take part in a debate with me over the issue. Although this distinguished chair was previously held by Dumas Malone and Merrill Peterson—each widely regarded as the nation's preeminent Jefferson scholar of their time—Professor Onuf has been a strong critic of Jefferson and has endorsed the view that there was a decades-long sexual relationship between Thomas Jefferson and Sally Hemings that produced several children. But in response to the debate invitation, Professor Onuf replied later that same day: "I'm afraid I will have to decline your invitation: the controversy has long since ceased to be interesting to me."

It was at this program that I had my first (and, thus far, only) opportunity to speak personally with Dr. Holowchak, who was one of the speakers. When he overheard that the Heritage Society had been unable to find a senior professor to present the pro-paternity viewpoint, his face perked up and he exclaimed: "Debate! I'll debate!" He was prepared to take on anyone from the pro-paternity camp, or to debate me if we could find an issue on which there was sufficient disagreement. After you have read the pages that follow, I suspect you will understand his willingness—nay, his *enthusiasm*—for a free and open public exchange of views on the issue. You may also understand why some on the other side of the issue are reluctant to see such a debate. Enjoy the book.

Professor Robert F. Turner
Chairman, Jefferson-Hemings Scholars Commission

# PREFACE

*Truths necessary for our own character, must not be
suppressed out of tenderness to its calumniators.*
—TJ TO PRESIDENT JAMES MADISON, MARCH 23, 1815

*I*magine a time in the not-too-distant future where a famous American personage is accused of some misdeed, based on thin evidence. Stories of the misdeed, which initially vary from reporter to reporter, soon gain currency in one particular form. All other variations drop out. The story is thereafter inseparably linked to the personage just as the lion's skin and club are linked with Hercules; and baggy pants, oversized shoes, cane, and derby are linked with Charlie Chaplin.

We are at that time in the not-too-distant future when it comes to Thomas Jefferson. It is now assumed as fact, without sufficient warrant, that Jefferson had a sexual relationship with one of his slaves—a handsome, much younger woman by the name of Sally Hemings. Moreover, it is said that he carried out the relationship for thirty-eight years and that he had several children with her, without anyone being the wiser. It is an arresting story—an intriguing story—made all the more arresting and intriguing because there is not much evidence for it. At the current stage of historical and scientific investigation, it can be neither verified, nor disconfirmed. That allows true believers—and this book is a book about true believers—to spin their yarn and fashion a tapestry, depicting a legend, irrespective of truth, for tomorrow's true believers.

Since 1802, when noted calumniator James Callender made widespread the story, there has been the rumor, fueled by political opponents during his two terms as president, that Thomas Jefferson had a sexual relationship with Hemings. As was his habit, Jefferson did not respond to the rumor, but at least on one occasion he denied the relationship and on another chortled upon hearing of it.

After his stint as president, the rumor of his mistress-slave was kept alive by northern abolitionists and hostile British, though it tended to fall on deaf ears for most Americans, for whom such a relationship was unthinkable. It was inconceivable, Americans thought, that one of the most prominent founding fathers, the third president of the United States, the author of the Declaration of Independence, and a man of steadfast character would have taken one of his slaves as a sexual partner, continued to do so for several decades, and then have children by her.

In 1974, the rumor was rekindled in Fawn Brodie's book *Thomas Jefferson: An Intimate History*. Important questions to be answered, she noted, were these: Why were there so few references to Sally Hemings in any of Jefferson's writings, when it is clear he had a lengthy affair with her? Why did Jefferson not list Tom Hemings, his alleged first child by Sally Hemings, in his *Farm Book*? Why did Jefferson continue his alleged sexual relationship with Sally, once it was leaked to the press in 1802 by Callender? Why did Jefferson, who always expressed great love of family, virtually ignore his mulatto children? How could Jefferson have had a liaison with Hemings for thirty-eight years without anyone knowing? Those questions, she acknowledged, were intriguing. Of course, by Occam's razor, they could readily be answered by the nonexistence of a liaison, but that was not Brodie's tack. Having psychoanalytic insight into Jefferson's writings and proceeding on feeling and not just fact, she attempted to provide provocative answers to those beguiling questions.

Brodie was severely criticized, even ridiculed, by most serious scholars for her answers, which were given gossamer support. Yet the book sold well, just as Brodie prophesied, and gave rise to Chase-Riboud's *Sally Hemings: A Novel* (1979), the film *Jefferson in Paris* (1995), and the long-suppressed CBS miniseries *Sally Hemings: An American Scandal* (2000). The legend was taking root among a gullible, scandal-loving American public.

In 1997, Annette Gordon-Reed published *Thomas Jefferson and Sally Hemings: An American Controversy*. In an effort to show that a liaison between the two was possible, she charged prior historians, all white males, with racism. They refused to consider the possibility of a liaison, she stated, because sex with a black woman would be an unspeakable defilement of Jefferson's character. The implicit sentiment is racist history.

A DNA study was soon undertaken, and its results were published in *Nature* in 1998. The study, misleadingly titled "Jefferson Fathered Slave's Last Child," showed, among other things, that Jefferson, or someone else with the Jefferson Y-chromosome, fathered Eston Hemings—Sally Hemings's last child. Though the researchers implicated Jefferson in the study—he was considered the simplest and most probable father of all of Hemings's children—there were roughly twenty-five chromosomal matches at the time. The Thomas Jefferson Memorial Foundation (TJMF) thereafter examined the DNA findings in conjunction with the historical data that had a bearing on paternity and agreed with the conclusions of the scientists.

Using Monte-Carlo statistical analysis and a Bayesian argument, Fraser Neiman, a member of the Thomas Jefferson Memorial Foundation panel of experts, published a study to show that it was next to impossible that anyone other than Jefferson fathered each of Hemings's children. Due to unfamiliarity with Monte-Carlo analysis and Bayesian induction, many scholars, assuming anything mathematical must be decisive, took this to be the final nail in Jefferson's coffin. Mathematics had aligned itself with physiological science and history. Only Jefferson could be the father of all of Hemings's children.

Defenders of Jefferson's character jumped ship. Historian Andrew Burstein was one. In *The Inner Jefferson* (1995), Burstein wrote Jefferson was a passionate man, whose love and dedication to his family made a liaison with Sally Hemings virtually impossible. Yet he published "Jefferson's Rationalizations" in 2000 and *Jefferson's Secrets* in 2005. As the titles of both works suggest, Burstein argued that Jefferson had a lengthy, secretive sexual relationship with Hemings (for reasons of health) that he could keep from others, even his family, only because he had a supranormal capacity to separate his public and private image.

Gordon-Reed published the award-winning *The Hemingses of Monticello* in 2008 and possibility morphed into fact. She not only considered the liaison factual, she also filled in many of the details of that liaison in an "artful" reconstruction of events that gave Sally Hemings the dignity that she deserved and brought down Jefferson from Mount Rushmore. Jefferson was given his comeuppance.

As of this writing, it is accepted by most scholars with some familiarity of the issue not only that Jefferson had a lengthy affair with Hemings that resulted in his fathering several children with Hemings—Harriet (1795–1797); Beverly (1798–1873); an unnamed daughter who died in infancy (b. 1799); a second Harriet (1801–ca. 1865); Madison (1805–1877); Eston (1808–1856); and possibly Tom, who was born just after Jefferson returned home from Paris in 1789—but also that Jefferson, because of that affair, was a hypocrite and a racist. The evidential pattern such scholars often follow is uncritical reference principally to Gordon-Reed's work and secondarily to the DNA study as well as the TJMF's analysis of it and of the relevant historical evidence. R. B. Bernstein[1] typifies that approach. Gordon-Reed, who in 1997 complained of white male scholars "controlling the discourse," now controls the discourse. It is no exaggeration to say that many, if not most, Jeffersonian scholars merely cite her work as the final word on the subject. It is a scholarly unhealthy and frightening state of affairs.

In spite of the massive shift on the issue, the fact remains that the DNA evidence is inconclusive and does not show it likely that Jefferson was the father of Eston, or any, of Sally Hemings's other children. Moreover, as I aim to show, there are remarkable flaws with the leading scholarship in defense of a liaison.

This book is composed of two parts, each with three chapters. The first part, "Three Prominent Spins," comprises a critical examination of the works of a prominent biographer, a professor of law, and a prominent historian: Fawn Brodie, Annette Gordon-Reed, and Andrew Burstein. The second part, "Unframing the Legend," comprises chapters on the much-vitiated argument from character, the sloppy science and the revisionist tendency to treat history as a normative discipline, and the issue of Jefferson's avowed racism.

Brodie's book, *Thomas Jefferson: An Intimate History*, is the subject of chapter 1. Brodie makes the case for a thirty-eight-year sexual relationship between Jefferson and Hemings through her often-inane psychoanalytic conclusions from Jefferson's writings, her selective use of evidence, and her tendency to fill in evidentiary gaps with ungrounded speculation. Because the book sold well and opened the gates to consideration of the possibility of a relationship between Jefferson and Hemings among the American public, it set the standard—and a squalid one—for much of the scholarship that followed.

Chapter 2 examines chiefly Annette Gordon-Reed's two books: *Thomas Jefferson and Sally Hemings* and *The Hemingses of Monticello*. In her first book, she argues merely for the modest claim that a liaison between Jefferson and Hemings is possible. By the writing of her second book, she not only claims to know that the two had a liaison, but also gives many of the details of that liaison. As I will demonstrate, *The Hemingses of Monticello* is fraught with fallacies, tendentious psychologizing, and paternalistic prosaisms, and her use of data is selective. She makes no attempt to address the leading literature that argues against her thesis. The reason for her selective approach to history, I show, is clear. Gordon-Reed has a social, not a historical, agenda—namely, to change the way blacks are viewed by historians. The agenda seems laudable, but it comes at expense of regard for historical truth. Thus, I argue, her books cannot be taken seriously.

Andrew Burstein's work on Jefferson is the topic of chapter 3. At the time of *The Inner Jefferson*, Burstein is convinced that Jefferson is incapable of a relationship because of his stalwart character. After Gordon-Reed's *Thomas Jefferson and Sally Hemings* and the DNA evidence, Burstein's man of stalwart character becomes, in effect, a deceitful rogue in *Jefferson's Secrets*. Burstein, however, argues against Brodie and Gordon-Reed—that is, against the notion that the liaison was loving and mutually beneficial. For Burstein, Jefferson is merely interested in physical and emotional health. Thus, he needs periodic sexual release with a youthful, handsome female. Hemings is preferable to a white alternative, just because she is a slave—that is, a no-strings-attached option. Burstein's argument, given no more than gauzy support, is grossly unpersuasive. At day's end, one wonders how anyone, so convinced of Jefferson's stalwart character at one time, could be equally convinced of Jefferson's duplicity years later. Such a radical shift requires a substantial explanation and Burstein's explanation, we shall see, is scrimpy.

Since much of the debate about the supposed liaison centers on Jefferson's character, chapter 4 is devoted to the argument from character. There is much from which to draw in the recent literature. I focus, once again, on Brodie, Gordon-Reed, and Burstein. I aim to show that Jefferson's character is not a "tiresome" issue, as a colleague had once told me, but a vital issue that makes for a strong argument against a liaison.

Chapter 5 comprises two parts: "Appeals to Science" and "The Canons of 'Normative History.'" The first part looks at Jefferson's detractors' attempts to marshal "scientific" evidence to demonstrate the existence of a lengthy relationship. I include analyses of the DNA evidence and the TJMF's report on the Jefferson-Hemings relationship. I argue that the DNA evidence does not show it is likely that Jefferson was the father of Eston Hemings, or any other of Hemings's children, and show that there is no reason to think the TJMF's report is credible. I include also an analysis of Fraser Neiman's Bayesian argument for Jefferson's paternity of all six of Hemings's children, as well as an analysis of the Toulminian, informal-reasoning model by James Golden and Alan Golden that implicates Jefferson in the paternity of Eston Hemings and perhaps all his other siblings. I show that Neiman's argument seems compelling only because it uses biased and insufficient data and that the Goldens' informal-reasoning model uncritically uptakes the conclusions of the scientists and the members of the TJMF. The second part is a critical examination of the "Aesopian" history concerning Jefferson. Critical analysis, for such historians, gives way to deconstruction, and these Jeffersonian historians turn to Jefferson's private life, about which so little is known. Their reconstructions are not just descriptive, but also morally evaluative. For them, it is insufficient to say *Jefferson acted in such and such manner at a particular time of his life*. One must add normatively *and that makes him a hypocrite, a misanthrope, and a villain*. Moreover, it is insufficient for understanding Jefferson to read carefully and literally his written lines. Jefferson was too clever to reveal much of himself in his thousands of writings. True Jeffersonian historians are bellwethers and revisionists. They go by feeling more than intellect. They read between the lines and deconstruct a masked and troubled personal life, inaccessible to historians wedded merely to rationality.

Finally, in chapter 6, I examine the all-too-frequent claim that Jefferson was racist and its implications for the possibility of a liaison with Hemings. Jefferson's most thorough examination of race is in his *Notes on the State of Virginia*. In the work, Jefferson is customarily slammed for his examination of blacks, which depicts them as less intelligent and less attractive than nonblacks, though the moral equals of nonblacks. Yet scrutiny of the book, Jefferson's only book, shows it has a decidedly empirical slant, and his examination of the morality, physicality, and intelligence of blacks in it is consistent with the empiricism of the book as a whole. In short, Jefferson's conclusions about blacks' defects are faulty not because of prejudice, but because of sloppy induction. Nonetheless, his view of black inferiority of body and mind would probably have been sufficient inducement for Jefferson never to have considered Hemings as a viable sexual outlet, even if he had had need of sexual outlet.

Overall, scholars, who accuse Jefferson of having had a lengthy liaison with Hemings as well as having been racist—at the forefront is Gordon-Reed—have gained control of the historical discourse and have molded public opinion concerning Jefferson in spite of the fact that there are no rationally persuasive reasons for such accusations. Thus, this book is an attempt to reopen the issue of Jefferson's paternity to rational—that is, evidence-based—discussion. It is an invitation for all interested persons, scholars especially, to weigh all the relevant evidence pertaining to the liaison. It is, in effect, an invitation for scholars to begin once again to do scholarship the correct way—to invite reason back into the scholars' arena. The success of this book, however, is to be determined not by scholarly disputation and intellectual argufying, but in a manner of which Jefferson would have most approved—namely, by appeal to the moral integrity and sound judgment of ordinary people, suitably stocked with all the relevant evidence surrounding the possibility of paternity.

Given that the effect of a relationship would be moral condemnation of Jefferson by vitiating his character—namely, he would be exposed as a liar, a hypocrite, and an unconcerned father—it is incumbent on accusers like Gordon-Reed and Burstein to show through incontrovertible evidence, not circumstantial evidence or hearsay, that Jefferson and Hemings had a liaison, before spinning yarns about the nature of their liaison. Lacking such evidence, it is morally reprehensible for scholars to state that a liaison occurred or was even probable. To do so is to blur the line between fact and fantasy, to place monetary gain or literary prizes in writing ahead of integrity, or to supplant regard for truth with a political or personal agenda.

That leads to a deeper issue, ignored by critics of such authors: the immorality of agenda-driven scholarship.

Research can be motivated by an agenda—I suspect that it always is—but once it begins, evidence must lead a researcher by the nose, as it were. Conclusions cannot be decided in advance of disclosure of evidence for them. Evidence contrary to one's thesis cannot merely be ignored. Historical scholars have a duty to aim at truth, not sales of books, literary prizes, or even vengeance.

Scholars, especially when drawing conclusions that alter a person's legacy for the worse, have a duty to weigh all available relevant evidence, to make sure there is sufficient evidence to secure "condemnation," and to be certain that the research is driven not by bias, but by evidence. Jefferson—whether as scientist, politician, philosopher, educational reformer, father, or friend—was a person who gave much of himself to his fellow human beings. Even staunch political rivals like John Adams and Alexander Hamilton recognized that. It is morally irresponsible for scholars to oppugn hastily Jefferson on gauzy, ambiguous evidence.

Finally, should it someday come to pass, against my own belief that no such relationship existed, that biological evidence surfaces that unfailingly (or nearly so) implicates Jefferson as the father of any or all of Hemings's children, that would not be an I-told-you-so moment. The reasons are three. First, most of the arguments I put forth in this book do not aim at exoneration of Jefferson concerning paternity. They modestly aim to show, among other things, that the arguments of three of the most commonly cited Jefferson-did-it scholars are inexcusably weak and, therefore, unpersuasive. Second, the argument I do give in an effort to exonerate Jefferson—the argument from character of chapter 4—I take to be strong, given the current state of evidentiary affairs—that is, the lack of evidence that implicates Jefferson in a liaison. If it should sometime be proven that Jefferson was the father of at least one of Hemings's children, Jefferson, for reasons given later in the book, would be exposed as a liar, a hypocrite, and an uncaring father. In defending Jefferson, I remain open to the possibility of that eventuality. Last and equally as important, that moment, if it should come to pass, would not vindicate the scholarship of historians like Brodie and Gordon-Reed. Drawing the right conclusion from a body of evidence that does not support that conclusion is like getting out of the Labyrinth but refusing to follow the thread of Ariadne. No scholar ought to be praised for irrationality.

All writings of Jefferson, unless otherwise specified, are from the Paul Leicester Ford's *The Writings of Thomas Jefferson.*

PART 1

# THREE PROMINENT SPINS

# CHAPTER 1

# MINING JEFFERSON'S ORE

## Jefferson's Forbidden Females

A passion for politics stems usually from an insatiable need, either for power, or for friendship and adulation, or a combination of both. Any man who leaves a legacy of 18,000 letters in his own hand, most of them written with a wrist that was crippled and stiffened in an accident, has a desperate need of friendship.

—FAWN BRODIE, *THOMAS JEFFERSON*

Fawn Brodie writes metaphorically in *Thomas Jefferson: An Intimate History*, "Despite hundreds of volumes about Thomas Jefferson, there remain unexpected reserves of unmined ore, particularly in relation to the *connections* between his public life and his inner life, as well as his intimate life."[1] The quote suggests that Brodie aims to disclose the "inner" as well as the "intimate" Jefferson in her book. The two, she says without amplification, are not the same. "To illuminate this relationship, however, requires certain biographical techniques that make some historians uncomfortable. One must look for feeling as well as fact, for nuance and metaphor as well as idea and action."[2]

What is unique to Brodie's approach is "what in these library collections has been passed over, or ignored because it did not fit into the traditional notions and preconceptions of Jefferson's character" as coolheaded, rational, and dispassionate. In addition, she includes two overlooked published reports by the Monticello slaves Madison Hemings and Israel Jefferson.[3] The implication is that the historical and biographical scholarship heretofore is contaminated because it has been selective.

31

Brodie aims to expose the real Jefferson, the intimate Jefferson, as a man whose intellect was keen but whose passions were also strong. Her reconstruction of the intimate Jefferson aims to show that he was involved in fulfilling a thirty-eight-year sexual relationship with a household slave that resulted in the birth of several mulatto children. The evidence of those two hitherto-overlooked reports is key to her reconstruction.

This chapter is a critical analysis of Brodie's book as it relates to the presumed Jefferson-Hemings relationship. I begin with a brief summary of her book, turn to a critique of her biography, and end with an examination of Brodie's "investigative" tactics and their rhetorical force.

## FEELING, NUANCE, AND METAPHOR

### Jefferson's Early Years

Brodie does much to tease out an account of Jefferson's early life, and the attempt is not without merit and substance. Overpassing any errors of fact on which numerous scholars have commented over the years, I rehash some of what she has written.

The son of Peter Jefferson and Jane Randolph, Jefferson was born in 1743 and was the oldest male of seven siblings. After the death of brother-in-law William Randolph, Peter Jefferson moved his family to Randolph's estate at Tuckahoe in 1745. Jefferson was two at the time. The Randolph children—a boy of four and two girls of seven and nine—were added to his siblings, who were then only three in number. Jefferson was doubtless bullied by the older boy but mollycoddled by his older sister Jane, who favored him. Brodie adds of the years at Tuckahoe, "All we know for certain . . . is that regret at separation from home, and hunger to return home, are two of the most ubiquitous and passionately expressed themes in all of Jefferson's intimate letters."[4] Thus, she concludes, the years at Tuckahoe could not have been happy.

Brodie takes it for granted that black children were among Jefferson's early friends, as she asserts blacks on plantations outnumbered whites by ten to one. It is likely he was confounded and disturbed by the separate treatment of blacks and whites. Only the latter had to go to school, which Jefferson hated. These early experiences shaped his lifelong ambivalence concerning blacks and unquestionably drove his thinking that blacks, when freed, should be schooled but expatriated—both at public expense.[5]

Brodie reveals something about Jefferson's religiosity in a short anecdote. In a story Jefferson related to his grandchildren, he tells of slipping out of the English school, reciting the Lord's Prayer, and requesting the cessation of school. Brodie generalizes, "Every child is sooner or later disillusioned by the impotence of his own prayers," and Jefferson learned "not to expect too much of Heaven."[6]

Peter Jefferson removed his family to Shadwell when Jefferson was nine. Thomas stayed behind to attend school at Dover Church near Tuckahoe to learn Greek, Latin, and French. He boarded with the family of Rev. William Douglas. Since nothing is known of that time—Jefferson's letters were lost in the fire at Shadwell—Brodie examines Jefferson's later letters to his children to give evidence of the sort of advice he, when young, must have received from his mother and father. She notes that Jefferson advises his daughters to be good and obedient. He uses loss of love as leverage. He cautions them against anger and idleness. His admonitions are "tangled with a subtle parental seduction," because daughter Martha is told that no one in the world can bring him happiness or misery as much as she can.[7] "What happens to a child who finds that love is made conditional upon good behavior?" Brodie says. "Any child so subtly tormented is likely to develop a continuing hunger for love that is never quite fulfilled, and also to confuse affection with esteem." That proved to be Jefferson's fate. "Few presidents have been so thin-skinned, few made so wretched by expressions of political and personal antipathy."[8]

Jefferson's sense of closeness to family as well as his notion of "family" as extendable were conditioned by his father, who had seven children and was responsible, with the death of William Randolph, for Randolph's four children. Thomas encouraged marriage within the extended family and always hungered, when away from Monticello, for his "Elysian fields"— that is, to return to his "family." In effect, "[He] was [forever] trapped in his family and by his family."[9]

Upon the death of Peter Jefferson in 1757, Thomas was granted some 2,500 acres of land on the Rivanna River and some thirty slaves. He was responsible for the education of the younger children and the distribution of his sisters' portions of land, and he was in charge of all expenses related to Shadwell. He was, Brodie emphasizes, given prodigious responsibility, though he was too young to have power.[10] The responsibility-without-power theme is one to which she returns often and puts to use often.

Jefferson went to school in Fredericksville and was taught by Anglican clergyman James Maury, with whom he boarded during the week. Jefferson wrote nothing about Maury other than he was a "correct classical scholar"—a "clear indication of dislike," when contrasted with his abundant praise of certain teachers at William and Mary College. Maury, Brodie adds, was a self-righteous Anglican bigot. He hated the Virginian Scots and members of rival religious sects that threatened the Anglican domination of Virginia. As Jefferson lived with Maury when fourteen and fifteen years of age, he doubtless fashioned considerable detestation of the minister and everything for which he stood: conservatism, aristocracy, immaterialism, Anglicanism, bigotry, and self-righteousness. Nonetheless, he was thankful at least for learning aright both Greek and Latin.[11]

It was under George Wythe's tutelage, Brodie says, that Jefferson began to flourish as a scholar. Wythe, sixteen years Jefferson's senior, took the young man under his wing and apprenticed him in law for five years. Jefferson studied with Wythe not only law but also political philosophy, Greek and Latin authors, and English literature. Thus, the apprenticeship was not so much "an apprenticeship for law as an apprenticeship for greatness." Wythe ignited in Jefferson the "passion to make all knowledge his province" and Jefferson patterned his life in such a way to make that come to fruition.[12]

Overall, Jefferson's early years—characterized, as Brodie is wont to say, by responsibility without power—were a time of enslavement or suffocation. She writes of the farrago of Jefferson's internal tensions.

[Jefferson's] humanity was comprised of [sic] more than his loves and his hatred; there was his fear of enslavement clashing with his habits of benevolent despotism, his affection for power tempered by his extraordinary guilt over its abuse, his normal need for sexual fulfillment coupled with his attraction for the forbidden, his hunger for affection and esteem assuaged not only by his multiple friendships and several loves but also by his fanatical obedience to his larger fantasies of what constituted his duty to state. His passion, guilt, indignation, and despair, even his weakness, were all tempered by his intellect. They also served to mold and direct it.[13]

In a nutshell, Jefferson's ambivalences were "in the most extraordinary fashion harnessed to creative endeavour" in his visions of perfection: the perfect state, the perfect constitution, the perfect home, the perfect garden, and the perfect university. She sums with metaphors, aplenty and mixed, "The Jefferson legacy, then, may be looked at as a fountain of dazzling complexity, its beauty compounded by the sunlight of his rare intelligence, but its sources of power—including the rewarding but intermittently tragic secret loves—hidden and deep in the earth."[14]

## JEFFERSON'S FORBIDDEN FEMALES

The large mistake of traditional scholars, says Brodie, is to see Jefferson as a "monkish, abstemious, continent, and virtually passionless person"—someone indifferent. She adds, "One of the important reasons that Jefferson's true nature has remained elusive is the insistence of all his previous biographers that after the death of his wife he never felt any lasting affection again for any woman."[15]

It is here that Brodie develops the Freudian/Eriksonian motivation for her thesis.

But does a man's sexuality atrophy at thirty-nine, especially if he has already demonstrated that he was capable of very great passion? And if he is by nature or upbringing cold and impotent, is not this significantly reflected in his entire personal and political life? All the clinical evidence of our own time suggests a negative answer to the first question, and an affirmative answer to the second. It is true that Jefferson never married again, and the reasons why have been a subject of careful searching in this book. But this searching has been based on the premise that a man's sexuality remains largely undiminished through the years unless it has been badly warped in childhood. Of such warping there is no evidence in Jefferson's life.[16]

The argument, therein contained, might be phrased as follows:

1. One's sexuality does not much diminish throughout the years, without early warping.
2. Jefferson was in his early years a highly sexual person.
3. So, Jefferson, upon the death of his wife, was still a highly sexual person. (1 and 2)
[4. So, Jefferson, upon the death of his wife, acted on his sexuality.] (3)

The conclusion, implicit (hence, the brackets around claim 4) in claim 3, is that Jefferson had to act on his libido. Otherwise, he would have drowned in it. That is a queer conclusion, given Brodie's psychoanalytic bent, for it ignores one alternative in keeping with the tenets of psychoanalysis: heightened sublimation.

That Jefferson was highly sexual is not to say that he was not robustly intellectual. Brodie states, "It is true that Jefferson more than most men did seek to guide his actions by intellect and reason, but he was no less pulled by affection or driven by indignation and rage than the other revolutionaries of his time."[17] She quotes a letter to Maria Cosway (October 12, 1786), in which Jefferson says that the American revolutionaries, had they been guided by their heads, not their hearts, would have been hanging on gallows. Yet that is not necessarily to say that the revolutionary actions were guided by unbridled passion (e.g., raw rage and lust) but instead that they were the result of a sort of indignation, fueled by the "judgment" of the moral-sense faculty, unaided by reason. For Jefferson, the human heart is either the organ that houses the moral-sense faculty or, what is more likely, a metaphor for man's innate moral sensibility.[18]

The remainder of Brodie's work is, in a sense, an exploration of the four "forbidden" women of Jefferson's life: Betsy Walker, wife of his good friend John Walker; his own wife, Martha Wayles, a widower with a child; Maria Cosway, coquettish wife of the English artist Richard Cosway; and Sally Hemings, a slave at Monticello and presumed half-sister of Martha Wayles. I cover each in turn.

First there was Jefferson's early "affair" with Betsy Walker. Brodie suggests that Jefferson's affair with Walker might have "set a new pattern of secrecy for Jefferson in matters of the heart" and effected a "separation of chastity from morality," which probably remained with him till his death. She notes that Foley in his estimable work *The Jefferson Cyclopedia* has a heading for *morality* and *virtue*, and many passages under each, but no heading for *chastity*. She says, "Jefferson in his writings stayed clear of the word, though the idea was implicit in an occasional discussion of morality." She adds, "From age twenty-six to sixty-six many things happened to condition Jefferson's feelings about the value or nonvalue of continence and chastity." He doubtless learned of many instances of sexual contact between white males and black females in his law practice and might even have seen or participated in sexual contact with black females as a youth. Nonetheless, there is no evidence of promiscuity or that he was casual with his passions. On the contrary, he fell in love "only a few times" and it seems "always with great intensity."[19]

Betsy Walker was the wife of John Walker, a neighbor and intimate friend of Jefferson. In the summer of 1768, John Walker went to Fort Stanwix to help fashion a treaty with American Indians. He asked Jefferson to look after his wife and child in his absence. He even prepared a will and made Jefferson its executor in the event of his failure to return. Jefferson apparently did more than look after Walker's wife. Rumors of an affair eventually leaked to the press during Jefferson's presidency in 1802, and Walker eventually replied to the rumors in 1805.[20] Jefferson did not respond publicly to the accusations, but he did admit to one attempt at seduction, which was "unpremeditated" and "accidental." Brodie quotes Jefferson in a cover letter to Robert Smith (July 1, 1805), secretary of the navy: "You will perceive that I plead guilty to one of their charges, that when young and single I offered love to a handsome lady. I acknolege [*sic*] its incorrectness."

Brodie makes much of Jefferson's use of "incorrectness." That particular word connotes behavior at odds with established social conventions and not vice—namely, a peccadillo, not a peccancy. That shows Jefferson felt "no overwhelming remorse." Coveting his neighbor's wife was not a crime; getting caught was. Jefferson's behavior was not sinful, but a mere breach of decorum.[21]

Brodie then castigates biographers such as Dumas Malone and Merrill Peterson for making light of the affair.[22] "Why have Jefferson biographers been so intent on minimizing these 'scrapes,' or indeed effacing them altogether," she asks. She does admit, at the chapter's end, that there is no way to know precisely what happened between Jefferson and Betsy Walker.[23] Brodie's point, however, is that the affair gives evidence of Jefferson's libido at work and, most significant, his interest in forbidden women.

Jefferson's letter to Robert Smith—a cover letter to a lost letter of denial to Attorney General Levi Lincoln—was written nearly forty years after the incident. That one should express "overwhelming remorse" at an indiscretion that occurred some forty years earlier is pathological, in that it shows incapacity to come to terms with or, at least, escape one's past. It would be strange for a man, whose moral faculty has matured, to express overwhelming remorse some forty years later, especially in light of Jefferson's Stoic-like demeanor and his purchase of intellectual and moral progressivism.[24] Jefferson's mind-set was future-focused, not past-focused.

The second forbidden woman was his wife, Martha Wayles Skelton. Jefferson fell for her in 1770 at the age of twenty-seven. She was "forbidden," Brodie claims unconvincingly, because there is "slight evidence" that Jefferson's mother disapproved of the marriage and Martha was "matured by marriage, sexually experienced, and also scarred by the tragedy of her husband's death [Bathurst Skelton]." According to the "testimony" of Madison Hemings, son of Jefferson's slave Sally Hemings, Martha's father John Wayles also took one of his slaves, Elizabeth Hemings, as concubine and had by her six children, one of whom was Sally Hemings. Brodie writes, "In matters of miscegenation John Wayles was an important parental model in [Jefferson's] life."[25] He paved the way for Jefferson's relationship with Sally Hemings.

There are difficulties here. First, John Wayles's paternity of Elizabeth Hemings's children is evidenced only by Madison Hemings's account and, as we shall see in the next chapter, there are good reasons to doubt the truth of many components of the account, so it cannot be taken at face value. Second, Wayles is known to have been involved in slave trading. Why was Wayles for Jefferson an "important parental model" concerning miscegenation and not concerning other things? For instance, why did Jefferson also not involve himself in slave trading as did Wayles? Third, if Wayles's promiscuity was a model for Jefferson, then one can reason likewise that Elizabeth Hemings's promiscuity would similarly have been a model for daughter Sally Hemings. Yet Brodie—and this applies as well to almost all the pro-liaison scholars—is adamant that all six of Sally's children were fathered by Jefferson. Sally was not promiscuous, they affirm.

Jefferson's third forbidden woman was Maria Cosway, wife of artist Richard Cosway. Brodie writes that the correspondence between Jefferson and Cosway comprises "missives of . . . ineffable tenderness." She is at a loss why almost all scholars dismiss them as flirtatious, instead of recognizing their seriousness.

> So overwhelming is the evidence that Jefferson's affection for Maria Cosway was not casual at all that one must conclude that the historians and biographers refuse to believe the evidence only because they do not want to. It upsets their conviction that Jefferson was a man whose heart was always rigidly controlled by his head; it destroys their image of the supreme man of reason; and, more important, it shatters the tenacious myth out of childhood that the father loves only the mother, and the corollary sentimental legend that one great passion fills a whole live [sic] until death.[26]

I have read through the epistolary exchange between Jefferson and Cosway, and I fail to see the "ineffable tenderness." Jefferson never loses himself completely to his emotions in his letters. Even his most vulnerable moment, the billet-doux of October 12, 1786, is a dialog between Head and Heart, as if Heart cannot have its say, unless it duels with Head. In that famous letter, Heart's seeming victory over Head occurs only through the language of Head. Heart, as it were, reasons it out with Head and thereby wins the day. Yet the victory is short-lived. Heart may have won a battle, but Head wins the war, as later letters to Cosway indicate. Jefferson soon comes to recognize that marriage to or a long-term relationship with Cosway is impossible.

Jefferson's effusions in his Head-and-Heart letter and several other letters leave little reason to doubt that he was in love with Cosway. Moreover, there is no question that Cosway was emotionally overwhelmed by Jefferson's Head-and-Heart letter. Subsequent letters attest to that.[27] Yet, was Cosway in love with Jefferson or was this relationship one of unrequited love?

Jefferson's reserve in most of his missives to Cosway suggests unrequited love. Cosway flirted with Jefferson in cat-and-mouse fashion, as she did with other men. She loved to have men, especially men of power or esteem, vie for her attention and affection. On the morning of December 8, 1787, the two were supposed to meet for breakfast before Cosway was to leave for Calais, with Jefferson accompanying her part of the way. Cosway left prior to the planned breakfast. She explains in a letter (December 10, 1787) that she was "confused and distracted." On Christmas Day of the same year, she writes that she left without seeing Jefferson because seeing him again would have been too painful. Months later, she states to Jefferson (April 29, 1788): "There are but four people I could wish to pass all my time with. Is this too great a number? when [*sic*] you are one, even if you don't guess the others I am sure you would not object to."

In agreement with Brodie, Jefferson's letters give evidence of knowing of Cosway's coquetry and being powerless in the face of it. Jefferson (January 31, 1788) complains that the only way to enjoy Cosway's company is "*en petite comité*" ("among intimate friends"). He adds: "You make everybody love you. You are sought and surrounded therefore by all. Your domestic cortege was so numerous, *et si imposante* [and so imposing], that one could not approach you quite at their ease." Months later, Jefferson writes (July 30, 1788): "I am sure if the comparison could be fairly made of how much I think of you, or you of me, the former scale would greatly preponderate. Of this I have no right to complain, nor do I complain. You esteem me as much as I deserve. If I love you more, it is because you deserve more."

## CONDEMNED TO SECRECY

Jefferson's final forbidden female, slave Sally Hemings, deserves her own section.

The way people think about Jefferson, Brodie says, is the result not only of what historians have written about him, but also of the "inner needs of the reader in search of a hero." One must ask whether Jefferson was a celibate, coolheaded Irish clergyman or a casual debaucher of female slaves, she says in black-and-white fashion. "[However,] there remains a third alternative: that he was a man richly endowed with warmth and passion but trapped in a society which savagely punished miscegenation, a man, moreover, whose psychic fate it was to fall in love with the forbidden woman"—his comely slave. Jefferson is not to be faulted, she adds. He was a product of the "society which condemned him to secrecy."[28]

In such a manner, Brodie has a felicitous and ready explanation for Jefferson's cooling of his fiery passion for Cosway: Jefferson in France turned his attention to his fourteen-year-old slave, Sally Hemings.

It is with her reconstruction of Jefferson's years in Paris that the book takes an odd turn. As Mary-Jo Kline says, despite certain oversimplifications in her psychological generalizations, Brodie "does not serve her readers badly in the first half of her book." It is when she turns to Jefferson's years in France that Brodie goes astray.

> But the device [of generalization] falters with Jefferson's years in France. Since the course of his negotiations in Europe cannot be easily tied to incidents in his "intimate" life, his performance as a diplomat is ignored, even though this would seem an obvious reflection of a man's "inner" strengths. Instead, Mrs. Brodie devotes herself to an analysis of Jefferson's relations with Maria Cosway and Sally Hemings. And it is

Sally Hemings and her children who finally destroy the balance achieved earlier in the biography.[29]

For Kline, what Brodie assumes is her pièce de résistance, the Jefferson-Hemings relationship, is ultimately what diminishes the work.

Kline understates the destruction of balance. Cautious readers eventually come to recognize that there never was balance, because Brodie's "intimate history" is really only about exposing Jefferson's relationship with Hemings. Everything that Brodie has written about Jefferson's early life—his separation anxiety, feelings of entrapment and torment, use of loss of love as leverage, responsibility without power, and desire for omniscience, and so on—was written in an effort to explain his attraction to and undying need of his forbidden slave. What is worse, everything written thereafter seems unneeded. Brodie, it seems, has flimflammed her readers.

Brodie begins, "The evidence that the real rival was the comely little slave from Monticello, and that their affection began to bloom early in 1788, is complicated and subtle."[30] Her phrasing is a red flag that her use of "evidence" will prove disturbing to traditional, fact-based scholarship.

Much of the evidence for a relationship is an 1873 "interview" with Madison Hemings, son of Sally Hemings, by editor Samuel Wetmore in the *Pike County Republican* in Pee Pee, Pike County, Ohio. I give only a small selection of this interview (see Appendix B):

When Mr. Jefferson went to France [his daughter] Martha was a young woman grown; my mother was about her age, and Maria was just budding into womanhood. Their stay (my mother and Maria's) was about eighteen months. But during that time my mother became Mr. Jefferson's concubine, and when he was called home she was *enciente* [*sic*; *enceinte* or "pregnant"] by him. He desired to bring my mother back to Virginia with him but she demurred. She was just beginning to understand the French language well, and in France she was free, while if she returned to Virginia she would be re-enslaved. So she refused to return with him. To induce her to do so he promised her extraordinary privileges, and made a solemn pledge that her children would be freed at the age of twenty-one years. In consequence of his promises, on which she implicitly relied, she returned with him to Virginia. Soon after their arrival she gave birth to a child, of whom Thomas Jefferson was the father. It lived but a short time. She gave birth to four others, and Jefferson was the father of all of them.[31]

Brodie draws plentifully from this "testimony"[32] in her book. It is clear that she takes it at face value, as she uses it to trump any testimonial evidence to the contrary, and there is considerable testimonial evidence to the contrary. Yet there are many difficulties with the account, considered in its entirety, not the least of which is that oral tradition is hearsay, which is dubious and inadmissible in court because it is insubstantial. Thus, it does not take the place of genealogical documentation and meticulous historical reconstruction therefrom.[33]

First, there is Sally's pregnancy and her refusal to return to Monticello. "The notion that a sixteen-year-old slave [Sally was sixteen when Jefferson would return to America from France] would defy her master and seek to drive a hard bargain with him is incredible on its face," writes Pulitzer Prize winner Virginius Dabney, author of *The Jefferson Scandals*. "And there is no evidence that Sally was granted 'extraordinary privileges' on her return; actually, there is every reason to believe that her position at Monticello was the same as that of the other house servants. . . . There is no convincing evidence to support [her pregnancy] either."[34]

Next, there is the blanket statement that Jefferson was Madison's father as well as the father of three others, excluding the child she was supposedly carrying on her return to Monticello. Madison states, later in the account, that Jefferson "was not in the habit of showing partiality or fatherly affection" to him and his siblings, though he was "affectionate to his white grandchildren."[35] Dabney says, "It is inconceivable that a man of Jefferson's temperament, who showered affection and attention upon his white children and grandchildren to an almost excessive degree, would have ignored his 'black children' by a woman with whom he was alleged to have been deeply in love for more than a third of a century."[36] Dabney is right. How could the relationship have brought Sally, in Brodie's words, "much private happiness," if Jefferson neglected their children? In such a scenario of neglect, Sally would have been miserable.

Moreover, there is the consideration of motives. Brodie never considers the premise that Madison Hemings would have had good motivation for prevaricating. Being not merely a black man, but promoting himself as the son of Thomas Jefferson, he would have had much to gain. She merely says: "How long the desire to tell the story festered in him one cannot know; it may have begun very early. But it was not until 1873 that he found a newspaperman willing to believe, and to publish what he had written."[37] It is queer that Madison Hemings could not have found a willing reporter for his story, if he had been chomping at the bit to tell it for so many years. Scandalous reports about Jefferson were published readily throughout his life, especially during his years as president, in Federalist newspapers. The lengthy delay gives good reason to believe that the story is a canard.

Furthermore, it is strange that Madison, in his published report, says nothing about Jefferson's relationship to his mother Sally. To all children, fathers and mothers are seen as a couple, howsoever unequal the relationship might be. Speaking on behalf of him and his siblings, Madison does speak of his father and mother as "our parents." How, then, did Jefferson treat Madison's mother? Given the two's sexual intimacy on at least six occasions, it is strange that Madison gives no evidence of any public displays of intimacy, however subtle, between his parents. To think that Sally Hemings and Jefferson could have had a clandestine relationship for thirty-eight years that yielded no memorable moments to Madison is incredible. That his mother would not at some point have related any stories about the tender bonds of affection that existed between Jefferson and his mother is also incredible.

Again, there is Madison's statement that Jefferson had "but little taste or care for agricultural pursuits." The overwhelming evidence of Jefferson's passion for husbandry shows Madison's statement is manifestly false.[38] One questions how intimate his knowledge of Jefferson was.

In addition, there is the issue of Madison's literacy. Madison said he learned to read "by inducing white children to teach [him] the letters and something more" and later "picked up here and there till [he could] read and write."[39] Yet Madison's published account, considered in full, shows considerable command of the English language. There is little reason to doubt that the account was written by Samuel Wetmore, the editor of the paper, "a publication with political motives that were anti-Jefferson."[40]

Finally, what is most telling is that Madison says nothing of how he knows Jefferson is his father. The youngest of Sally Hemings's children next to Eston, Madison was born in 1805, so he could not have had direct knowledge of the births of the children prior to him. Moreover, he was three when Eston Hemings was born in 1808, so any early recollections of Eston's birth cannot be taken at face value. Writes Eyler Robert Coates Sr. in an insightful critique of the Thomas Jefferson Memorial Foundation's "Research Report" of 2000 (see chapter 5): "The statement made by Madison Hemings in 1873 . . . contained information that he could not have known firsthand, and that he had to have gotten from some other person. It contains nothing to indicate how he knew the things he was relating. . . . Apparently, Thomas Jefferson acted towards him in no way that would indicate that he was Madison's father."[41] In short, without some evidence of how Madison had come directly to know what he was reporting in his account (e.g., "I saw my mother and Thomas Jefferson kissing on such and such occasion") the account is hearsay.

Next, Brodie turns to what "one might call hard evidence as well as psychological evidence" for Jefferson's special treatment of Sally Hemings. In France, Jefferson paid 240 francs on November 6, 1787, for a smallpox vaccination for Sally. Sally and her brother James began to receive 24 francs a month in 1788 and 12 francs for the holiday season. Moreover, there are also records in Jefferson's account books of a "surprising amount of money" on Sally Hemings's clothes. Finally, on April 18, 1788, Brodie adds, Jefferson got a note from his daughter Martha, in which she requested permission to become a nun. Are the events coincidental? "One wonders if it ever occurred to him that Patsy [Jefferson's pet name for daughter Martha] upon coming home from school on Sunday would look upon the spectacle of her maid newly dressed in stylish Parisian clothes with absolute incomprehension."[42] Patsy knew of her father's secret affair, Brodie says, and the nunnery was her response.

Cynthia Burton, author of *Jefferson Vindicated*, writes, "There is absolutely no evidence to suggest that Sally Hemings and her children received better treatment than other members of the Hemings family."[43] Moreover, it is not surprising that Sally Hemings, as Patsy's maid, would have to be well dressed. Jefferson was ambassador to France. That Jefferson should vaccinate Hemings is also no surprise. Why would he wish her or anyone of his party to fall ill? Finally, that Patsy's request to enter the nunnery was designed to get her father's attention—perhaps even to anger him—is not unreasonable. That it is linked to recognition that her father was having an affair with Hemings is unsupported by evidence and, thus, bosh.

Brodie also states, following noted Jeffersonian scholar Julian Boyd, that in 1788, the year Jefferson went to Holland and Germany, many of Jefferson's letters are missing. Brodie states they might have been destroyed because of references to Sally Hemings. "This raises the question whether or not someone at some time went through Jefferson's papers systematically eliminating every possible reference to Sally Hemings. . . . [N]o letters or notes exchanged between Sally Hemings and Thomas Jefferson have as yet ever found their way into the public record."[44]

There are difficulties with the suggestion. Dabney notes that those missing letters were destroyed by Jefferson's grandson—Thomas Jefferson Randolph—not by Jefferson. They could not have been objectionable to Jefferson, Dabney adds, if he had preserved them for numerous years and his grandson destroyed them many years after his death.[45] Dabney's claim is reasonable.

## BACK IN AMERICA

Jefferson wrote constantly of his excitement of the prospect of returning to America and his home, Monticello. Nonetheless, when it was time to return to America, Brodie, again following Madison Hemings's account, says Sally was reluctant and pregnant: Sally refused flatly to return with Jefferson until he promised to free her children, upon each reaching the age of twenty-one. Jefferson agreed.[46]

Jefferson left France on September 28, 1789, to return home. Once again basing her account on Madison Hemings's interview, Brodie asserts that he returned to Monticello to great aplomb. His slaves treated him like "a medieval prince returning from a crusade." Sally, "big with child," was also likely in the homecoming carriage. The child was born, according to Madison Hemings, "soon after" Sally returned.

Madison Hemings reported, we recall, that the child "lived but a short time."[47] Yet according to the report of James Callender in 1802, the son, Tom, did not die as an infant, and as an adolescent the boy strikingly resembled Jefferson.

> It is well known that the man, whom it delighteth the people to honor, keeps and for many years has kept, as his concubine, one of his slaves. Her name is SALLY. The name of his eldest son is Tom. His features are said to bear a striking though sable resemblance to those of the president himself. The boy is ten or twelve years of age. His mother went to France in the same vessel with Mr. Jefferson and his two daughters. The delicacy of this arrangement must strike every portion of common sensibility. What a sublime pattern for an American ambassador to place before the eyes of two young ladies! . . . By this wench Sally, our president has had several children. There is not an individual in the neighbourhood of Charlottesville who does not believe the story, and not a few who know it.[48]

Callender's report is based on a Charlottesville rumor. No evidence for the rumor, prior to his report, has been found.[49] Moreover, it is widely known that James Callender was a seedy character—a professional blackmailer[50] who was given to drink and universally detested. Why should Callender's report count as credible evidence? He was, after all, wedded to gross exaggeration and prevarication.

As if to deflect any objection that Callender was an unreliable source —even though Brodie too devotes considerable ink to Callender's misshapen character—she adds that the story was corroborated by the editors of the *Frederic-Town Herald* and Lynchburg's *Virginia Gazette*.[51] Apparently Callender was a scurrilous rogue, a self-centered opportunist, and a maligner, but he was also a first-rate reporter who backed all of his calumnies. That she finds no grounds for doubting his "reports," hyperbolies and all (e.g., "There is not an individual in the neighbourhood of Charlottesville who does not believe the story"), is unbelievable.

Brodie says little about the mysterious Tom Hemings, Sally's first child and who was mentioned by Madison Hemings and Callender. It is worth noting that Tom Hemings's birth was not recorded in Jefferson's *Farm Book*. "This absence has been cited as evidence that Tom did not exist, that he was a mere creature of the poisonous imagination of James Thomson Callender," she states. "It may also be evidence that Jefferson chose to consider him free from birth, either because he had been conceived on the free soil of France, or because Jefferson had promised his mother." After considering the options, she concludes without evidence that "it seems likely" Tom was a light-skinned runaway, whom Jefferson allowed to leave "probably shortly after the story of his mother's relationship with Jefferson broke into the press in 1802."[52] She adds, "Perhaps his mother chose not to discuss this son with anyone after his departure and made every effort to protect his identity in the white society by a mantle of silence." The "account" flounders in possibility claims. The most plausible explanation, as many prominent historians have concluded, might be the simplest—Tom Hemings never existed.[53]

Brodie asks, How did Jefferson's daughters react to Sally's pregnancy? "Is there any evidence of anguish and jealousy on the part of Jefferson's daughters? What kind of accommodation was made?" Patsy did not enter the nunnery, but she "rushed impetuously into marriage" and "the haste is suggestive."[54] Such impetuosity and haste are certainly strong signifiers that she must have been aware Sally Hemings was her father's mistress, Brodie claims.

## REASON, INGENUOUSNESS, AND CLARITY

### Was Jefferson Highly Sexual?

As we saw above, Brodie's case for a relationship between Jefferson and Hemings is predicated both on the accounts of Madison Hemings and

James Callender and on the argument that Jefferson was a highly sexual person throughout his life.

That Jefferson had four "forbidden relationships" scarcely shows great sexuality. Jefferson was certainly in love with his wife, as is evidenced by his excessive grieving on her passing. However, the case for Martha being "forbidden," because she was previously married, seems strained. Moreover, I grant that Jefferson loved Maria Cosway, the artist whom Jefferson met while in France, but I suspect that the love went unrequited and that the affair was never sexually consummated. Cosway, the coquette, continually flirted with Jefferson, the diplomat, but she continually flirted with many other highly visible men. At some point, Jefferson recognized that nothing would come of the "friendship." Cosway probably never had any intention of leaving her husband for him and of changing her way of life.

Jefferson was clearly gauche when verbally expressing himself in front of other men. He shied away from debate and public speeches. His presidential addresses were scarcely audible. He preferred expressing himself through his quill and he did so remarkably well through a prodigious quantity of writings, evidencing a substantial acumen. One can only assume that such awkwardness was redoubled around attractive women. His letters to Cosway offer stark evidence of that.

Given his clumsiness with Cosway, one cannot merely assume that Jefferson was a Lothario when it came to his early-life indiscretion with his friend's wife, Betsy Walker. Overall, we know too little about the indiscretion and Jefferson's early life to form a categorical judgment, or even a firm judgment.

What of Jefferson's youthful passion for Rebecca Burwell, a young woman with whom he fell irretrievably in love circa 1762, who was not forbidden? Under the spell of Burwell, whom he called "Belinda," Jefferson longed to travel to Williamsburg and propose to her. He tarried, presumably because of inner fear and because of express plans for travel. His letters to boyhood friend John Page show Jefferson to be no Lothario, suave and versed in the ways of women. He is instead inelegant, maladroit, and lay-it-on-the-line. In one letter to Page (July 15, 1763), he writes: "If I am to meet with a disappointment, the sooner I know it, the more of life I shall have to wear it off. . . . If Belinda will not accept of my service, it will never be offered to another." When Jefferson finally found the nerve to propose to her, he practiced his proposal, but the result, when face-to-face with Rebecca, was disastrous. He tells Page (October 7, 1763), "A few broken sentences, uttered in great disorder, and interrupted with pauses of uncommon length were the too visible marks of my strange confusion." Belinda, perplexed, did not grasp his intent. Jefferson rehearsed his proposal for another day. This time the proposal was "too clear and too logical," for it seemed more of an ultimatum than proposal of marriage. She announced weeks later her betrothal to another. Jeffersonian scholar Gilbert Chinard sums, "This was the typical Jeffersonian way of presenting his own wishes, of letting the others decide after he had stated the pros and cons; clearly he was not made to win personal triumphs, either in love or in politics."[55]

Would Jefferson have been graceless and gauche around his handsome, youthful slave? Perhaps he would not have been, one could argue, because of her status as servant and slave.

Nonetheless, certain factors would have made a relationship difficult, if not impossible. Jefferson's health and activities were issues at the time of the conception of Eston Hemings in 1807. Letters evince he was likely suffering from chronic diarrhea, periodic migraines, rheumatoid and osteoarthritis, prostatitis, and sciatica at the time, among other things. Again, there were numerous activities at and around Monticello, among them, rebuilding mills along the river and renovations at and of Monticello. Moreover, when Jefferson was home, he was almost always swamped with guests—from ten to thirty visitors beyond his immediate family—and busily engaged in writing letters each day.[56]

Following on the work of Cynthia Burton, lawyer William G. Hyland Jr. makes the case that Jefferson's presumed exceptional health must be taken with a grain of salt. There is, he asserts in keeping with Burton's account, considerable reason to believe his health, during the last two decades of his life, was in steady decline. In addition, his mental health waned. His memory began to falter greatly and he suffered emotional stress from continued concerns over bankruptcy. So debilitated was Jefferson that he was impotent, "within a reasonable degree of medical certainty."[57]

It is difficult to assess the argument from declining health, for though Jefferson listed problems with his health in numerous letters, there are numerous indications to suggest Jefferson was blessed with better health all of his life than most others of his day. Foremost among these are his testimonies in his letters—for example, his letter to John Adams (December 18, 1825) concerning his willingness to relive his life again, save the last seven years of declining health, were there the opportunity. As biographer Dumas Malone notes, Jefferson outgrew his migraines, only had infrequent colds, rarely suffered from indigestion, and was unusually active: "Not until he was entering his eighty-third year did he gravely decline."[58] I think it safer to conclude the steady decline assumed by Hyland cannot be presumed, only that, as Burton asserts, periodic health problems would have made steady sexual interest improbable and engagement in a multiplicity of other activities would have made a liaison improbable.

## A Case for Hypersublimation

I cannot agree with Hyland and the critical historians who dismiss Brodie's work because of her "pseudo-psychological explanations," given often in Freudian language. I have critically addressed Freud's work in numerous publications[59] and have taken especial issue with his tendency toward "metapsychological" or metempirical explanation. Nonetheless, his work on ego-psychology and defense mechanisms might at least be heuristically profitable.[60] Overall, that Brodie, like Freud, examines what is known of Jefferson's childhood and searches for insight into how he became the person he was seems laudable, not condemnable. Furthermore, that she examines psychologically his use of language is unobjectionable. Moreover, her assertion that one's sexuality is a relatively stable disposition of a person throughout life is reasonable. What I take issue with are the haste with which she tends to examine Jefferson's use of language and her conclusion—given her reconstruction of Jefferson's four "forbidden" affairs—that Jefferson acted on his sexuality because he was a highly sexual person.

Many of Freud's insights on defense mechanisms are still taken seriously today by psychologists—especially ego psychologists—and are so commonly known that they have become part of everyday language. One of those mechanisms is sublimation—the mechanism for diverting psycho-sexual energy from its principal outlets (sexual exchanges, from highly casual to highly intimate, with other persons) and deploying it in constructive or socially accepted ways. That Freud's particular metapsychological explanation of sublimation is dubious seems clear. What seems indubitable, however, is that something like sublimation actually occurs in human beings (i.e., a highly sexual person who engages in frequent sexual activity does not just cease all such activities without repercussions). That, of course, is Brodie's point. The death of Jefferson's wife, Martha Jefferson, could not have signified the death of Jefferson's sexuality. He had to find other outlets.

That follows only if Jefferson was a highly sexual person with frequent opportunities for sexual involvement. Nothing inevitably points to that. Yet, even if one grants that Jefferson was highly sexual throughout his life, it is unreasonable to conclude that that sexuality manifested itself starkly in four "forbidden" relationships.

Readers will pardon me for continuing in Freudian language, if only to give the surface structure of an explanation, without countenancing the dynamics of it, concerning what must have been the case with Jefferson. I do not challenge Brodie's reconstruction of Jefferson's childhood. On the whole, it seems plausible and I know too little of his childhood to be a viable psychoanalytic critic. I assume it, in its broadest sketch, to be accurate. Instead, I argue that Jefferson's desire early in life to learn everything he could learn was, if anything, manifestation of an early expression of a lifelong tendency to sublimate sexual impulses. In Freudian parlance, Jefferson was dutiful, punctual, orderly, prolific, polymathic, and forward looking, because his libido was forced into the direction of productivity, not sexual activity. In modern parlance, he was an abundantly intelligent geek at the expense of his sexual activity.

No better illustration exists than Jefferson's keen interest in science, broadly construed. Jefferson was inordinately interested in nearly all branches of useful sciences and was routinely ridiculed for that interest. He recorded meteorological data punctiliously at 4 a.m. and 4 p.m. for some fifty years. He collected fossilized remains of extinct creatures. He worked on a dictionary of American-Indian terms and collected American-Indian artifacts. He introduced numerous new plants and even some animals to America from Europe. He dabbled in philology and enjoyed throughout his life classical authors in Greek and Latin. He endorsed and participated in scientific invention. He met and exchanged letters with many of the greatest scientists of his day. He founded and oversaw construction of the University of Virginia. He was an avid member of the American Philosophical Society and numerous other scientific societies. I could go on, but that would be overkill.

Many books have been written about Jefferson's interest in science. Many more need to be written, as this is an underexplored and underappreciated dimension of Jefferson the person. So completely absorbed was he in learning and its advance that it is highly unlikely that he could have been a Lothario even in the limited sense of carrying on a lengthy relationship with one of his slaves. His time was dutifully parsed out each day to increase efficiency and maximize production. Such efficient, productive persons are efficient and productive at expense of libidinal interests. Thus, Jefferson's keen activity in science testifies to heightened sexuality that has been diverted from its normal outlets. It testifies to heightened sublimation.

It is also commonly understood that Jefferson was not comfortable in expressing himself emotionally. For instance, Jefferson biographer Dumas Malone cites an incident after the death of Jefferson's dear friend Dabney Carr. When Jefferson observed the two men he had set to grub a plot of land for Dabney Carr's grave, he noted the time it took to grub the land and concluded that one laborer could grub one acre of land in four days. He noted also that the first peas were ready for the table in what was a forward spring. "He was never one to give free expression to his emotions; and he was quite in character in turning for relief to figures, to garden peas and the weather, to the prosaic affairs of every day. This strong, strange man did not wear his heart upon his sleeve."[61]

Finally, certain of Jefferson's letters betray a Platonic or Epicurean contempt for sexual licentiousness. To Charles Bellini, an émigré living in Virginia at the time, he expresses repugnance of French culture (September

30, 1785). The young are preoccupied by "intrigues of love." "Conjugal love" and "domestic happiness," he adds, do not exist. The French "nourish and invigorate all our bad passions," which sustain them by brief stints of ecstasy, at the expense of the "tranquil, permanent felicity" of American domesticity. To lifelong friend John Banister (October 15, 1785), Jefferson asserts that a youth sent to Europe to be educated is "led by the strongest of all the human passions, into a spirit of female intrigue, destructive of his own and others' happiness, or a passion for whores, destructive of his health." The gist of such letters is in keeping with Plato's link of "erotic love" with "anarchy" and "lawlessness"[62] and Epicurus's notion that sexual love "never actually benefits anyone."[63] In sum, if Jefferson was highly sexual, his sexuality was massively sublimated.

## Jefferson's Progressive Demeanor

Brodie's psychoanalytic assumption that one is a product of one's childhood is plausible. That is a claim that Greek philosopher Aristotle and the Greek and Roman Stoics acknowledged millennia ago. What she disacknowledges is that Jefferson's demeanor was, in the main, not remorseful. Though he did worry much about the truth of calumny and reproaches, he was mindful of damage control. He seldom directly replied to calumniators, in the belief that to fan an ember was to create a fire or, in some cases, a conflagration—that is, to make substantive what was frivolous or baseless. Ever the progressivist, Jefferson was content to look forward, not backward. He acknowledged that he should have his say on important matters, but not necessarily the final word on them. He satisfied himself with doing his part to nudge things forward without feeling the need to do everything.[64]

There is no doubt that Jefferson exhibited distinct pathological tendencies, which in Freudian terminology would be "anal" (e.g., tidiness and orderliness), yet he also exhibited what ego-psychologists would dub great adjustment to reality. For instance, he did not press the issue of slavery when he believed it premature (see chapter 6). The country was too divided and his energies would best be spent otherwise. Again Jefferson did not dwell on the past but looked to the future. He counted on the slow progressive march, evidenced by history, of intelligence and morality; and he did what he could politically, morally, and scientifically to expedite that march. Furthermore, Jefferson did not address slanderers, but constantly ignored reproaches.[65] So great were the number of his slanderers that were he to address their calumny, he would have been left with no time for worthwhile pursuits like serving his state or country, farming, science, reading, letter writing, entertaining visitors, and enjoying his family. Moreover, Jefferson recognized that liberty came with a price—service to one's country. Though he expressed on numerous occasions his wish to retire from public service and spend his time with family at Monticello,[66] he had spent his salad years in service to the American nation. Though he recognized, as did the Roman Stoic Seneca, that one could ask only so much of a person, that at some point it was time for others to do their part, he acknowledged that one could still modestly serve one's state in retirement.[67] He more than modestly served his state in retirement. He was a dutiful letter writer—an important service to his fellow citizens as well as his human beings—and almost daily oversaw construction of his pet project in retirement—the University of Virginia. Although manifestly "anal," he showed superordinary adjustment to reality—a sure indication that he was not a person bedazzled by libidinal distractions.

## BRODIE'S "INVESTIGATIVE" TACTICS

### Psychologizing

Brodie's work has been roundly criticized by historians for its conclusions, based on flights of fancy: innuendo and not fact. Sally Hemings, a minor historical figure about whom nothing is certainly known, becomes in her artful, Machiavellian imagination a significant historical figure who had a marked influence on late eighteenth-century and early nineteenth-century happenings through a thirty-eight-year relationship with Thomas Jefferson. Historian John C. Miller in *The Wolf by the Ears* writes that Brodie is "piling implausibility upon implausibility."[68] Other scholars agree. Clifford Egan writes, "To Brodie's factual errors, contradictions and cavalier use of evidence must be added another sin—the injection of contemporary issues into evaluating the past"[69]—what I call in chapter 2 the "fallacy of historical anachronism." Holman Hamilton says, "The book contains many errors of fact or of judgment involving a wide historical spectrum." It is "long on speculation and suggestion" and reflects Brodie's continued "strainings for the conjectural."[70] Garry Wills notes Brodie's ingenuity as well as her ignorance. "She has managed to write a long and complex study of Jefferson without displaying any acquaintance with eighteenth century plantation conditions, political thought, literary conventions, or scientific categories."[71] William G. Hyland Jr. writes:

> In Brodie's enthusiasm to find a link between Jefferson and Hemings, she misread language and invoked pseudo-psychological explanations to over interpret unconscious patterns in Jefferson's writing. Brodie wove a tale of psychological interpretation based upon selected letters written by Jefferson. Though her book received poor reviews from historians for its eccentric psychological ruminations, its allegations of deceit of a Founding Father made it a bestseller.[72]

Brodie has also been criticized severely because of her Freudian bent. Jefferson biographer Merrill Peterson dismisses the psychologizing and says the book leaves us as ignorant as we began. "I see no need to charge off in defense of Jefferson's integrity when we have no solid grounds for doubting it."[73] Dumas Malone, perhaps the greatest authority on Jefferson, writes, "This determined woman carries psychological speculation to the point of absurdity. . . . But to me the man she describes in her more titillating passages is unrecognizable."[74]

I have stated above that I am not against psychologizing historical figures. Many of her conclusions concerning Jefferson's inner life ought not to be unrestrictedly dismissed, just because they are of the psychological sort, but ought to be given fuller consideration. The difficulty is that much of Brodie's psychologizing is recklessly speculative or undersupported. I offer several examples.

Jefferson's daily journal, kept while traveling through France, Germany, and Holland in 1788, gives a clue to his "special preoccupation" with Sally Hemings, writes Brodie. In twenty-five pages, the word *mulatto* appears eight times, whereas in his tour of southern France one year earlier, he uses the word once in forty-eight pages. She goes on to list each citation.[75]

Many scholars use this example as illustration of Brodie's overventuresome psychologizing. Yet let us take the bait, as it were, and grant the inordinate use suggests a preoccupation with *mulatto*. It is not an unreasonable claim. One would then expect, if the preoccupation was driven by sexual attraction for Sally Hemings, that *mulatto* would in each instance be linked with *fertility*, *richness*, *beauty*, or similar terms, in keeping with Jefferson's high estimation of Hemings's budding attractiveness. Yet only three of the eight references are cognizable as sexual attraction (my italics throughout below).

> The road goes thro' the plains of the Maine, which are *mulatto* and *very fine*. . . .
>
> These plains are sometimes black, sometimes *mulatto*, always *rich*. . . .
>
> [T]he valley of the Rhine . . . varies in quality, sometimes a *rich mulatto* loam, sometimes a poor sand. . . .

Three of the references are manifestly inconsistent with sexual attraction:

> It has a good Southern aspect, the soil a *barren mulatto* clay. . . .
>
> It is the South Western aspect, *very poor*, sometimes gray, sometimes *mulatto*. . . .
>
> *Meagre mulatto* clay mixt with small broken stones. . . .

Two other references seem neutral:

> [T]he plains are generally mulatto. . . .
>
> [T]he hills are mulatto, but also whitish. . . .

Thus, it might be that Brodie is correct to note Jefferson's preoccupation with *mulatto* in 1788, but the evidence suggests that that preoccupation is not due to sexual attraction to Sally Hemings. Brodie is grasping at straws.

A second instance of overventuresome psychologizing occurs with respect to Jefferson's wife. Brodie writes of Jefferson's famous "usufruct" letter to James Madison (September 6, 1789). In that letter, Jefferson argues that one generation of men has no right to bind the next—especially through public debts. The debts of one generation are not the responsibility of the next. A generation, Jefferson defines as nineteen years. Brodie asks, Why nineteen years instead of twenty or twenty-five? "Did it mean anything that the year was 1789, exactly nineteen years since he had met and fallen in love with Martha Wayles?"[76]

A careful reading of Jefferson's letter to Madison (September 6, 1789) shows that there is no psychological significance to "19." That number Jefferson derives from actuarial tables of French naturalist Comte de Buffon. The scientist gives 23,994 deaths at varied ages. Jefferson supposes the existence of a society in which the same number of people are born each year and whose people live to the ages in Buffon's table. That society, consisting of 617,703 persons at any time, will have (1) at any point of time, one half of all persons dead in 24 years and eight months; (2) each year, 10,675 persons attain the age of 21; (3) always 348,417 persons over the age of 21; and, (4) at any point of time, one half of them over 21 years dying in 18 years and eight months or, roughly, 19 years. "Then 19. [*sic*] years is the term beyond which neither the representatives of a nation," Jefferson sums, "nor even the whole nation itself assembled, can validly extend a debt."[77] Once again, the conclusion, implicit in her rhetorical question, is incautious and silly.

Third, soon after daughter Martha Jefferson wed Thomas Mann Randolph Jr., Randolph Jr.'s father decided to marry a teenage girl, Gabriella Harvie. His bride-to-be requested to increase the price of his Edgehill land, which his son wished to purchase. Martha wrote her father and Jefferson replied, Brodie writes, in a curiously clever and guarded manner. So ensconced in his troubles with the youthful Sally was Jefferson that he advised Martha to wish her father-in-law well on his new marriage and to avoid other troubles. Misapprehension, Jefferson says, might prove to be a "canker-worm corroding eternally on your minds." Brodie states that the "powerful metaphor" of "canker-worm" was "profoundly appropriate for what was happening at Monticello." Jefferson also advises his daughter, she notes, to love and cherish what is good in people and neglect what is bad, as no one—especially Jefferson—is perfect. Martha must be the "link of love, union, and peace for the whole family." To Brodie, Jefferson is clearly masking his affair with Hemings. How she derives that from what she quotes of the letter is unclear.

Just what was happening between Jefferson and Hemings at Monticello? Brodie never says. Yet his advice to love what is good in others and neglect what is bad, for Brodie, can only be an unconscious cover for and evidence of Jefferson's own misdeeds. However, there is a simpler explanation. Could it not be that Jefferson's ethical views, drawing from Christ's teachings and Stoicism, were nonconfrontational and benevolence-based and that Jefferson aimed to live an ethically sound life?[78] Brodie's unwillingness to consider that scenario underscores a problem with depth-psychology explanations. There is the tendency to go beyond the obvious and, in doing so, one can seldom, if ever, simply say that so-and-so is merely a good person for good reasons. Goodness, when psychoanalyzed, burns like butter on a sizzling skillet. Jefferson himself iterates a similar sentiment in a letter to Martin van Buren, "If no action is to be deemed virtuous for which malice can imagine a sinister motive, then there never was a virtuous action; no, not even in the life of our Saviour himself." That sentiment, he counters thus, "But he has taught us to judge the tree by its fruit, and to leave motives to him who can alone see into them" (June 29, 1824).

Fourth, there is Jefferson's preoccupation with Jesus. It begins, Brodie notes, conveniently at the zenith of the Hemings crisis, during his first term as president. "It was much more of an attempt at a resolution of a shattering personal dilemma [than a defense of Jefferson's religiosity]." She adds, "One sees him wrestling with his own sense of betrayal and crucifixion."[79]

Nonetheless, Jefferson's interest in Jesus begins perhaps as early as

1786, when he meets Richard Price in London, after writing him the year before. Learning of Price's preoccupation with divinity and morality, Jefferson writes Price in 1789 to learn more about the latter's Unitarianism and his conception of deity. Fascination with Jesus takes root thereafter when Jefferson reads Joseph Priestley's *An History of the Corruptions of Christianity* in 1793.[80] Thus, preoccupation with Jesus begins much earlier that Brodie says it begins.

Brodie makes much of Jefferson's opening statement in his "Syllabus"—a brief, critical comparison of Jesus's ethical views with those of the ancient philosophers and the Jews. "In a comparative view of the Ethics of the enlightened nations of antiquity, of the Jews and of Jesus, no notice should be taken of the corruptions of reason among the ancients, to wit, the idolatry and superstition of the vulgar, nor of the corruptions of Christianity by the learned among its professors." What perplexes Brodie? She answers with a question, "Could the repetition of the word 'corruption' suggest that he was not so much contemplating the 'corruptions of Christianity' or the 'corruptions of reason' as the corruptions of Thomas Jefferson?"[81] Brodie's "suggestion" here is hopelessly strained to the point of absurdity. Moreover it is, once again, ineffectually couched in the modality of possibility.

There is, I repeat, nothing in principle deplorable about exposing historical figures to psychological analysis. What is deplorable is psychological analysis done by biographers, not by competent psychologists. In a review of Brodie's book, historian Bruce Mazlish writes:

> While not impossible, certainly . . . Jefferson's character and views do mitigate against the Hemings connection. A compulsively controlled man, Jefferson was convinced that miscegenation meant "degradation": can readers believe that he would have conceived five children, one of them in the interval when he returned to Monticello for his daughter's funeral, not as a matter of exceptional passion but of continuing calculation, guiltlessly pursued? Brodie's analysis of the psychological situation is simply not convincing—which is not to say that her conclusion may not be right—though she then takes as bedrock what is still the shifting sands of speculation.[82]

## Sexual Psychologizing

One must also note the most disturbing feature of Brodie's "reconstruction"—her tendency to psycho-*sexualize* what is not straightforwardly sexual. Like Freud, she finds sex in the most unexpected places.

When Brodie cites several of Jefferson's letters concerning his delight at having returned to Monticello from France in 1789, Brodie gives those letters a sexual exegesis. "Infinitely the happier, totally absorbed, ardor, infinite appetite," writes Brodie of Jefferson's language in those letters, "these are strong words with the unmistakable flavor of sexuality. They suggest that satisfactions of the body at Monticello were real."[83]

Brodie's interpretation is strange and strained. What satisfactions of the body did Jefferson experience at Monticello prior to going to France? Did not Brodie state that it was in France where Jefferson's interest in his comely slave began? Why should he necessarily pine for Monticello? One would fully expect that the opportunities for sexual consummation would be less at Monticello, due to the perennial throng of people in and around the mansion, which was not all that large, and the high probability of exposure of his liaison over the years.

Brodie notices sexual tension between Jefferson and his daughters—especially Martha. Jefferson, in a reply to a letter to Patsy (March 22, 1792), writes: "The ensuing year will be the longest of my life, and the last of such hateful labours. The next we will sow our cabbages together." The reply, Brodie relates farcically, contains "as much yearning as if he were writing to a mistress."[84]

Later, Brodie states vaguely, "Something in the nature of the accommodation Jefferson's daughters made is revealed in the nuances of their correspondence with their father." Martha responded to her father's indiscretions with Sally Hemings with "heightened and almost palpable seduction of her father in her letters, a seduction that was as innocent as it was unconscious."[85] She devised the "elaborate fiction" of her father's "solitude and gloom" without her—Jefferson's "solitary fire side."[86] Elsewhere, Brodie speaks of the "unconscious seduction" between Jefferson and younger daughter Maria. "How . . . much pain it gives me to think of the unsafe and solitary manner in which you sleep upstairs," Maria writes to her father.[87] Brodie comments, "Unsafe indeed had Jefferson's bedroom proved to be at Monticello!"[88] The fiction, of course, was an unconscious defensive posture that shielded recognition that Jefferson loved another—moreover, a slave—more than either of his daughters. Daughter Martha eventually came to entertain the accommodating fiction that Hemings's children were fathered by the Carr brothers. "The fact that Sally's oldest son had been conceived in France seems to have been conveniently forgotten."[89] Yet as we have already seen, the infamous Tom Hemings might never have existed.

Other letters to his daughters, during his first retirement, express Jefferson's longing for family and are to her equally libidinal. Of such letters, Brodie writes, "One has only to repeat the warm phrases—motion of my blood, in the lap and love of my family, affection in every breath that blows around me, cut off from everything I love—to see that these are the longing of a man truly deprived of love, and that this special deprivation had only incidentally to do with his daughter."[90] The phrases, Brodie believes, unmistakably refer to longing for Sally Hemings, and that is outright nonsense.

One illustration of such a letter is in a letter from Jefferson to his daughter Martha. When Jefferson's daughter Maria intended to wed her cousin Jack Eppes, she could tell her father only through her sister Martha. Jefferson was hurt and wrote to Martha: "I now see a fireside formed into a groupe, no member of which has a fibre in their composition which can ever produce any jarring or jealousies among us. No irregular passions, no dangerous bias, which may render problematical the future fortunes and happiness of our descendants." Of "the reference to the 'irregular passion' [sic], the 'dangerous bias,'" Brodie adds, "who but himself was guilty?" We have, of course, another oblique reference to Sally Hemings.[91]

Another illustration is in a letter to Maria. Once Maria married, Jefferson wrote to her and bid her to spend time at Monticello, while he was away. "The servants will be here under your commands and such supplies as the house affords," wrote Jefferson (April 11, 1801). "Maria," Brodie states, with reference to her reply of April 18, 1801, "had responded with

great delicacy. 'The servants we shall carry up will be more than sufficient for ourselves and you would perhaps prefer yours being employed
in some way or other.'" Brodie ties Maria's delicate reply to recognition
that to employ all her father's servants to her own needs would be sexual
encroachment. Sally Hemings was "in charge of Jefferson's 'chamber and
wardrobe'"[92] and Maria knew she had no right to steal away Sally from
her father.

A third illustration occurs in a letter to John Trumbull. Concerning
Maria Cosway's letters to her husband and friends, Jefferson writes of the
"many infidelities in the postoffice," caused by the rumors of war. Brodie
replies, "Here, it would seem, he came very close to saying what was really
bothering him—*So many complaints of our infidelities are coming through
the postoffice.*"[93] That is another ridiculous inference.

## The Argument from Omission

Brodie makes much of Jefferson's guardedness concerning his "intimate
life." She calls his autobiography an "exercise in self-concealment" and
adds, "Why he abandoned his memoir at the precise point he did—after
describing his five years in France—is in itself a clue to his continuing
need for secrecy concerning his private life."[94] The suggestion, of course,
is that in France he consummated a relationship with Hemings.[95] Later,
when she writes of Jefferson meeting James Madison after France, she
says, "Whether he confided in Madison his affection for Sally Hemings,
or instead went to great lengths to preserve his façade of secrecy and
evasion, one cannot know for certain, though the latter seems the much
more likely."[96] She concludes, "Jefferson's secrecy about his intimate life
pervades every kind of document he left behind."[97] That in effect is just
another way of saying that there is no evidence of a relationship between
Jefferson and Sally Hemings.

When Martha wrote to her father, in Philadelphia, of the viruses
that infected many at Monticello, she mentioned the death of "poor little
Harriet," another of Jefferson's putative children by Hemings. Brodie says
that Jefferson, who likely wrote to Sally of the little girl's death (though

the letter does not exist), wrote immediately an "altogether extraordinary letter" to Martha. In the letter, Jefferson completely ignored Harriet's death and focused on his great affection for Martha and Maria. In doing so, he was "denying by omission the importance of what she had written to him [concerning the death of Harriet]." Brodie adds in concession, "Martha might well have misinterpreted the letter to read what she fondly hoped, that the death of this child had had no special impact on her father."[98] Again, lack of reference to Harriet and Sally are given as proof of Jefferson's preoccupation of them in his thoughts.

Brodie adds that Sally Hemings is surprisingly absent from Jefferson's *Farm Book*.[99] "The extent to which Jefferson kept Sally Hemings and her children relatively anonymous in his *Farm Book* would seem to be symbolic of his entire relationship with her. It was a kind of automatic denial, in the written record, that this slave woman and her children were important to him."[100]

We begin to notice abundant use of what might be dubbed the "argument from omission." The general form of this argument from omission begins to take shape.

(1) Jefferson writes little of Sally Hemings (and her children) in his writings.
(2) Absence of references is evidence of denial of a relationship.
(3) So, there is a strong sense of denial of a relationship in Jefferson.

It should be clear to anyone of self-possessed thought that the argument, as given, is pathetically weak: Absence of evidence for some claim is taken as evidence for the truth of that claim, via denial. No evidence of concern for Hemings is, if anything, evidence of noninvolvement with Hemings. The argument, to be forceful, needs an additional premise added—*Jefferson had a thirty-eight-year relationship with Hemings*. Adding that premise, however, is circular reasoning, as it proves the conclusion at which Brodie ultimately aims—the existence of a relationship.

Yet Brodie is clear that absence of references to Sally and her children in the *Farm Book* is offered in some sense as positive evidence—evidence by omission or "psychological" evidence—of their relationship.[101] If so, then we are in position to assert as true the following general claim: *For any person* p, *if* p *neglects some subject* s, *then* p *is psychologically preoccupied with* s. That is too ridiculous to entertain seriously, and no reasonable psychotherapist would countenance it, without additional confirmatory evidence of deep-rooted repression, which Brodie does not supply. Is that the "feeling" or "nuance" of which Brodie warned we must be aware?

It is here that one can put Freud to use effectively against Brodie. For Freud, there is no such thing as concealment. He writes, "He that has eyes to see and ears to hear may convince himself that no mortal can keep a secret. If his lips are silent, he chatters with his finger-tips; betrayal oozes out of him at every pore."[102] The only surefire, effective means of concealment is not having something to conceal in the first place. That is why I find it perplexing that Madison Hemings in his published account did not adduce even one episode of intimacy between his "parents"—not even a story related to him by his mother—in the twenty-one years he was to know his "father" and the many more years he was to know his mother. That is why I find it perplexing that Jefferson, according to Brodie, could have had a perfectly concealed thirty-eight-year liaison with Sally Hemings. Finally, Brodie's own attempts at psychoanalytic disclosure, I have already shown, are unpersuasive or massively underdeveloped and would be balked at by any competent psychotherapist.

Of course, the ploy of secrecy is critical for Brodie. There are no letters between Jefferson and Hemings in Jefferson's writings. Jefferson seldom mentions her in any of his extant writings. Instead of concluding what seems obvious to most—*Sally Hemings was a sprat to Jefferson*—Brodie concludes that Jefferson was a master of suppressing his intimate life, because of a clamant need for secrecy. He magnificently succeeded in allowing no manifest trace of intimacy between him and Sally Hemings in any of his writings for thirty-eight years. Only Brodie, through her sort of psychoanalytic investigation, is capable of exhuming those secrets.

Overall, Brodie's attempt to find psychological or psychosexual evidence in Jefferson's writings of an affair with Hemings through "omission" is ridiculously lame.

## Brodian Swamping

The most disingenuous feature of Brodie's "scholarship" is the tossing out of possibility claims to effect historical explanation. Page after page of her reconstruction of Jefferson's putative relationship with Hemings is fraught with sentences to which the modality of possibility is added. According to Jeffersonian historian Julian Boyd, Brodie's biography consists of "her pyramiding of conjecture upon conjecture and then regarding the result as incontrovertibly proven facts, to be employed thereafter as the basis for still further piling on of inferences."[103] An exhaustive listing would be exhausting, so I offer merely a small sampling. All italics below are my own.

When Beverly Hemings was born to Sally on April 1, 1798, Jefferson was in Philadelphia, but wrote in his account book. "Gave Laurence Allwine ord on Barnes for 26 D. for a stick sopha and mattras [*sic*]." States Brodie, "*It is possible that* the sofa and mattress were ordered for Sally Hemings in anticipation of the birth."[104]

As vice president, Jefferson wrote to politician Edward Rutledge, "Tranquillity [*sic*] is an old man's milk. I go to enjoy it in a few days, and to exchange the roar and tumult of bulls and bears, for the prattle of my grand-children and senile rest." Writes Brodie, "His metaphor of 'old man's milk' *could distantly suggest* a young breast on which to lay his head."[105] (Note here the ambiguity of "distantly," which can express the distance between Philadelphia and Monticello or mean "indirectly," "roughly," or "vaguely.")

Recall Brodie's metaphor-filled and metaphor-mixed summary of Jefferson's legacy, "The Jefferson legacy, then, *may be looked at* as a fountain of dazzling complexity, its beauty compounded by the sunlight of his rare intelligence, but its sources of power—including the rewarding but intermittently tragic secret loves—hidden and deep in the earth."[106]

Brodie writes of the absence of Tom Hemings from Jefferson's *Farm Book*, "This absence has been cited as evidence that Tom did not exist. . . . *It may also be evidence* that Jefferson chose to consider him free from birth, either because he had been conceived on the free soil of France, or because Jefferson had promised his mother." She adds, "Since Jefferson mentioned three 'runaways' in his *Farm Book*, two of whom, Beverly and

Harriet Hemings, were Sally Hemings's children, *it seems likely that* the fourth was Tom Hemings, and that he left Monticello at a relatively early age, *probably* [here a slightly stronger modality] shortly after the story of his mother's relationship with Jefferson broke into the press in 1802. *Perhaps* his mother chose not to discuss this son with anyone after his departure and made every effort to protect his identity in the white society by a mantle of silence."[107]

The cumulative effect of those possibility claims—a rhetorical tack used similarly and equally disingenuously by law professor Annette Gordon-Reed (the focus of chapter 2)—is to overwhelm readers with a dizzying array of possibilities, most of which are sizeable improbabilities. By book's end, readers are swamped with possibilities, which titillate quixotic minds, but, taken together, amount to nothing to discerning readers in search of historical truth, not chimera.

## Glossing Over

Finally, I note Brodie's tendency to gloss over disconfirmatory evidence.

After the death of Maria at the age of twenty-five, Jefferson was devastated and wrote, months later, to his friend John Page (June 25, 1804). "Others may lose of their abundance, but I, of my want, have lost even the half of all I had. My evening prospects now hang on the slender thread of a single life. . . . But whatever is to be our destiny, wisdom, as well as duty, dictates that we should acquiesce in the will of Him whose it is to give and take away, and be contented in the enjoyment of those who are still permitted to be with us."

Doing the math, the letter suggests Jefferson has not fathered children by Hemings, but only daughters Martha and Maria by his wife Martha. Yet Brodie is undaunted. She tendentiously argues that Jefferson, in such a moment of despair, "may have . . . taken refuge in denial and rejection of the children conceived by his dark and secret mistress." She adds that there is "important evidence"—Jefferson's use of "those still with us"—that Jefferson found solace in the "young black mother, the source of continuing life."[108] It is disquieting and perplexing that Brodie can claim that "those still with us" is "important evidence" or even an oblique reference to Sally Hemings.

Finally, there is the testimony of Edmund Bacon, overseer at Monticello. In his memoirs, he reported that speculation concerning one beautiful mulatto being Jefferson's daughter was false. "I have seen him come out of her mother's room many a morning when I went up to Monticello very early."[109] Why the testimony of Bacon, who had no clear motive for prevarication, should be quickly dismissed by Brodie, other than that it creates problems for her thesis, is unclear. Bacon, Brodie states baldly, was merely "supporting the 'family denial.'"[110]

## ADDENDUM: BRODIE VINDICATED?

To end this chapter, I turn to Jennifer Jensen Wallach's "The Vindication of Fawn Brodie" (2002). She states, "[Brodie's] biography . . . is immune from the racism that unconsciously infiltrated the interpretations of many Jefferson scholars who could not believe that the builder of Monticello and founder of the University of Virginia could have stooped so low as to have had sexual relations with, or perhaps worse, romantic attachments to a black woman."[111]

There are two alternatives, Wallach says. There is the white oral tradition and the black oral tradition. White male historians have had a decided preference for the white tradition. Inclusion of "white" and "male" here imply that skin color and gender influence rationality and that there are no canons of proper reasoning. Wallach, as does Brodie, takes the account of Madison Hemings as irrefutable.[112]

Wallach then turns to the reporting of the infamous James Callender. Scholars, she subtly states, take his message to be false because of his faulty character. "Jefferson enthusiasts, unwilling to believe this testimony which substantiates Madison Hemings's claims, have consistently disparaged the messenger as a means of discrediting the message." She cites, as example, historian Virginius Dabney's account of Callender. Dabney says Callender was "a morose and ill-tempered individual who resorted all too often to strong drink [and] seemed unable to get along with anybody." Wallach contrasts that to Brodie's account. Brodie says Callender was a "notorious defamer of the great" and adds that he was also a "talented writer, and a generally accurate reporter, and Jefferson's former friend."[113]

To contrast two accounts of Callender's personhood is ridiculous. Was he a "talented writer"? Ed Anger is a talented writer for the *Weekly World News*, by the gossipy, tongue-in-cheek standards of that publication. Is he a "generally accurate reporter"? The term is too vague to be availing, but it is included, of course, to leave open the possibility of the accuracy of his report on Jefferson. Hogwash!

Yet there are certain unquestioned facts about Callender that Wallach conveniently disacknowledges. First, he was never a friend of Jefferson. Jefferson was, early on, amicably disposed to Callender, when he recognized that Callender might be of some service to the republican cause. That amicable disposition soon ceased, as Jefferson quickly realized that Callender was not the sort of person who could be trusted by anyone for anything, as he was merely out to advance his own cause.

Moreover, Callender had a throat inclined to strong drink and a nose inclined to sensationalism, and he used both for personal advantage. In short, he was a drunkard and an unprincipled blackmailer—and I use the terms here descriptively and not pejoratively—the sort of person who would turn against his mother, if it might prove favorable. Everything points to Callender being no mere messenger. He was incapable of delivering any message without slanting it to harm another. This is no ad hominem attack on Callender. Callender was an incredulous witness. As lawyer William G. Hyland Jr. says, "The charges against Jefferson were suspect from the beginning because they issued from the vengeful pen of an unscrupulous man and were promulgated in the spirit of bitter, political partisanship." He was an "alcoholic, tabloid journalist."[114] Such claims are not pejorative. They are factual.

There follows by Wallach a vain attempt to vindicate Brodie's "psychobiography." Psychobiography, Wallach says cryptically, is "something of a cousin to the broader field of 'psychohistory.'" Here she follows psychohistorian Henry Lawton, who states that psychohistory tries to explain why someone has acted as he has by using the principles of psychoanalysis. Thus, psychobiography can be seen as an attempt to "discover why an individual historical agent behaved in a certain way." Following psychohistorian Peter Loewenberg, she says both disciplines are "hermeneutic—they're sciences of meaning—not random. The patient makes a slip, or presents a dream, and together we explore its meaning. The same thing is true in history."[115]

Wallach says nothing more to help confused readers discern just what hermeneuticism is and to show how history and psychoanalysis are hermeneutic. I suspect she, given complete reliance on what she quotes of Loewenberg's inchoate sketch on hermeneuticism, is fully perplexed and reduced merely to taking Loewenberg as a reliable authority on the topic. In spite of the utterances of certain historians, history is not a hermeneutic discipline; it is instead etiological. Hermeneuticism is too flimsy to explain anything through appeal to causes. Psychoanalysis is only said to be hermeneutic, a claim made famous by philosopher Paul Ricoeur, because attempts to substantiate psychoanalytic claims as genuinely causal have failed—that is, hermeneuticism is a way of conceding the efficacy of psychoanalysis as a clinical method without subjecting psychoanalytic claims to the rigors of the hypothetico-deductive method, according to which scientific generalizations are put to the test through predictive consequences that either confirm or disconfirm the generalization.[116]

Wallach quickly leaves the uncomfortable subject of hermeneutically practiced history—whatever that might entail for her—by stating that Brodie did not utilize psychohistory as an inductive tool. "After compiling oral and circumstantial evidence that confirmed the affair, she interpreted the rest of Jefferson's life in light of this revelation. Her attempts to 'psychoanalyze' Jefferson are designed to bolster the rest of her evidence and not to stand-alone."[117]

The sentences show profound bafflement. First, she writes of confirmation as if it were proof—the affair is "confirmed," period. Confirmation in science is not absolute, but a matter of degrees. What degree of confirmatory support does the oral and circumstantial evidence give? Oral testimonies are greatly suspect, and the circumstantial evidence is based on gossamery inferences. Second, just how does psychobiography "bolster the rest of her evidence"? "Bolstering" has the general meaning of "supporting." Offering support to the oral and circumstantial evidence can only be taken to mean providing additional inductive evidence. Otherwise, it is senseless. So, in effect, Wallach is stating that Brodie both inductively used psychohistory as evidence and did not use it as evidence!

Yet there is a difficulty with that take on Wallach. She says plainly that Brodie had first come to the realization of an affair in light of the oral and circumstantial evidence, which is thin. The psychobiographical "evidence," then, was translated, as it were, in light of her realization. Given that, it *has* to agree with the oral and circumstantial evidence. If so, it does not bolster it in the least, for it was culled *ad hoc*.

Wallach next turns to Brodie's take on Jefferson's "silences." Brodie writes, "In any President's life the silences can reverberate as loudly as the speeches." Jefferson's silence of the paternity charges, she thinks, cannot be taken as denial. "Instead, [Brodie] saw in these silences evidence of a pragmatic man determined to free his slave children and continue loving Sally." By keeping a low profile, Jefferson was best able do those things. Disowning his slave family was not an option.[118]

Yet according to Madison Hemings's own account, Jefferson showed especial attention to his white daughters and white grandchildren, but almost completely ignored his "slave family." One cannot keep a low profile concerning a woman and family one presumably loves—especially not for thirty-eight years. To do that Jefferson would have had to be a superman of sublimation. Jefferson's low profile concerning his slave family is fully and cleanly explained by use of Occam's razor: He did not have a slave family.

Overall, Wallach lauds Brodie for her historical integrity. She says, "It was always Brodie's contention that she did not launch the biographical project *in* order to 'prove' the Hemings affair but instead discovered evidence for the affair, which she was unable to ignore, in the process of her research." She quotes Brodie: "The good historian tries not to manipulate deliberately but to let the material shape itself . . . it is a little like building a mosaic: you don't create the materials, the materials are there."[119]

The analogy of building a mosaic is horribly misleading on at least three counts. First, artists often do create the materials for their mosaics. To make a finished mosaic come out the way an artist wishes it to come out, he often has to cut precisely specifically colored smaltos (pieces of glass used in mosaics) to fit his pattern. Second, even if an artist should construct a mosaic from a fixed number of preestablished smaltos, there are innumerable ways in which he can pattern them. Overall, there are an indescribably large number of possible patterns. Third and finally, he need not use all the smaltos at his disposal. If a pattern suggests itself once certain smaltos are put into place or if the artist has a preexisting pattern in mind prior to building the mosaic, then the artist will have to be selective—that is, certain smaltos will not form part of the finished product.

Brodie's approach to history is constructive and selective, not reconstructive and accommodating—the product of fancy, not fact. She is selective about the materials to be used (e.g., Madison Hemings's account trumps the numerous other contradictory testimonies of whites); she has a set pattern for those materials that requires that numerous other pieces of evidence cannot be used (e.g., she has decided, given Madison's account, that Jefferson must have had a relationship and disallows any evidence to the contrary); and she fashions the pieces of evidence to be used (e.g., she uses a rather incautious approach to psychoanalytic explanation). The finished mosaic is wildly unhistorical and explanatorily empty.

Wallach then turns to a critique of the "Jefferson Establishment." She notes that Merrill Peterson, who as a Jefferson biographer is part of that establishment, warned of the difficulties of segregating Jefferson the man from Jefferson the symbol. Thus, "The historian's obligation to historical truth is compromised, in some degree, by his sense of obligation to the Jefferson symbol." She contrasts Peterson's approach in *The Jefferson Image in the American Mind* to Brodie's. Brodie, she boasts, placed concern for truth above concern for "Jefferson the symbol."[120] Wallach—whose knowledge of Peterson's biographical sketch in his nearly 550-page book comes through a paper by Jeffersonian scholar Douglas Wilson[121] and not through reading the book!—astonishingly fails to realize that Peterson was not stating that the best a historian can do is effect a compromise between truth and the symbol. He was stating that the quest for truth is made especially difficult because of the symbol. Furthermore, to put Brodie at the same level of scholarship as Peterson, let alone at a higher level, is criminal, given the body and quality of work Peterson has contributed toward understanding Jefferson compared to that of Brodie as well as their divergent approaches to history.

Overall, the "Jefferson Establishment" is guilty of circular reasoning, Wallach claims. She quotes approvingly historian Max Beloff, "They assume that Jefferson was incapable of having a relationship of this kind and thus dismiss the evidence for it as irrelevant."[122] To be guilty of circular reasoning is to be guilty of assuming the very claim to be proven. *Jefferson was incapable of having a relationship of this kind, since he was incapable of having a relationship of this kind* is circular reasoning. Beloff's reconstruction is not circular. The problem for the "Establishment" is that evidence for a relationship is wanting and that Jefferson's character seems grossly inconsistent with a relationship.

Wallach notes that in Brodie's day, before the DNA evidence, proponents and opponents of a relationship were split along color lines. Black Americans were proponents; white Americans were opponents. Yet the blacks, falling upon their black oral tradition, knew Jefferson had a relationship with Hemings and, she adds, they were correct. Oral traditions, presumably, cannot be mistaken. Yet Homer's *Iliad* and *Odyssey* are the products of an oral tradition. Few critical scholars take the details of those works—including deeds of divine intervention and of superhuman strength—as literal truths. Again, there still exists in many Arabic countries an oral tradition concerning Alexander the Great being the son of the devil. Though he was plainly an unprincipled killer, I suspect fully that the oral tradition exaggerates apropos of his parentage. There is another difficulty. The black oral tradition is not monolithic. Other families of Hemings's descendants have an oral tradition—and this was likely the predominant tradition until Brodie's book and its backlash—where an uncle of Jefferson is the father.[123] Moreover, there is a loud oral tradition among the Woodsons that Tom Woodson was the mysterious, missing Tom Hemings. That loud tradition was proven wrong by DNA testing in 1998.

Tom Woodson was shown not to have been fathered by Thomas Jefferson.

Wallach somewhat mawkishly quotes Julian Boyd, who merely "intuitively knew" there was a relationship between Jefferson and Hemings.

> Through all my life, as long as I have known there was a Thomas Jefferson, I have known there was a Sally Hemings. And I have known, not in . . . a scholarly way. . . . I know this relationship existed and while, I cannot prove it, I don't find it at all odd that it might have, or could have, or actually did happen. A man who owns slaves is not far away from one who will sleep with his slave.[124]

It is unbelievable that an incredulous Wallach would include the passage as *evidence* for a relationship. Boyd just knew and "not in . . . a scholarly way." It is even more astonishing that an editor would not demand that the passage, which makes light of historical scholarship done aright, be excised. It seems highly unlikely that Boyd would have approved of anyone attempting to use that passage as evidence of a liaison.

The debate continues today, Wallach notes, even though "Fawn Brodie was right." She appeals to the DNA evidence and the experts' response to it.[125] As is well known to anyone familiar with the DNA evidence (see chapter 5), it nowise implicates Jefferson as the father of any of Sally Hemings's children.

Brodie has not been and will never be vindicated—at least, not in the minds of scholars who affirm that history ought to be evidence based, not conjectural. Why? Even if incontrovertible evidence does someday surface to implicate Jefferson in a relationship with Hemings, it will not show Brodie to be a prophet. Drawing the right conclusions for all the wrong reasons might indicate, as Plato states in *Meno*,[126] a certain god-given inspiration, but it betrays no knowledge and, thus, is worth about as much evidence to a serious scholar as is Boyd's unscholarly feeling.

CHAPTER 2

# CONTROLLING THE DISCOURSE

### Cutting Down Jefferson to Size

> Symbolically, it's tremendously important for people—
> as a way of inclusion. Nathan Huggins said that the
> Sally Hemings' story was a way of establishing black
> people's birthright to America. If you look at the flip
> side of it, rejecting the story is a part of the rejection
> of black people's birthright and claims to America. So
> people invest a lot in the topic and the subject.
>
> —ANNETTE GORDON-REED,
> PBS *FRONTLINE* INTERVIEW

Gordon-Reed, in her books *Thomas Jefferson and Sally Hemings* and *The Hemingses of Monticello*, follows in the footsteps of Fawn Brodie. Both argue for a lengthy, mutually fulfilling relationship between Jefferson and Hemings. Each accuses the great Jeffersonian scholars of bias; each makes tendentious use of psychological generalizations; each has a selective approach to historical data; and each tends to react to resistance to their work as vindication of it. Brodie's trump card seems to be gender. The great Jeffersonian scholars, all males, have failed to accommodate feeling, nuance, and metaphor in their assessment of Jefferson. Gordon-Reed's trump card is unquestionably race. The great Jeffersonian scholars, all white, have refused to accept the "testimony" of a black slave, Madison Hemings, at face value. Still, for all she owes Brodie, Gordon-Reed mentions her just as one scholar among many in a list of revisionists. For example, in *Understanding Thomas Jefferson* E. M. Halliday, long-

time senior editor of American Heritage, states that Gordon-Reed's work—
there is reference only to Gordon-Reed's first book since Halliday's book
was published in 2001—merely reinforces that of Brodie.

> Brodie had written the most original Jefferson biography of the century.
> She, more than anyone else, cleared away the cloud of ignorance, obfus-
> cation, and denial that had enveloped the story of Jefferson's long liaison
> with Sally Hemings, bringing into the light the convincing evidence that
> supported its validity. Although it took nearly a quarter of a century of
> debate, plus the hugely reinforcing impact of Annette Gordon-Reed's
> *Thomas Jefferson and Sally Hemings: An American Controversy* and,
> finally, the DNA results in 1998 to vindicate Brodie in the eyes of most
> of the academic community, the fact is that she already had presented all
> the basic points of evidence needed to justify belief in the liaison. But
> beyond that, Brodie's biography is a complete study of Jefferson's career
> in all its aspect, thoroughly researched, well written, and meticulously
> documented. It deserves to be considered as one of the very best single-
> volume biographies of Jefferson ever written.[1]

Moreover, Gordon-Reed is critical of Brodie's approach. Although she
lauds Brodie for disclosure of details that had never been disclosed and for
raising issues that had never been raised, she chides Brodie for overstating her
case by psychologizing history—a crime of which she too, I show, is guilty.[2]

In this chapter, I begin with Gordon-Reed's *Thomas Jefferson and
Sally Hemings*, whose thesis is modest—to show that a liaison between
Jefferson and Hemings was not impossible. I then turn to her award-
winning *The Hemingses of Monticello*. Here Gordon-Reed sheds her
modesty and aims to show not only that the two had a liaison, but, like
Brodie, that it was a relationship of mutual love. She draws plentifully
from the published testimony of Madison Hemings in 1873 to drive her
reconstruction of the liaison and merely overpasses the numerous difficulties with that testimony.[3] The issue of race uncomfortably drives both
works. The historical issue of the truth or untruth of an actual liaison takes
second spot to the sociological issue of giving blacks a sense of legitimacy
concerning the founding of the American nation.

## IT IS NOT IMPOSSIBLE THAT . . .

Gordon-Reed in *Thomas Jefferson and Sally Hemings: An American Controversy* gives us a title that leads readers to believe in the existence of a relationship between the two—one that was more than master and slave. Just linking the two names in the title is radical—as Sally Hemings's name almost never appears in any of Jefferson's writings—and inclusion of *controversy* strongly suggests scandal of some sort.

Yet Gordon-Reed, trained in law, is not out to demonstrate that Jefferson and Sally Hemings did have a liaison in this book but to offer "a critique of the defense that has been mounted to counter the notion of a Jefferson-Hemings liaison."[4] Thus, her leitmotif is an attack on the presumed "impossibility" of a liaison, because of Jefferson's lofty character and Hemings's lowly status. "In order to maintain the claim of impossibility, or even to discuss the matter in those terms, one has to make Thomas Jefferson so high as to have been something more than human and one has to make Sally Hemings so low as to have been something less than human." The suggestion here already in this early book is that scholars have made out Jefferson to be something more than a human and Hemings less than a human.

The difficulty is not so much what amounts to proof, but rather "controlling public impressions of the amount and the nature of the evidence."[5] Nonetheless, in her roundabout critique of the received view, Gordon-Reed does offer some insight into the nature of "proof" by giving an analogy to shed light on how "proof" differs from "evidence." Evidence can be likened to bricks and proof can be likened to the wall comprising them. "Some scholars and commentators, who almost invariably approach the subject of Thomas Jefferson and Sally Hemings in a defensive posture," she writes, "have demanded that every brick of evidence that the two might have had a relationship amount to its own individual wall of proof."

What precisely the brick-wall analogy purports to show is unsettled. However, the analogy is misleading in at least two respects.

First, evidence and proof are qualitatively different: the former admits of degrees, while the latter does not. Deductive arguments are proofs.

When the premises of a deductive argument are true, the conclusion must be true, because the conclusion never oversteps the bounds of the premises. Inductive arguments, in contrast, are assessed by evidence and admit of degrees of strength. The conclusion always oversteps the bounds of the premises. Arguing historically for a liaison or its lack is merely a matter of evidence; proof factors in nowise. One cannot prove, for instance, that a liaison occurred. Even the most inflexible historical evidence for the truth of a claim can be vitiated, if incompatible evidence shows up that gives strong evidence of the falsity of the claim. Thus, the existence of a liaison must be determined inductively by amount and relevancy of evidence garnered. Moreover, all the relevant evidence must be considered and weighed. Evidence incompatible with one's claim cannot simply be ignored. To ignore incompatible evidence is to have a selective approach to evidence and a biased approach to historical scholarship.

Second, to speak of every brick as an "individual wall of proof" is unavailing. What does Gordon-Reed mean by that? A discerning reader will ask for a clarifying explication of the wishy-washy claim. The clarifying explication, once given, makes superfluous the brick-wall analogy in the first place.

Gordon-Reed is clear about one thing: Her enterprise is one of showing that a liaison is possible—not that one occurred. She says plausibly, "The evidence must be considered as a whole before a realistic and fair assessment of the possible truth of this story can be made."[6] Her thesis, then, is a valuable contribution to the literature, only if the critics she is addressing—and she is generally silent about who they are—have literally and unquestionably argued for the impossibility of such a liaison. No one, I suspect, would be inclined to rule out the literal possibility of a liaison, because the issue is empirical, not a priori, and historians are in the empirical business. New evidence is always a possibility and new evidence can readily make a conclusion that is strongly supported by evidence a conclusion that is weakly supported by evidence.

Consider the following argument for claim *c*: *All the US pennies in my pocket are made of copper.*

(1) All the US pennies in my pocket, on close inspection, seem to be made of copper.

(2) So, all the US pennies in my pocket are made of copper.

The framer of this argument for *c* would seem to be on firm inductive grounds, assuming the "close inspection" involves, say, having tested the surface of each penny for the existence of copper and having found, after testing, each surface to be of copper.

Now assume a friend, later in the day, relates to the framer of the penny argument the disquieting fact that all US pennies minted after 1982 are over 95 percent zinc, with merely a coating of copper, while all those created prior to 1983 are 95 percent copper.[7] Unnerved by the news that *c* might be false, the man checks the pennies in his pocket and notices that five of the seven were minted post-1982. With the introduction of that new evidence, he is now committed to the following inductive argument.

(1) All the US pennies in my pocket, on close inspection, seem to be made of copper.

(2) Some of the pennies in my pocket were minted post-1982.

(3) So, *not* all the US pennies in my pocket are made of copper.

A seemingly inductively cogent argument for *c*, *All the US pennies in my pocket are made of copper*, has instantly become a deductively sound argument for ~*c*, *Not all the US pennies in my pocket are made of copper*.

The point of the illustration is to show that additional evidence can always make what was taken to be a cogent (that is, well-supported inductive) argument at one time an uncogent (that is, bad inductive) argument at another time. First-rate historians, I suspect, are amply aware of that and, thus, no first-rate historian would go out on a limb and argue that some event is categorically impossible. That just makes no sense, so one must be charitable. Historians who argue, for instance, that a liaison with Hemings would have been impossible because of Jefferson's character are merely asserting that a liaison is extraordinarily improbable.

What precisely does it mean to say that some event is *possible*? When one adds the modality of possibility to a standard declarative sentence, one weakens the assertion tremendously. Consider two claims:

(1)  Jefferson had a liaison with Sally Hemings.
(2)  It is possible that Jefferson had a liaison with Sally Hemings.

Claim 1 is making a substantive assertion that requires substantial relevant evidence. By adding the modality of possibility to it, as in claim 2, one weakens greatly the assertion. In effect, claim 2 asserts that a liaison is not an impossible state of affairs—namely, that there is no contradiction in asserting it—and that is to assert next to nothing. Thus, possibility claims, in effect, are vacuous, as they make no demands on reality other than what is asserted must not be an impossible (i.e., logically impossible) state of affairs.

To grasp why, let us consider the following sentences—claims 2 through 5.

(2)  It is possible that Jefferson had a liaison with Sally Hemings.
(3)  It is possible that Jefferson had a liaison with his daughter Martha.
(4)  It is possible that Jefferson had a liaison with his nephew Peter Carr.
(5)  It is possible that Jefferson had a liaison with one of his books.

Given our current knowledge of Jefferson's history, we are in no position to say claim 2 is false—there is, as we shall see in chapter 5, DNA evidence consistent with it—yet we are in no position to say claims 3 through 5 are false, either. Moreover, there is "evidence" for each. Jefferson often spoke of his love for his daughter Martha in letters. Brodie, recall, made much of the unconscious seducing between the two in letters. How do we *know* that the seducing was never consummated? Perhaps key letters between the two were destroyed. Moreover, it is well-documented that Jefferson was especially fond of his nephew Peter Carr. Did his fondness morph into sexual activity? He was, given the testimony of Brodie, a highly libidinal man who could not suppress his sexuality. Finally, since Jefferson wrote to John Adams (June 10, 1815), "I cannot live without books" and had, throughout his life, two extraordinary collections of them, one could conclude that he had an especially perverse attraction for paper, bounded by leather. That claim is silly, but it is not impossible.

Because they assert little, in common parlance possibility claims are seldom very significant and seldom insightful. They are significant only in certain cases: for example, when a certain state of affairs is, for whatever reason, construed as impossible—literally, *not* logically impossible—and when evidence for a claim is wanting or ambiguous. First, consider the possibility claim *a*, *Moderate amounts of alcohol can contribute to enhanced physical health*. That claim is significant only because it has been taken as gospel for years that consumption of alcohol in any amount is deleterious. Second, consider the claims *p* and *g* respectively: *The nearest planet to Earth has life-forms on it* and *Consumption of raw garlic reduces blood pressure*. Evidence for *p* is lacking; evidence for *g* is ambiguous. Thus, it is legitimate to express both claims as possibility claims to show our uncertainty concerning their veracity. The evidence for a liaison between Jefferson and Hemings is both very scant and, at best, ambiguous, thus the modality of possibility is justified. The statement *Jefferson had a liaison with Hemings*, lacking unambiguous evidence, is unjustified. The statement *Jefferson could have had a liaison with Hemings*, given the lack of unambiguous evidence, is justified, though perhaps vacuous.

Yet one might object, the statement *Jefferson did not have a liaison with Hemings* is also unjustified, as it, too, lacks unambiguous evidence. That goes without saying. As Gordon-Reed admits, the burden of proof is on those who make the positive claim, the "proponents of a Jefferson-Hemings liaison," and that is how it should be. In that, stating *Jefferson had a liaison with Sally Hemings* is like claiming *Santa Claus exists*; *Aliens visit Kalamazoo, Michigan, every 777 years*; and *Submicroscopic strings are what ultimately bind together all cosmic phenomena*. Those who make existential claims, lacking evidence, must provide at some point substantive and relevant evidence for those claims. Overall, absence of evidence cannot be taken as evidence of absence; however, it is even more absurd to take it, as does Brodie in *Thomas Jefferson* and as does Gordon-Reed in her later book *The Hemingses of Monticello* as evidence of existence.

Both assert flatly that lack of direct evidence of intimacy between the two
is a mystery.

At day's end, Gordon-Reed admits to agnosticism concerning a
liaison. "I cannot say that I definitely believe the story is true, but I can
say that I believe that it is not the open-and-shut case that those bent on
'defending' Thomas Jefferson at all costs would have the public think."[8]
Given Gordon-Reed's express agnosticism and the relative vacuity of her
thesis, one must question the significance of the book and its contribution
to the secondary literature.

## "A MAJOR SHIFT"

Gordon-Reed begins chapter 13 of *The Hemingses of Monticello*, written
eleven years after *Thomas Jefferson and Sally Hemings*, with a "major
shift" in the relations between the Hemingses and Jeffersons. Following
Brodie nearly to the letter, she asserts that at some point in their trip
to France Sally became Jefferson's "concubine," though there is "no
elaboration on how that happened or exactly when." The only marker
of that supposed shift is the 1790 birth of the infamous and elusive Tom
Hemings. Allegedly, the father was Jefferson and the conception likely
occurred while the two were still in France—Jefferson, from 1785 to 1789;
Hemings, from 1787 to 1789.

It is difficult to know precisely what happened, Gordon-Reed says, as any
letters between Jefferson and Hemings, as well as any letters with the name of
Sally in them, are "missing."[9] She asks, "How is it possible to get at the nature
of a relationship between a man and a woman like Jefferson and Hemings
when neither party specifically writes or speaks to others about that relationship or their feelings?"[10] She is unwilling to consider the obvious: Lack of
verbal or written testimony is readily explicated by the nonexistence of a relationship. The account of Madison Hemings, it seems, is unshakeable. Lack of
evidence notwithstanding, she is determined to get at the nature of their liaison.

Gordon-Reed offers "a mere glance" of the circumstances that obtained
at L'Hôtel de Langeac, where Jefferson stayed when he arrived in France in

1785, and where Gordon-Reed assumes Hemings stayed when she arrived in France in 1787. It is "a mere glance," I suppose, because we know next to nothing of who Sally was, let alone what Sally did or where she stayed in her twenty-six months in France. We do know that Jefferson's daughters stayed at the convent Abbaye Royale de Panthemont. Gordon-Reed assumes as fact that Hemings did not go with them but stayed with Jefferson at the hotel. That critical assumption opens up a cornucopia of erotic possibilities for her.[11] Yet given that Hemings accompanied Jefferson's daughter Maria on the boat to England and was considered Maria's attendant, it is likely that Hemings would have gone with Jefferson's daughters to the convent to attend to Maria's and perhaps Martha's needs.[12] Still, even if she did stay at L'Hôtel de Langeac with Jefferson, there would have been little opportunity for a liaison, as the residence was "flowing over with visitors, guests, tutors, and servants."[13] There were three bedrooms—one used by Jefferson, another by William Short (Jefferson's secretary), and the third for guests—and a large oval office. Where would Hemings have stayed? The inconvenient fact of the cramped circumstances is not addressed by Gordon-Reed.

Staying with Hemings, Gordon-Reed goes on to say, the forty-seven-year-old Jefferson tried to win over the sixteen-year-old woman. She does not entertain the possibilities of Hemings trying to seduce Jefferson, of mutual seduction, or of nothing happening. Note also that Sally was fourteen when she arrived in France with Maria. Why did Jefferson wait until just before he was slated to return to the United States to seduce Hemings?

The story continues. Once pregnant with Jefferson's child, Hemings threatens to remain in France, where she will be free. Here, once again, she follows the lead of Fawn Brodie, who takes the newspaper account of Madison Hemings at face value. Hemings negotiates with Jefferson. She agrees to return with him on the condition that he frees her children upon the age of twenty-one. What *children*? Either Jefferson is planning to have several children with Hemings or the two are preparing for any contingencies of a long-term sexual relationship.

Jefferson and Hemings return to America and Sally is pregnant with Jefferson's child, to be named "Tom." I iterate some of the difficulties in assuming Sally Hemings's pregnancy and the existence of the mysterious

Tom Hemings. James Callender, who first mentioned the boy in 1802, wrote of Tom as being ten or twelve years old and being a sable resemblance to Jefferson. Jefferson makes no mention of the boy in his *Farm Book*, in which he lists all of Sally's children. The first mention of any child by Sally in the book is in 1795, not 1789. Madison Hemings, we recall, wrote that Tom Hemings did not live long. Moreover, if pregnant on her return to Virginia, Tom Hemings would have been born sometime early in 1790 and the two, amorously linked, would have no more children for about six years, for the remaining six children were born between 1795 and 1808. Why such a long respite after the supposed first child? As historian and Virginia native Virginius Dabney has noted, the historians Winthrop Jordan, Garry Wills, Merrill Peterson, James Bear, and Douglass Adair have concluded that Tom Hemings, conveniently named, was merely "another figment of calumniatory James Callender's fertile imagination" in his quest to humiliate the president.[14] That conclusion is plausible.

Note, at this point, how far Gordon-Reed has gone on mere assumption—Hemings stayed with Jefferson at the hotel in France; Jefferson seduced Hemings; Hemings became pregnant; a sixteen-year-old [presumably illiterate] slave negotiated with the ambassador to France; the child resulting from that pregnancy was named Tom, etc.—for failure to address difficulties with sixty-eight-year-old Madison Hemings's "testimony," which is hearsay, is to go on assumption. It is astonishing that Gordon-Reed does not address the numerous concerns of critics like Virginius Dabney, Cynthia Burton, and the many other scholars who have contributed articles to the Thomas Jefferson Heritage Society's *The Jefferson-Hemings Myth*—and explain them within the confines of her hypothesis. That is a concern of considerable size—symptomatic, as it were, of her view of how history is to be done. Gordon-Reed does not once mention the works of either Dabney or Burton in her most recent book, even though she acknowledges in her earlier book that the burden of proof is on the one making the case of paternity. Nonetheless, she ought to address the leading literature of the time, explain away claims to the contrary, and argue that her view is the most probable, given all the available relevant evidence. That is how proper history is done. Dabney does that. So too do Burton, Eyler Robert

Coates Sr.,[15] and lawyers Richard Dixon[16] and William G. Hyland Jr. Moreover, Gordon-Reed does not address problems with her reconstruction, and failure to address problems is another practice eschewed by all first-tier scholars. Historical reconstructions are never airtight, and responsible scholars willfully point out defects in their own work to be addressed later, perhaps by other scholars.

In science, when a new theory tries to replace the received view—for example, when the relativity essayed to supplant Newtonian dynamics— adherents of the new theory need to show why it is preferable to the old. The new theory should at least explain all that the previous theory explained. It helps also if it is simpler, more fruitful, and consistent with significant and empirically bolstered claims of other sciences of the day. For instance, relativity theory showed its superiority to Newtonian dynamics by its greater explanatory power and fruitfulness. It explained everything that Isaac Newton's theory explained, and more—for instance, time dilation and length contraction as well as a slight anomaly in the orbit of Mercury.[17]

Gordon-Reed, in *The Hemingses of Monticello*, makes no effort to explain why her hypothesis, that there was a mutually fulfilling liaison between Jefferson and Sally Hemings, is preferable to what was then the received view: the nonexistence of a liaison. She cold-shoulders hypotheses inconsistent with her view, instead of explaining them away.

## MOUNTING ANECDOTAL EVIDENCE

Upon the return of the "lovers" to America, Gordon-Reed gives a laundry list of anecdotes about the couple. They are too numerous and, for the most part, too far-fetched to address. Here I also admit freely to a sort of distaste for critical engagement with such dreamy, quixotic speculating. Nonetheless, when historians and textbooks on history treat the putative "liaison" as fact and when more college students know Jefferson as the father of Hemings's children than they do Jefferson as the author of the Declaration of Independence, critical engagement is needed to set the record straight; hence the motivation for this undertaking.

In *The Hemingses of Monticello*, never has one done so much from so little, it might be said. Historical reconstruction, as chapters 13 through 16 show, is reducible to creative fiction masquerading as history. Gordon-Reed's "reconstruction" is fraught with outlandish stories. No longer is she arguing, as she did in her first book, that p *is possible—Jefferson could have had a liaison with Hemings*—a minimal and perhaps vacuous assertion; she has gone on in her second book to give *p*, without the modality of possibility, a life of its own—*Jefferson did have a liaison with Hemings*. Possibility has insidiously morphed into fact. She speaks, for illustration, in chapter 16, of the pain Hemings must have felt on being both slave to and lover of Jefferson: "She would appear a less sympathetic version of the lead character in the opera *Aria*, who sings an impassioned and heartrending aria about the pain of being in thrall to a man who was her lover *and* also the determining enemy of her own people." At most times, her outlandish "deconstructing" is no better than that of Brodie. Again, Gordon-Reed writes of a letter from Jefferson's granddaughter Ellen Wayles Randolph Coolidge to her husband James Coolidge (October 24, 1858). Writes Ellen, "No female domestic ever entered his chambers except at hours when he was known not to be there and none could have entered without being exposed to public gaze." Gordon-Reed in the manner of Brodie states, "What she wanted to assert, but could not do so explicitly, was, *The woman everyone is talking about, Sally Hemings, was my grandfather's chambermaid, but she never went into his room when he was there, and if she did everyone would have seen her* [Hemings]."

Gordon-Reed has much to say about the nature of the liaison between Jefferson and Hemings, a figure, I repeat, about whom almost next to nothing is known. Following Madison Hemings's testimony, she goes on to weave a fanciful account of the probable nature of their relationship over the years. In doing so, she creates a chimerical narrative, as misleading as it is delusory, concerning the probable course of events between Jefferson and Hemings, insofar as she can reconstruct them.

What is the problem with that? Is not historical reconstruction in some sense an imaginative discipline? Does not imagination allow for possible avenues of historical research?

Historical reconstruction does allow for *some* creativity and imagination. However, the problem is that Gordon-Reed habitually presents speculation as historical fact. In effect, we are told by Gordon-Reed that a series of events unfolded—say, from α to ω—and that each event is probable, given the occurrence of the event prior to it. Let us arbitrarily and most generously assign a probability of 0.75 to event α—the occurrence of a liaison [$p$ (α) = 0.75]—as well as a probability of 0.75 to every event thereafter, conditioned on the prior occurrence of the event before it [e.g., $p$ (β/α) = 0.75]. Thus, we come up with the following sequence: [$p$ (α) = 0.75] & [$p$ (β/α) = 0.75] & [$p$ (γ/β) = 0.75] & . . . & [$p$ (ω/ψ) = 0.75]. Doing the math, as it were, we see quickly that the probability of the whole sequence of events is close to zero. Thus, the probability that the sequence of events unfolded precisely in the manner Gordon-Reed suggests it had unfolded is almost zero.

If that in itself is not devastating, one can question whether any of the reconstructive *steps* of Gordon-Reed can be said to be probable, given the truth of the event assumed prior to it. I suspect that the probability of a liaison between the two—the triggering event α (the existence of a sexual relationship)—is in the first place quite low and that, by itself, makes the whole sequence extraordinarily improbable. It is bewildering that her reconstructive "history" is taken so seriously by prominent historians—for example, Onuf, Burstein, Freeman, and Bernstein.

Overall, Gordon-Reed's preference for fabulizing in the chapters relating to the presumed liaison makes it impossible to know what to take seriously of the rest of the book. That is unfortunate, because it might have important insights into the Hemings family.

## GENERAL CRITIQUE OF GORDON-REED'S WORK

### Fitting an Argument in a Preexisting Frame

In a review of *The Hemingses of Monticello*, prominent American historian Eric Foner lauds Gordon-Reed's admission that too little is known of James

Hemings, Sally's brother, to speculate on why he, when freed by Jefferson after returning from France, took his own life. From scant evidence of James's life, it is scholarly irresponsible to propose speculation as fact. Gordon-Reed wisely suspends judgment.

Yet when it comes to Jefferson and Sally Hemings, Gordon-Reed has much to say about the inner dimension of Jefferson's life. Scant evidence of Sally's life leads to a cornucopia of details of the lives and thoughts of the two—Jefferson especially. Foner says, "Gordon-Reed is determined to prove that theirs was a consensual relationship based on love."[18] In short, she begins the book with the conclusion she wants to "prove" and then sifts through historical documents to find evidence for that conclusion.

> Sometimes even the most skilled researcher comes up empty. At that point, the better part of valor may be simply to state that a question is unanswerable. Gordon-Reed's portrait of an enduring romance between Hemings and Jefferson is one possible reading of the limited evidence. Others are equally plausible. Gordon-Reed, however, refuses to acknowledge this possibility. She sets up a series of straw men and proceeds to demolish them—those who believe that in the context of slavery, love between black and white people was impossible; that black female sexuality was "inherently degraded" and thus Jefferson could not have had genuine feelings for Hemings; that any black woman who consented to sex with a white man during slavery was a "traitor" to her people. She cites no current historians who hold these views, but is adamant in criticizing anyone who, given the vast gap in age (thirty years) and power between them, views the Jefferson-Hemings connection as sexual exploitation.

Engaging in a selective approach to culling evidence is, of course, biased and brash, and I leave it to discerning readers to judge its ethical status. Beginning with a dubious premise—the existence of a liaison between Jefferson and Hemings—Gordon-Reed fills in countless details of that liaison, some of which are scandalously and unremorsefully ad hoc. For instance, in trying to explicate why Jefferson did not often bring Hemings to Washington while he was president, she writes, "Living with her anyplace other than Monticello would have caused all sorts of complications, not the least of them cute babies running around who looked just like him."[19] In short, she has a preexisting frame and she must create a picture of Jefferson that neatly fits the frame, irrespective of the final likeness.

That is a practice that Jefferson himself abhorred. For instance, in a letter to John Adams (June 11, 1812), he excoriated the French missionary Joseph-François Lafitau for his "observations" concerning American Indians.

> Lafitau had in his head a preconcieved [*sic*] theory on the mythology, manners, institutions and government of the antient [*sic*] nations of Europe, Asia, and Africa, and seems to have entered on those of America only to fit them into the same frame, and to draw from them a confirmation of this general theory. He keeps up a perpetual parallel, in all those articles, between the Indians of America, and the antients [*sic*] of the other quarters of the globe. He selects therefore all the facts, and adopts all the falsehoods which favor his theory, and very gravely retails [*sic*] such absurdities as zeal for a theory could anyone swallow.

Jefferson's critique of Lafitau's perspective on American Indians seems to fit neatly Gordon-Reed's approach to the alleged Jefferson-Hemings relationship.

In *The Hemingses of Monticello*, Gordon-Reed's "evidence" is contaminated, as she handles the possibility of a liaison as probability and, often, even as fact, in spite of a paucity of evidence. Because she treats speculation as fact, it is difficult to say what, from the research she clearly has done, is salvageable. An unfortunate consequence of following such an approach to history, I repeat, is that it throws into doubt the validity of her other work. Analogously, when one finds mold in a bowl of chili, one seldom tries to remove the mold and salvage the chili. Mold has an insidious way of creeping into other parts of the dish. The wisest plan is to throw out the chili.

Despite following a questionable approach to history in her research methods, Gordon-Reed had the impudence to state in a *New York Times* interview in 1998, "A more disciplined, rigorous and less prejudiced application of historical method [by prior white historians] could have yielded the same answer [as did the DNA results]."[20] Yet the DNA results, she fails to add, have yielded nothing definitive—nothing on which one can hang one's hat.

## Gordon-Reed's "Racistism"

The prefaces to both of her books, as they relate to Jefferson and Hemings, show why Gordon-Reed employs such a selective and fanciful approach to history. History texts have ignored black figures and, when they have not, they have marginalized or misrepresented them. She writes, "In the beginning, blacks were something less than human, and then over the years, some of them changed."[21] In contrast, "there never was a time when whites were not bright, curious, and attractive beings." She is not shy about letting her readers know that she is not merely an historian, but a black historian with an agenda to set the record straight on blacks as they have historically been portrayed.

There is nothing necessarily wrong with one's work being agenda driven. In fact, it seems hard to imagine that anyone can be highly motivated to pursue research without some agenda. Gordon-Reed's agenda even seems, in some sense, to be laudable. Blacks *have* been historically marginalized and misrepresented, and she is to be commended for recognizing those facts and trying to do something about them.

Yet Gordon-Reed's leitmotif of racism in history seems to preclude objectivity. In a PBS interview after publication of *Thomas Jefferson and Sally Hemings*, Gordon-Reed says unabashedly of the Jefferson-Hemings liaison:

> Symbolically, it's tremendously important for people—as a way of inclusion. Nathan Huggins said that the Sally Hemings' story was a way of establishing black people's birthright to America. If you look at the flip side of it, rejecting the story is a part of the rejection of black people's birthright and claims to America. So people invest a lot in the topic and the subject.[22]

The response here is troublesome, as it suggests that what motivates her research—I include her among "people," as she especially has a large investment in the topic—is social change, not historical accuracy. There is much to be gained by blacks in America in corroborating Callender's remarks, she believes, however vicious and hate-filled they might have been toward Thomas Jefferson. Jefferson seems to be a convenient sacrificial lamb for the cause of social change.

Additional evidence that Gordon-Reed has social change and not truth as her objective also comes out in her 2000 essay "Engaging Jefferson." She says, "The rejection of the Sally Hemings story can be seen as a denial of black ties to the founding of the nation and a rejection of black birthright claims."[23] Both claims are empty. They suggest that a link to Jefferson's blood gives African Americans legitimacy—namely that blacks need some link to the founding of the nation to be construed legitimate American citizens. Blacks do not need Jefferson's blood for legitimacy any more than American citizens of Eastern descent need Jefferson's blood for legitimacy. Yet the only "evidence" she cites for a liaison comprises the DNA tests, which are horribly inconclusive, and the black oral tradition—and anyone who questions that tradition is racially insensitive.

As an illustration for her seeming disregard for historical accuracy, I return to the issue of the doubtfulness of Madison Hemings's account.[24] Madison could readily have had a self-aggrandizing agenda. Psychological studies indicate that humans tend to remember selectively. They also remember things in a manner consistent with the image they have framed of themselves, which is generally not negative (e.g., the Forer effect). Moreover, there is a high likelihood of errors slipping into stories that are told and retold over decades. Madison Hemings was sixty-eight at the time of the newspaper story, and the account indeed contained several errors— for instance, Jefferson's dislike of farming. Furthermore, there is the added problem of knowing how much to attribute to Madison Hemings and how much to attribute to the editor Samuel Wetmore, who had both personal and political motivations for an anti-Jefferson story.[25] In addition, "there is no evidence of an oral tradition corroborating the assertions attributed to Madison Hemings which antedates the publication of the 1873 Pike County *Republican* story."[26] Other families of Hemings's descendants have an oral tradition in which an uncle of Jefferson is the father, not Jefferson himself. Given those facts, it is historically irresponsible for Gordon-Reed to dis-acknowledge the difficulties with Madison Hemings's account and not to engage in a critical analysis of works, like Dabney's and Burton's, that list numerous difficulties.

Uncritical acceptance of Madison Hemings's testimony drives *The*

*Hemingses of Monticello*. That is the book's undoing. Yet Sally Hemings left behind no evidence of a liaison. It is the same with her children, other than Madison. Besides the account of Madison, Gordon-Reed gives no evidence other than nonevidence—that is, the historical marginalization of blacks in America by white Jeffersonian scholars with a racist agenda. Is it that a black man, because he has been marginalized, is incapable of lying? Marginalization, if anything, is a good reason for lying. Madison would have had much to gain by claiming to be a son of Jefferson—not the least of which was legitimacy in the eyes of others.[27]

Moreover, in accepting Madison Hemings's testimony at face value, we have to reject the testimonies of numerous other credible witnesses— of which Jefferson is one—who state categorically that Jefferson did not have a relationship with Hemings or could not have had a relationship with Hemings. Failure to weigh Madison Hemings's account, which is hearsay, against the testimonies of those persons on behalf of Jefferson, who happen to be white (e.g., Monticello overseer Edmund Bacon, Jefferson's daughter Martha, his grandchildren, and numerous others who knew Jefferson intimately) is biased scholarship—a point recognized by Jefferson biographer Dumas Malone. He states, "At all events, [Sally's claim] must be weighed against the testimony of Jefferson's grandchildren, his categorical denial of the alleged liaison, and his own character."[28] It is not, as Gordon-Reed has made it out to be, a white-versus-black issue. It is an issue of rationally assessing data, and rational assessment is blind to skin color. Gordon-Reed's work could be deemed, I dare say, racist or, perhaps more fittingly, *racistist*—that is, racially driven in a nonhateful manner.

Gordon-Reed's racistism infects her work to such an extent that it becomes tedious. Others who dismiss or ignore her work, the suggestion is, are racist.[29] Eric Foner writes of the tedium of Gordon-Reed's obsession with race:

> As a black female scholar, Gordon-Reed is undoubtedly more sensitive than many other academics to the subtleties of language regarding race. But to question the likelihood of a long-term romantic attachment between Jefferson and Hemings is hardly to collaborate in what she calls "the erasure of individual black lives" from history. Gordon-Reed even

suggests that "opponents of racism" who emphasize the prevalence of rape in the Old South occupy "common ground" with racists who despise black women, because both see sex with female slaves as "degraded." This, quite simply, is outrageous.[30]

David Mayer writes that a "McCarthy-like inquisition" ready to pounce on anyone who challenges the liaison currently exists in Jefferson scholarship. Anyone challenging the liaison is "racially 'insensitive'" or "racist."[31]

Online reviews of Gordon-Reed's book iterate the point that the themes of racism and of the evils of slavery oppress readers. Writes one: "I . . . felt manipulated while reading. I do not need to be reminded over and over again about how morally wrong, cruel and degrading slavery was—I possessed this opinion long before I picked up this book." Writes a second: "The author constantly brought up the fact that Sally Hemings and her family were 'human chattel,' but that they were human beings as worthwhile as any other human being. Clearly this is true, and mentioning it once or twice wouldn't be a problem, but it came up time and time again." Writes a third: "Once I agree with that sentiment [the evils of slavery] and espouse it wholeheartedly, I don't need to be beat over the head with it again and again. No, Jefferson was not a perfect man, and anyone who immortalizes him as such is flat-out wrong. But many, many people had slaves during his time, and the fact that he did have slaves does not immediately put him into the 'shit pile' either. There is a middle ground between saint and ass, I promise." A fourth writes: "i know that slavery was bad. all sane people know it. anybody who would read a book like this knows it. the fact that the author could not help adding little lectures to us, struck me as, well, a bit immature. that such a flawed book won both the pulitzer prize and the national book award is just plain silly. it seems topic matter triumphs over actual artistic merit these days."[32] I could go on, for there are a large number of other reviews that echo the point that the book has a racial, not a historical, agenda.[33]

Gordon-Reed's pressing sociological agenda behind *The Hemingses of Monticello* suffocates readers. She writes that all white historians prior to her work have treated black persons as "lumps of clay to be fashioned and molded into whatever image the given historian feels is necessary in order to make his point."[34] That claim is unsustainable, historically implausible, and racist. It is one thing to note and clear up inaccuracies in prior research, which perhaps has marginalized blacks. It is another to malign first-rank scholars, like Malone and Peterson, who have demonstrated their scholarly integrity over the years. One wonders why more critics have not taken her to task for hurling racial stones at others. There is fear of being labeled "racist" in doing so. Gordon-Reed, then, uses race to her advantage. It is sad when scholarship is driven more by controversy and fear than by concern for truth and accuracy.

## Controlling the Discourse

If the scholars about whom Gordon-Reed has been critical, she asserts in her first book, *Thomas Jefferson and Sally Hemings*, would have merely said, "I don't believe that Thomas Jefferson and Sally Hemings had a relationship . . . [b]ut there is no proof one way or another," then "that would have been acceptable."[35] The problem is that scholars go the extra step and add, "Now let me tell you why the story cannot be true."

Nonetheless, Gordon-Reed is also troubled by scholarly neglect of the liaison in her early book. "It is my belief that those who are considered Jefferson scholars have never made a serious and objective attempt to get at the truth of [the Jefferson-Hemings] matter."[36] Why have scholars tended to neglect the Jefferson-Hemings chapter of Jefferson's life?

Gordon-Reed, like Brodie, astonishingly disacknowledges that lack of proof "one way or another" is itself sufficient explanation for scholarly neglect. For Brodie, scholarly neglect is a sign that the evidence is subtle, often psychological, and that scholars, dreading the fall of their hero, have had no wish to disclose the deep subtleties and see their hero fall. Yet for Gordon-Reed in *Thomas Jefferson and Sally Hemings*, the evidence is not subtle; it is wanting, as "there is no proof one way or another." Nonetheless, for her, scholarly neglect is a sign that scholars refuse to consider even the possibility of a liaison. Yet is not absence of evidence for some claim itself sufficient reason for scholarly neglect of it? Scholarship is, after all, about evidence. One can concoct multiple billions of possibility claims that are consistent with current historical knowledge. For instance, one online reviewer writes perhaps seriously of a speculative opportunity Gordon-Reed has missed:

> For all the speculation that was included [in *The Hemingses of Monticello*] there was some surprising speculation missing. One of Sally's older brothers [James] who was also in Paris, trained to be chef, was a good looking man who had great friendships and "fallings out" with other men never married, never any hint of a relationship with a woman, was wracked with personal issues when emancipated—he was a talented but troubled drama queen who sadly killed himself. For any reader this screams the question, was he gay? It could have lead [*sic*] to a fresh avenue of exploration, exploring the impact of homosexuality. Yet the author stubbornly avoids this. Given one of the biggest issues of the book is the free white-defined members of Jefferson's family refusal to mention or talk about the taboo of Sally's enduring relationship with Jefferson, to avoid speculating about someone's sexuality almost seems like repeating the mistake of deliberate omission.[37]

The overwhelming majority of possibility claims concerning any noteworthy historical figure are not worth pursuing. Evidence must factor into responsible research. Otherwise, anything goes.

Yet for Gordon-Reed, the issue is one of control or be controlled. Most Jeffersonian scholars, she asserts, have decided beforehand that the story of a liaison was false. She concludes, "The goal has been . . . to restrict knowledge as a way of controlling the allowable discourse on this subject."[38]

Nonetheless, is not control in some sense an important scholarly necessity? Science, for instance, has controls and those controls exist for good reasons. History too has controls. That is why the peer-review process is critical: It is intended to weed out flimsy scholarship; it requires historians to keep up with and build upon current research; it awards priority of disclosure; and so on.

The control of which Gordon-Reed speaks is racial marginalization, not suppression of truth. Her aim is to change the way blacks, as historical figures, are viewed. To a large extent, her sociological agenda is to show that Sally Hemings is an important historical figure, while cutting down Jefferson to size.

Nonetheless, is not Gordon-Reed trying to control the discourse by her fixation with race, not evidence? For her, it is better to dismiss the numerous testimonies on behalf of Jefferson's character than the single hearsay account of Madison Hemings, with its flaws and difficulties. Otherwise, scholars will be participating in the marginalization of a black historical figure. Moreover, as she has admitted in her PBS interview, black Americans would seem to have much to gain if her thesis should gain currency, and it has.

Perhaps because of people's preference for fable and not fact, the overall effect of Gordon-Reed's books, papers, and interviews has been that a liaison, in spite of lack of evidence, has become the received view. Some of the largest contemporary historians of Jeffersonian scholarship— for example, Peter J. Onuf[39] and Andrew Burstein—are intimate friends who are on the Jefferson-did-it and Jefferson-was-racist bandwagons. Jefferson-bashing sells books. Moreover, Gordon-Reed has won numerous prizes, including a Pulitzer Prize, for *The Hemingses of Monticello*. She cannot be writing gibberish, can she? I am, I admit frankly, at a loss.

As a result of Gordon-Reed's racistist agenda, historians who have not fully investigated the issue simply acknowledge cavalierly that the liaison is fact. In doing so, they merely cite Gordon-Reed as the decisive authority concerning the historical data.[40] Perusal of the historical literature indi- cates that. By skillfully playing the race card—and references to race and racism fill a dizzying number of pages of her two books (and the works of most other Jefferson historians)—Gordon-Reed has accomplished what she has accused white historians of doing: controlling the allowable dis- course. That is morally unconscionable: History is about rationality; and rationality, I repeat, is blind to skin color.

### Fallacies and Sophistries

This final section examines certain rhetorical devices employed by Gordon-Reed. Their use to promote her racistist agenda indicates plainly her training in law.

## *Fallacy of Significance through False Attribution*

Gordon-Reed is obsessed with showing that Sally Hemings "must be seen as a figure of historical importance" for a "multiplicity of reasons." Unfortunately, she lists only three: that "her name and life entered the public record during the run-up to a presidential election," that she and her siblings were used as political pawns throughout and after Jefferson's life, and that Hemings's story has had an effect on Jefferson's "white family."[41]

The fallacy behind that line of reasoning—a sort of fallacy of significance through false attribution—is manifest. I sketch out the fallacy as follows:

(1) Many persons have become historically popular through attribution of deed(s) they have not done.

(2) Those canards have had a significant influence on history.

(3) Therefore, those persons have had a significant influence on history (1 and 2).

(4) Anyone who has had a significant influence on history is worth writing about.

(5) Sally Hemings has had a significant influence on history.

(6) Therefore, Sally Hemings is worth writing about (4 and 5).

It is clear that the second syllogism, comprising claims 4 through 6, is deductively valid. The question is whether claim 5 is true.

The obvious difficulty here is that statement 3 does not follow from premises 1 and 2. The fact that *canards* about a person have had an influence on history does not show that *the person* has. If it is the case that Hemings did not have an affair with Jefferson, no historian of sane mind would pick her out as someone who "*must be seen* as a figure of historical importance." She becomes merely a person worthy of historical study in the manner that any other nonfamous person is worthy of study. That, of course, is up to the discretion of any historian, who is presumably free to pursue research on any person and then, as it were, roll the dice and hope for a good outcome. If it is the case that Hemings did have a lengthy affair with Jefferson, it is incumbent on historians to give incontrovertible evidence of that liaison, not hearsay, and to try to disclose her influence on the management of Jefferson's own public and private affairs.

Yet Gordon-Reed's racistist analysis of the Jefferson-Hemings liaison suggests that she has taken untoward and insidious scholarly liberties. In her presentation of the "evidence" for an affair between Jefferson and Hemings, she seems to have ignored significant data, colored the data she uses, and invented data to entice readership and other historians to promote her agenda. History ought to be grounded in fact, not fabulation.

### *Fallacy of Historical Anachronism*

Gordon-Reed admits that the Jefferson-Hemings story that began in France and ended with Jefferson's death offers, she says at the end of chapter 15, an "instructive window into the workings of a world that no longer exists but whose legacies are still with us."[42] That is a clear admission that the mores and values of Jefferson's day have since changed.

It is strange, then, that Gordon-Reed has no difficulty in judging Jefferson by the standards of our day. In *Thomas Jefferson and Sally Hemings*, she writes:

> It is not good enough to say with regard to this question, "Well, we live in the twentieth century and Thomas Jefferson lived in the eighteenth and nineteenth centuries." People had internal conflicts during those periods as well as today, probably more regarding the question of race and sex. Whites and blacks in the South often lived and interacted with one another under a system that made them, at once, enemies and intimates.[43]

Gordon-Reed here commits what I call the fallacy of historical anachronism. That occurs when one forms a judgment of a historical event or figure in an argument by using contemporary standards that were not in place during the epoch of that event or figure, or when one forms a judgment of a contemporary event or figure by recourse to the standards of the past that are no longer in place today. For instance, to call Jefferson "racist," because he owned slaves or because he tended to believe in black inferiority of body and mind, is to commit the fallacy. One might as well call him "sexist" because he believed women should have nothing more than a domestic role. It would be presumptuous for Gordon-Reed to assert that she, if she had been a white male Virginian who owned a large estate in Jefferson's day, would not have owned black slaves. It is very likely that she, like anyone else projected into that counterfactual scenario, would have. Slavery was an accepted part of Southern culture at that time. It is the exceptions among the Southern gentry that need to be explained.

It is not necessarily the case that in embracing the fallacy of historical anachronism, one is embracing historical relativism. Jefferson, for instance, was not a relativist about either knowledge or morality but a progressivist.[44] From the progressivist perch, the fallacy occurs precisely because a modern-day historian has the advantage of progress—for example, consider the global progress on gender and race in the last three hundred years—and that advantage makes normative judgments unfair. Why today's historians feel compelled to pass striking normative judgments is another issue, covered in chapter 5.

## Fallacy of False Alternatives/Fallacy of Complexity

Gordon-Reed turns to the issue of Jefferson's massive debts and considers law historian Herbert Sloan's argument that exaggerated virtues were the reason for them. It was Jefferson's kindness, hospitability, and goodness that increased his debts, writes Sloan.[45] He could not turn away visitors. Against Sloan, Gordon-Reed maintains that it was not exaggerated virtues, but inattention to monetary matters and, thus, derogation of duty to his family that increased Jefferson's debts. In short, it is not his virtues, but certain of his vices.[46]

Gordon-Reed then asks rhetorically, "Why . . . does the idea that Jefferson, widowed at thirty-eight and sworn to a promise not to remarry, might have taken a slave mistress appear so awful that it denotes a lack of love for his family?"[47] The question is out of the blue. Gordon-Reed is, of course, ready with an answer to her question. It is a matter of competing value judgments: either Jefferson was morally culpable because of financial neglect[48] or Jefferson was morally culpable because of fornication and miscegenation. She writes, "If one's horror at the thought of miscegenation and fornication outweighs one's horror at the thought of a person allowing his family to slide into financial ruin and onto public charity, then the answer is clear."[49] Thus she takes herself to have blocked Sloan's exaggerated-virtues thesis. Virtue is out of the question. Jefferson's express embrace of virtue in numerous writings is mere hypocrisy, it seems.

To showcase her "humaneness," Gordon-Reed rejects both alternatives. The "strongest case" is that neither "can be taken as a measure [exclusive measure?] of his love for his family."[50] She adds, "Humans are far too complex for such a simplistic calculus. The conflict between our personal needs and our sense of duty to others . . . is a chief contributor to that complexity, and the manner in which we resolve the inevitable conflicts that arise often will be unpredictable and highly idiosyncratic." Here Gordon-Reed, who readily chastised Brodie for offering rash insights into human nature, which for her *always* escapes subsumption under generalizations, seems to have humans figured out, when the experts, the psychologists, have failed. The fact that almost everything we know of Jefferson seems to fit a simple etiological pattern is irrelevant. Chaotic complexity reigns; and that is good, because from chaotic complexity, anything follows.[51]

Gordon-Reed's turn here leaves much to be desired ethically. She tries to show that there is no room for consideration of virtue concerning Jefferson's massive debt. Vice is the only option. Cast into disjunctive-syllogism form:

(1) Massive debt can only be explained by exaggerated virtues or exaggerated vices.

(2) Jefferson's virtue is out of the question.

(3) So, Jefferson is exaggeratedly vicious (1 and 2).

However, out of sheer generosity, she recants. Humans are far too complex for such a simplistic either-or depiction. The argument is a false dilemma.

The maneuver is transparently disingenuous because the damage has already occurred. Her recanting comes only after she has gotten in her jab—that is, had her say about virtues being out of the question. Anyone, like Sloan, who thinks Jefferson can be acquitted because of exaggerated virtues is a fool, she says.

We are left with another fallacy—what might be called the fallacy of complexity, which assumes the etiological complexity of human behavior for the sake of blocking the possibility of a simpler causal explanation.

(1) Human behavior in all (or almost all instances) is inordinately etiologically complex.
(2) Jefferson's words and behavior fit simple patterns of etiological explanation.
(3) So the simple patterns of etiological explanation cannot explain Jefferson's words and behavior (1 and 2).

Occam, thus, is turned on his head.

## Racial Bullying

Gordon-Reed is to be applauded for recognizing that history has tended to marginalize blacks and treat them as nonentities, through denigrating them and ignoring their stories. The various Hemingses stories are worth reconstructing and iterating to the extent that they can be known. For Gordon-Reed, they are not to be forgotten, because Jefferson's wife, according to the testimony of Madison Hemings, was Sally Hemings's half sister and because of Jefferson's lengthy liaison with Sally Hemings. These "connections" ensured that the Hemingses would be remembered, though that is "certainly not what Jefferson and his white family wanted." The reasons presumably are the taint of miscegenation on the family's legacy and, she adds, the family's racism. Yet memories, love, and strength of his black family overcame the blight of law.[52]

Two questions redound: Why did Gordon-Reed choose the Hemingses and not some other family of slaves? Are not other black families' stories equally worth telling?

The conclusion is obvious. In praising the Hemingses—Sally especially—Gordon-Reed can at the same time indict Jefferson for opportunism, hypocrisy, and racism. Recall Gordon-Reed's statement in *Thomas Jefferson and Sally Hemings* about the possibility of a liaison. "In order to maintain the claim of impossibility, or even to discuss the matter in those terms, one has to make Thomas Jefferson so high as to have been something more than human and one has to make Sally Hemings so low as to have been something less than human."[53]

In an article called "Engaging Jefferson," Gordon-Reed points out the tendency of whites who believe in a liaison to see it as rape and of blacks who believe in a liaison to see it as mutual affection. She says, "If affection existed between Jefferson and Hemings, Hemings would necessarily have gained some measure of power over Jefferson, in the way the women typically exert power over heterosexual males."[54] Referring to the novel *Sally Hemings*, written by Barbara Chase-Riboud, in which such an affectionate relationship is given, Gordon-Reed adds: "In a small but important way, the humanity of Hemings [in the novel] is reemphasized. Jefferson's humanity comes back into focus too. She is raised. He is cut down to size. Thus, two of the major requirements of black progress (restoration of black humanity and obliteration of the cult of the godlike white person) are fulfilled." In telling the Hemingses' stories, Jefferson gets his comeuppance. Being "cut down to size"—and her choices of language here is telling—he loses his Triton-among-the-minnows status and earns the labels of opportunist, hypocrite, and racist. At this juncture, Gordon-Reed's racial agenda seems to preclude the possibility of scholarly objectivity.

If comeuppance is a large part of the motivation of Gordon-Reed, as I suspect it is for her, then what of the ethical implications of spinning yarns with gauzy thread? Are not evidence and all the evidence supposed to factor into a historical account? Are not alternative, inconsistent accounts supposed to be entertained and explained away? Is not such an agenda-driven approach to "historical research" racist or, at least, racistist?

## *Psychologizing*

In *Thomas Jefferson and Sally Hemings*, Gordon-Reed castigates Fawn Brodie for her psychologizing. In a passage that I examine more completely in chapter 4, Gordon-Reed dismisses all psychological generalizations because they are "untrustworthy."

People who are compulsive about making lists have no interests in sex or romance. People who hold their emotions severely in check have no interest in sex or romance. People who are extremely clean have no interest in sex or romance. None of this follows. It is not even remotely a fact that a person who possesses all of these traits—even in abundance—is without sexual passion or romantic yearnings.[55]

Moreover, when writing of enslaved women's vulnerability to rape, she cautions against generalizing. "This view describes the way things were between enslaved women and white men generally, but deserves greater scrutiny when one takes on the responsibility of seeking to understand and present the story of one individual's life."[56] She adds, "It would be intellectually unsound to ignore evidence, or skip over reasonable inferences, in order to return to the presumption based upon the experiences of the overall group of enslaved women."[57]

The avowed modus operandi of Gordon-Reed is to examine the particulars of the Jefferson-Hemings story through examination of Jefferson's life and tendencies as well as Hemings's life and tendencies and then to draw more guarded and secure conclusions than past historians. For such historians, following the path of generalization, "it is unnecessary to pay attention to details, discern patterns, and note sometimes even sharp distinctions between given situations, putting one on a more comforting voyage of reiteration rather than one of potentially disconcerting discovery."[58] Her use of metaphor here is spellbinding. Other historians—the white males who have refused to acknowledge a liaison—are on the "comforting voyage of reiteration." Blind to the drudgery of investigative historical research, they work from theoretical presuppositions that taint their research. She, a black female law professor, is on a voyage leading to "disconcerting discovery." Eyes fully open and with the work ethic of a Trojan, she works from meticulous observation, without theoretical biases—especially concerning race. Her training in law, it seems, enables her, and her alone, to sift out fact from fiction.

Nonetheless, she is no stranger to psychological generalization when it suits her cause. I give two illustrations: one lengthy, one short.

On assumption that the two were together and Jefferson had time alone with Hemings in France, Gordon-Reed says Jefferson was in the position of master to Hemings's position of slave—that is, Jefferson was in a position of power. Did he force himself on her? In an effort to block the impossibility of forced sex—Gordon-Reed wishes to consider it possible, though not probable, if only to illustrate the wickedness of slavery—she writes pedantically, "Not *all* of anyone ever *always* [*sic*] does anything."[59] The catachrestic generalization is a psychological triumph in that it trumps all other psychological generalizations. What is the rub? It is hopelessly mired in ambiguity. What is the "all of everyone"—all parts of any one person? Are we to assume a fight between Head and Heart, in Jefferson's words? To what does "anything" refer? Does it refer to any one *particular* action, such as strolling through the woods on one specific afternoon in late autumn? If so, she presumably means that there is never any one action that any person does that is done without some measure of internal dissonance—a particular claim. Does it refer to any one kind of action in general, such as strolling? If so, she presumably means that there is never any particular kind of action that any person does that is done without some measure of internal dissonance—a generic claim. Moreover, "*always*" is not enough; we are told "ever *always*." Stripped of catachresis, we arrive at the following psychological insight: *No person always (always) does any one [particular or general?] thing from complete internal consonance.* That might be true—and I suspect it is, though philosophers like Aristotle, the Stoics, and Kant would disagree—but how aidful is it in showing the likelihood of forced sex?[60]

Elsewhere in *The Hemingses of Monticello*, she writes: "It is a cliché that revolutions in societies occur not at the point of maximum misery but during periods of rising expectations. The same can be said of individuals."[61]

In sum, though she castigates Brodie for needless psychologizing, Gordon-Reed too is not averse to it when she has need of it to advance her thesis.

### Jefferson's Bookishness

In an essay on Jefferson and Madison, Gordon-Reed mentions Jefferson's "habit of delving into books and finding (and believing) the sometimes outlandish stories told in them about things like the sexual preferences of orangutans in tropical jungles—an animal he knew nothing about, from a place he never visited."[62] The claim is supposed to expose Jefferson as credulous and gullible.

Jefferson did believe some outlandish things. It is virtually impossible to have his scientific attitude toward phenomena and not believe some outlandish things, if only provisionally. Nonetheless, she fails to acknowledge that he, sequestered at Monticello, generally had nothing else but books. In that, he was remarkably like many other American scholars of his time.

Moreover, Gordon-Reed fails to take Jefferson's comment about orangutans within the context of eighteenth-century thought. He says in his *Notes on the State of Virginia* that blacks prefer whites in much the same way that the male "Oranootan" prefers black women to females of his own species.[63] The orangutan to the eighteenth-century mind was a fictive creature, much like Bigfoot today, that was said to be some seven feet tall, to live in West Africa, and to molest black girls and women and to keep them as slaves. In doing so, the orangutan was merely acting pursuant to natural inclinations. According to the Great-Chain-of-Being biology of the day, inferior creatures strived to raise themselves in the chain of creatures through sex with animals similar but superior to themselves. To say that orangutans preferred black women and that blacks preferred whites was to say that orangutans were inferior to blacks and blacks were inferior to whites and that both species were striving to perfect themselves. That explains fully Jefferson's cavalier statement that the offspring of a black and white is improved "in body and mind, in the first instance."[64] Jefferson's "observations" were derived from reading accounts of biologists like Lord Monboddo and James Burnett.[65]

In sum, Jefferson was no more gullible than other science-loving scholars of his day. That he drew information from books and believed what he read is no indication of credulity or foolishness. The scientists of his day made purchase of what we recognize today to be some rather foolish claims. The same will be said apropos of the science of our day in years to come.

## *Jefferson's Secrecy*

One ploy of Jeffersonian revisionists is to argue that Jefferson's writings are contaminated, because Jefferson never fully reveals himself in any of his writings. Gordon-Reed takes this route concerning Jefferson's sexuality. "Despite the existence of a voluminous body of Jefferson's personal letters, very little is known about his private life that could tell us about his sexuality. In his own writings, Jefferson managed, as very private people often do, to impart a great deal of personal information without being particularly informative."[66] The second claim bespeaks the question: Just how does one impart a "great deal of personal information without being particularly informative"? Is not personal information what she seeks? If she means that in his writings we learn much about Jefferson the person, but little about his sexual life—specifically nothing about his putative liaison with Sally Hemings—then that is best explicable by there not having been a liaison. Gordon-Reed is undaunted. Following Brodie, once again, she goes on to say that Jefferson likely destroyed or had destroyed those letters that were most revelatory of his person such that "his true self was hidden from the world." Scholars are left with "a road map for how Thomas Jefferson wanted people to think of him."

The argument is unconvincing. Jefferson was indubitably cautious in his correspondence. That has been amply confirmed in the secondary literature[67] and he admits as much in several letters. It was also the propriety of his day. Yet he did not have absolute control of himself in the letters he had sent out, because he could not have had absolute control of himself in them, if only because Jefferson wrote thousands of letters during the course of his life. One cannot have a tight grip on thousands of letters.

# UPSHOT

Most scholars agree there is a consensus among historians that Jefferson had an affair with Sally Hemings. Consensus I suspect is true. Moreover, concerning scholarly matters, it is rational to accept a judgment based on scholarly consensus, when the consensus is reached by scholars on matters within their respective disciplines—for example, historians on historical matters. That is not to say that scholarly consensus is infallible—consider the shock waves felt with the Copernican and Darwinian theses—only that a scholarly consensus is the most reliable option.

Yet something has gone abundantly awry with Jeffersonian historical scholarship. Consensus on the Jefferson-Hemings liaison has been attained insidiously. Gordon-Reed has gained control of the discourse and has made the issue of paternity one that turns on race. To deny Jefferson's involvement with Hemings is to slight African Americans by denying them a sense of legitimacy they would otherwise not have in the founding of the United States. To slight African Americans is to be racist. The argument from authority—here, *Gordon-Reed asserts* c, *so* c *must be true*—has taken the place of disinterested and assiduous scholarship. In effect, consensus has been reached by fear rather than by evidence. That in itself is a frightening state of affairs for scholars who still believe that historical conclusions ought to be evidence-based, not based on a political or social agenda.

Where are we to turn when the so-called experts have let us down? Jefferson's answer perhaps would be this: to the sound judgments of the people.

Having read much of the professional literature on the relationship between Jefferson and Hemings—and there is a prodigious amount of such literature—and some of the nonprofessional literature through online reviews of Gordon-Reed's second book, I suspect that the popular assessment of *The Hemingses of Monticello*, though far from monolithic, is a better representation of the overall merit of Gordon-Reed's thesis than is the professional literature that refers to it. Why should that be so? Perhaps that is because, as Jefferson tells nephew Peter Carr (August 10, 1787), the average person's moral discernment—and the issue has an inescapable moral dimension—is as good as and often better than that of any professor or politician.

# CHAPTER 3

# RATIONALIZATIONS
# AND SECRETS

## Jefferson's Affair of Convenience

> Ultimately, the taboo of interracial sex meant less
> in this relationship, because the strict racial bound-
> aries that Jefferson prescribed in his *Notes on Virginia*
> were for America at large, and not for Jefferson in his
> private world.
>
> —ANDREW BURSTEIN, *Jefferson's Secrets*

ndrew Burstein, following up on the psycho-biographical trend of Brodie and Gordon-Reed, maintains in *The Inner Jefferson* (1995) that a relationship between Jefferson and Sally Hemings is highly unlikely. Scrutiny of his letters to family reveals a character that would not have consented to a relationship with a slave. Five years later, in a paper titled "Jefferson's Rationalizations," Burstein does an about-face and is now wholeheartedly committed to the existence of a thirty-eight-year, sex-only affair, because of Jefferson's tendency to rationalize. Mounting circumstantial evidence and the DNA tests have convinced him that Jefferson's letters to family gave him a limited, biased perspective. Jefferson's relationship with Hemings, he says, was a needed sexual outlet that helped to preserve his physical health.

In this chapter, I trace out the development of Burstein's thoughts over the years on the issue of a liaison and examine the reasons for his root-and-branch change of mind. I show that the circumstantial strands that Burstein weaves together to defend his thesis of a lengthy, sex-only affair are insubstantial. The finished tapestry is gossamery and threadbare. At day's end, the reasons for Burstein's remarkable shift of position tell us perhaps more about the inner Burstein than they do about the inner Jefferson.

## THE INNER BURSTEIN

In *The Inner Jefferson*, Andrew Burstein writes of Brodie's book on Jefferson:

> In *Thomas Jefferson: An Intimate History*, [Fawn Brodie] purported to have found what no previous scholars could, the telltale signs that Jefferson had fathered the children of a biracial slave named Sally Hemings, who might have been his deceased wife's half sister. In Brodie's enthusiasm to illustrate her point, she misread language, invoked currently fashionable psychological explanations to overinterpret unconscious patterns in Jefferson's writings, and construed psychic dilemmas without regard to eighteenth-century norms.[1]

Burstein's critique of Brodie gives us a blueprint for how history ought to be done that we can use to critique him. He is clearly aware of what I have dubbed the fallacy of historical anachronism.

Burstein's book, which neither "lavishly praises nor faithlessly scandalizes,"[2] aims at a depiction of the inner Jefferson by examination of his "familiar letters." Jefferson "examines life, nurtures an idealized vision of how it could be, and suffers from the knowledge that he may never break through the discord that persists among men." Burstein finds Jefferson to be a "lonely genius" and a "flawed poet."

Burstein also depicts Jefferson as a man of stout character who is irrevocably committed to his family and friends—a man who judges himself and others by temper. He writes that for Jefferson, one "becomes virtuous by discovering the softness of his inward nature, by drawing wisdom from his introspective moments, by finding in his Heart his sympathy toward humanity, and by acquiring nobility in taste."[3]

The fireside in Jefferson's letter to daughter Maria—the fireside that

Brodie takes to be linked with "irregular passion" and "dangerous bias," that is, sex—Burstein says merely symbolizes "family and friendship."[4] Whereas Brodie, like Freud, doubtless sees the flickering flames as phallic enticements,[5] Burstein sees the fireside as part of a "well-ordered dreamworld" in which "jarring and jealousies" and "irregular passions" have no place.

In *The Inner Jefferson*, Burstein devotes only a few pages to the Sally Hemings scandal. "As to the actual evidence in the matter of Sally Hemings, nothing fully satisfies," he writes.[6] He reviews briefly certain testimonies on behalf of Jefferson—that is, those of Thomas Jefferson Randolph; granddaughter Ellen Randolph Coolidge; and his daughter and "mistress of Monticello" Martha Jefferson Randolph. Against Jefferson, there is the testimony of Sally's son Madison Hemings. Burstein concludes:

> Knowing what we do about Jefferson's Heart and Head, that the first made him generous and the second ruled his actions, it seems highly unlikely that because light-skinned Sally Hemings bore light-skinned children at Monticello, they necessarily were fathered by Monticello's master. Moreover, Jefferson would have been uncharacteristically imprudent to be responsible for giving Sally Hemings the two children that she bore in the years after the charges surfaced, while he remained president.

Burstein seems to think an affair is implausible, yet his wording bespeaks discomfiture. Thus, he is committed to the proposition *It seems highly unlikely that Jefferson necessarily fathered Hemings's children*, and that is not the same claim as *It is highly unlikely that Jefferson fathered Hemings's children*. Inclusion of the words *seems* and *necessarily* in the first claim are significant. *Seems* shows Burstein has no more than a lukewarm commitment to a high unlikelihood. *Necessarily* shows that Burstein is lukewarmly committed to there being no options other than Jefferson fathering Hemings's children.

In an interview with PBS, Burstein repeats what he had written in *The Inner Jefferson*.

> The reason why it's highly unlikely that Jefferson could have fathered the children of Sally Hemings is that he was a moralist, but beyond that

he was a practical politician. And as President, he would not have been capable of giving Sally the two children that were born when Jefferson was a 60-year-old man and in the White House. Callender's revelations had surfaced.[7]

Note here that *seems* and *necessarily* are gone—the former is supplanted by *is*; latter is supplanted by *could*. Burstein is now committed to the much stronger proposition: *It is highly unlikely that Jefferson could have fathered Hemings's children.*

Let us contrast the two.

$B_{IJ}$: *It* seems *highly unlikely that Jefferson* necessarily fathered *Hemings's children.*

$B_{PBS}$: *It is highly unlikely that Jefferson* could have fathered *Hemings's children.*

Burstein in his PBS interview commits himself to existence of the high improbability of the *possibility* of a relationship—a decidedly stronger claim than the seeming high improbability of the *necessity* of a relationship. Here Burstein was either incautious about his use of language, or his use of language bespeaks an underlying ambivalence. Incautiousness, however, need not exclude ambivalence.

## JEFFERSON'S "RATIONALIZATIONS"

Ten years later, when asked in an interview about the possibility of an affair between Jefferson and Hemings, Burstein does an about-face. He acknowledges Jefferson's love of family in his letters to family, but now recognizes that those letters show only one side of Jefferson. Evidence outside of the letters to family shows a deceitful, protean Jefferson: He could write with love and tenderness to his daughters and grandchildren and then dissimulate or lie to them and to others about his long-term relationship with Hemings. Says Burstein:

We should not be surprised by the lie. Dabney is correct that it was not in Jefferson's character as he appears in his better-known texts—but those texts do not delineate the whole man. The more perplexing question at this point is whether members of the family who explicitly denied the relationship were complicit in the lie, or believed what they preferred to believe. Importantly, Jefferson was mocked by his enemies not for sexual immorality but for a social transgression—acting out the ordinary urges of an ordinary man, having sex with an alluring, lower-class woman when he appeared to all as a philosopher, immune to base urges. I offer *abundant evidence* [italics added] in the book that Jefferson could rationalize his behavior to himself on the basis of the medical authority of his age, which literally recommended for a widower like himself occasional sex with a young, healthy, fruitful, attractive female, in order to preserve his own mental and physical health.[8]

The interview is in response to Burstein's later book, *Jefferson's Secrets*, an expansion of his thoughts in a paper five years earlier, "Jefferson's Rationalizations." The paper might be a fleshing out of the thoughts of Gordon-Reed, who stated in 1997: "We know that Thomas Jefferson was capable of finding rationalizations for his sometimes contradictory beliefs and actions. A relationship with Sally Hemings would have been one of the easier ones for him to rationalize."[9]

Perhaps following Gordon-Reed, Burstein makes much of Jefferson's avowed rationalizations. Speaking on behalf of all modern Jeffersonian historians, he asks, How does a historian reconcile Jefferson's writings and his inconsistent actions? He answers:

To today's historian, Jefferson's writings and actions are irreconcilable, yet most interpreters of his character wish to resolve or explain his life of paradox. Jefferson could have been self-scrutinizing and yet willing to conceal certain feelings, remaining aware of his apparent deceptions— what we call rationalization. Addressing his nephew Peter Carr on how to act when faced with a moral decision, he urged in language that must now be read with great poignancy, "Ask yourself how you would act were all the world looking at you." Phrases like "most chaste honour," "virtuous dispositions," "good sense and prudence," and "innocent intentions" permeate his most personal documents. That he erected walls to shield himself from outside should not be seen solely as pathology. In Jefferson's public *and* private epistolary community, all writing involved concealment and rationalization—concealment, along with the *appearance* of honest self-exposure, is precisely how elites who wished to advance themselves were supposed to relate.[10]

There are several difficulties. It is not clear that Jefferson's actions and writings are irreconcilable. That works on assumption of a huge gap between them—something I believe is manifestly false. I, for instance, believe that they are largely reconcilable, and I have attempted to do just that in my book *Dutiful Correspondent*.[11] Next—and this is a point of "great poignancy"—that Jefferson habitually used moral language in his personal correspondence is strong evidence that he took moral issues seriously, not that he had something to hide. In that, he was no run-of-the-mill "elite." Moreover, he was unambiguous about there not being different moral codes for one's private and public personae: "I never did, or countenanced, in public life, a single act inconsistent with the strictest good faith; having never believed there was one code of morality for a public, and another for a private man."[12] He was, thus, committed to authenticity. So, the requirement to see beyond his moral language attends upon the truth of there being a large gap between his words and deeds. There was not. Finally, that "all [Jefferson's] writing involved concealment and rationalization" is an incautious generalization that bespeaks a slipshod use of language. For illustration, many of Jefferson's letters to Adams, in the later years especially, give no hints of any concealments or rationalizations.[13] Certainly, in a large number of Adams's letters to Jefferson, the worry of exposure nowise seems to exist.[14] It is clear that Jefferson's letters often show discretion and guardedness, but that is not to say that they *always* show discretion and guardedness. Note too Burstein's use of language, "Jefferson *could have been* self-scrutinizing and yet willing to conceal certain feelings, remaining aware of his apparent deceptions" (italics added). That argues for the possibility of rationalization, not the fact of rationalization—a claim too weak to be historically significant.

## UNEARTHING JEFFERSON'S SECRETS

In *Jefferson's Secrets*, Andrew Burstein continues scholarship along the lines of Brodie and Gordon-Reed that is designed to expose the man behind the words—Jefferson the hypocrite. He begins with three caveats. First, one must acknowledge that the emotional considerations of a mixed-race couple in Jefferson's day were markedly different from the emotions of a mixed-race couple in our day. Second, following Gordon-Reed's lead, he asserts one must not assume any universal generalizations about human sexuality, for "sexuality has a history." Last, breaking with Gordon-Reed, one must not aim to protect Jefferson and construct a history for Hemings by concluding the two were romantically, not just sexually, linked.[15]

Why is there such an about-face for Burstein—an antipodean shift in stance? Acknowledging the need of an explanation to readers, Burstein writes in chapter 5 of his book: "I allowed conventional notions of sexual propriety [in my early book] to describe the mind of Jefferson. Absence of information does not equal celibacy."[16] Moreover, new evidence has surfaced. The 1998 DNA evidence and the conclusions of the Thomas Jefferson Memorial Foundation panel of experts in 2000 (see chapter 5) have had a marked influence on his thinking.

"For most, Thomas Jefferson's paternity of Sally Hemings's children has now been convincingly established," he says, before adding paternalistically and in a manner that is reminiscent of Gordon-Reed's brick-wall analogy, "yet there are those who insist in reminding us that it has not been *absolutely* established."[17] There is one critical difficulty, related to the quantifier *most*: To whom does "most" refer? "Most Americans," as he notes on the previous page, or "most scholars"? The denotation is critical. If the former, Burstein commits the fallacy of consensus gentium—that is, an appeal to popular consensus for the truth of some historical claim, when evidence and expert testimony is needed. If the latter, it is far from clear that a full-fledged consensus has occurred and, if it has occurred, it cannot be by rational and dispassionate assessment of all the available relevant evidence (see especially chapters 4 and 5).

One critical difficulty for those committed to a relationship, admits

Burstein, concerns the births of Madison and Eston Hemings during Jefferson's two terms as president. They relate to one of the principal reasons he maintained in his earlier book that Jefferson did not father Madison and Eston Hemings, or any of Sally's other children: It would have been "uncharacteristically imprudent."[18] Why now does Burstein think Jefferson continued his relationship with Hemings after publication of Callender's malicious claims in 1802? To do so would mean the possibility of more and greater ridicule to which his children and grandchildren would be exposed for all of their lives. Burstein here does not satisfactorily answer that intriguing question. He merely and curtly lists love, sexual desire, and egoistic impulse as possible motivators, and he settles on sexual desire.

Burstein next turns to Thomas Jefferson Randolph's testimony that Peter Carr was the father of Hemings's children. This explanation, he writes, now "seems impossible," as "DNA eliminated the Carr family." The problem here is that the DNA evidence has eliminated the Carrs only from the possibility of fathering Eston Hemings, not from fathering any of the other children of Sally Hemings. Burstein is working from the house-of-cards assumption that Sally Hemings did not have more than one paramour. One cannot simply assume that, as it was not uncommon, though perhaps not customary, for black slave women who took on lovers to take on more than one lover.[19] Sally Hemings's mother, Betty, and her mother's sisters are known to have had multiple paramours of different races.[20] That is a pattern with which Sally would have been acquainted. Thus, the possibility of having multiple lovers cannot be cavalierly cold-shouldered.

Burstein takes up the notion that a Jefferson other than Thomas fathered Eston. He turns to the proposal that Randolph Jefferson, Thomas's brother, was the father of Eston: "The problem with this scenario, however, is that no one—no white Jefferson descendant, no historian—ever suggested Randolph's name until a defense of Thomas Jefferson's celibacy was mounted immediately after the DNA findings were published."[21] Randolph, it seems, was an ad hoc candidate; he was proposed only to save Thomas's reputation.

The difficulty with this ad hoc tack is fourfold.

There is evidence, not mentioned by Burstein, that makes Randolph a strong paternity candidate.[22] Foremost among that evidence is the testimony of Isaac Jefferson: "Old Master's brother, Mass Randall, was a might simple man: used to come out among black people, play the fiddle and dance half the night; hadn't much more sense than Isaac."[23] So even if Randolph is currently being explored as a possible father of Eston to save Jefferson's reputation, as Burstein says, lack of incontrovertible evidence implicating Jefferson demands that any scholar, seeking the truth and not content with a rough consensus among historians, explore thoroughly all avenues of explanation before arriving at a satisfactory conclusion. Burstein's ad hoc tack is dismissive and scholarly disregardful.

Moreover, scholars are fishing for alternative explanations not because they wish at all costs to save Jefferson's reputation, but because there are good reasons to believe Jefferson would not have had a relationship with Hemings.[24] Before implicating Jefferson on circumstantial evidence—and that is all that adherents of a relationship have—it is necessary to rule out all other plausible paternity candidates and all possible combinations of paternity candidates in the Jefferson bloodline. It is not sufficient to say one's motivation for defending Jefferson is ad hoc. Many ad hoc moves are undertaken for good reasons and wind up with favorable results. One has merely to consider the discovery of the planet Neptune. Uranus had a disturbance in its orbit—one at variance with Isaac Newton's dynamical laws and, thus, was disconfirmatory of Newton's theory—yet astronomers, reluctant to give up Newton's theory if only because they had nothing with which to replace it, posited ad hoc the existence of a perturbing planet outside of Uranus. The spurious move was taken to save Newton's theory. Calculations of the size, orbital rate, and position of the unseen planet were made, and the race was on to discover it. Urbain Leverrier, with the aid of German astronomers at the Berlin Observatory, soon discovered the perturbing planet and Newton's theory was not only saved but was afforded fresh confirmatory evidence.[25]

Furthermore, even if Jefferson, given the anecdotal evidence, is a priori the most plausible of all candidates for fathering Hemings's six children, it does not follow that it is probable that Jefferson fathered all or even any of Hemings's children. I illustrate by analogy. In one roll of two fair dice, the outcome *seven* is the most probable outcome of all possible outcomes: There is a 0.167 a priori probability of its occurrence, and that is higher than any other possible outcome (*two* through *six* and *eight* through *twelve*). Similarly, one cannot conclude that just because Jefferson's being the father of all (or any) of Hemings's children is the most probable a priori explanation—it is, in some sense, the simplest explanation—it does not follow that it is probable that Jefferson de facto fathered all (or any) of Hemings's children. Reality does not always prefer etiological simplicity.

Finally, in what sense is Jefferson as the father of all (or any) of Sally Hemings's children the simplest explanation? On assumption that all the children had one father, an assumption merely of scholarly convenience, it is the simplest explanation for historians insofar as it does not involve any historical digging, as it were. The simplicity here is that of convenience or, less directly, eliminating inconvenience. On assumption of one father for all the children and given that Jefferson's DNA matched that of Eston Hemings, claiming that Jefferson was the father eliminates the need of historians to do the dirty historical work of researching thoroughly all the other possible candidates. Exploring the possibility of more than one father makes matters even more historically inconvenient. The simplicity here, thus, is not Occam's. I return to this issue in chapter 5.

Like Brodie and Gordon-Reed, Burstein all too hastily falls back on Madison Hemings's newspaper account—the veracity of which we have found numerous reasons to question. Madison stated, Burstein says, that his mother became Jefferson's concubine in Paris, that he and his three siblings were the only children of Jefferson by a slave, and that Jefferson acted with indifference to his slave children, among other things. "That a key portion of Madison's testimony is now widely accepted as true, owing to the DNA results, strongly supports the pre-DNA argument of the law professor Annette Gordon-Reed that Madison Hemings was a man of veracity and sound memory."[26]

For Burstein, the case, apparently, is open-and-shut. We are concisely given three independent arguments—the wide acceptance of Madison's testimony (presumably by scholars, and note here he mentions only a portion of the testimony!), the DNA results, and Gordon-Reed's work. First, the argument from consensus is bunkum, if it is an appeal to the general American public. If not, it is simply falsely stated, as there is no wholesale consensus among Jeffersonian scholars. The 2001 Scholars' Commission Report, published in 2011 as *The Jefferson-Hemings Controversy: Report of the Scholars Commission* (see addendum), is sufficient proof of that. That several scholars have vitiated the pro-liaison arguments via appeal to evidence (and its want) is proof sufficient.[27] Second, the DNA results, as I show fully in chapter 5, nowise implicate Jefferson. It shows merely that *a* Jefferson fathered Eston Hemings, and there are many possible candidates. In addition, it says nothing about the other Hemingses to which Sally gave birth. Finally, to fall back on the expertise of law professor Gordon-Reed, as the lion's share of historians today do, is ad hoc in a harmful way. Her work, as I have shown, is as chimerical and unconvincing as that of Brodie. It is also agenda-driven, not truth-driven. Moreover, to give the testimony of *one* law professor on the veridicality of Madison's testimony—and I add there is good reason to question her authority, as racial bias abounds in her work—is a fallacious appeal to authority. Any argument based on authority, to be compelling, must show that, among authorities, a consensus, based on a thorough examination of all available relevant evidence, exists. William G. Hyland Jr. is a lawyer who has recently published on this issue and contends that the case for a liaison is "based on a pyramiding of inferences, wild speculation, conjecture, and witnesses whose credibility and memories have been severely impeached."[28] He adds, "The entire case is devoid of credible, corroborated evidence." Thus, trying to establish the truth of Madison Hemings's testimony by an appeal to Gordon-Reed's authority is unavailing.

Each of the three inductive arguments—and each is independent of the others—is weak. Three weak independent arguments do not add up to one strong argument.

In *Jefferson's Secrets*, Burstein has completely ignored the work of historians like Virginius Dabney, Cynthia Burton, and numerous other dissenters, and has given insubstantial reasons for his about-face. A change of mind that adversely affects public perception of one of the greatest figures of American history requires fuller explanation than Burstein seems willing to give. If Jefferson did have a relationship with Hemings that he continued after Callender's malicious slander in 1802, as Burstein says he did, then there is nothing more to say than Jefferson was an unheeding narcissist who thought more about sexual release than he did about the reputation of his family. That is highly unlikely. Why Burstein gives such matters short shrift is puzzling—one of *Burstein's* secrets.

## THE "TREATY OF PARIS"

Taking himself to have satisfactorily established that a relationship did exist, Burstein turns next to the nature of that relationship. Was it mutually fulfilling as Brodie and Gordon-Reed have stated?

Burstein examines Jefferson's *Notes on the State of Virginia* in an effort to show that Jefferson's view of black inferiority disallowed a genuine relationship of love between unequals.[29] Jefferson believed, if only provisionally, that blacks were inferior to whites in both mind and body. Burstein hedges on labeling Jefferson "racist," as the term, he admits, is anachronistic and, thus, inappropriate. In spite of his caveat, he makes use of the label in the next two paragraphs[30] and liberal use of it throughout the rest of the book. "Racism" as it relates to Jefferson is an anachronistic term, he admits; nonetheless he asserts baldly that Jefferson was a racist. Jefferson's view of black inferiority disallowed the sort of mutually fulfilling relationship for which Brodie and Gordon-Reed argued. I return to the issue of Jefferson's "racism" in the final chapter of this undertaking.

Burstein begins chapter 6: "We have established [in the previous chapters] that Jefferson's psychology was fundamentally different from ours, and that we cannot expect to understand his impulses by engaging with terms and concepts comfortable to the twenty-first century. Neither race nor sex was thought of precisely as we imagine; nor equality, nor virility."[31]

The argument given is patently a non sequitur—that is, the conclusion is poorly supported by the premise. Given that race, sex, equality, and virility in Jefferson's day were not thought of "precisely as we imagine," it does not follow that Jefferson's psychology was "fundamentally different from ours." Against Burstein, human sexuality is more whippy than it is protean. He seems to discount the influence of relatively stable biological considerations on human psychology. Freud, at least, got that correct.

Were the psychology of sexuality as protean as Burstein states it is, it would be difficult for historians to say anything about Jefferson's psychosexuality that would resonate with readers in the twenty-first century. Yet, for instance, readers of the Jefferson-Cosway correspondence are remarkably moved by the tenderness that underlies the sentiments of certain of Jefferson's letters to Cosway. They are also irked by Cosway's coquettishness. So too are readers moved by plays like *Agamemnon* and *Oedipus Rex*, written over two millennia ago, and the epic *Gilgamesh*, which dates back much farther. The human constitution has kept much the same over the millennia. The impulses have not changed; the milieu in which those impulses play out themselves has changed. Jefferson's psychology is not so far removed from us.

Burstein acknowledges that Jefferson had aimed to reserve his closest moral affections for his family: "Nothing in his life compared with the emotions he felt for his family."[32] Still he adds: "Yet male desire was just as 'real' to the people of his time and place as female self-control. So the bookish elder Jefferson, weighted down by a demanding schedule of intellectual work while writing to his learned friends around the world, presumably made it appear that he had had little time to develop emotional connections beyond those that bound him to his daughter and her children, his nephews and visiting cousins, and select young men of Albemarle County." Deceit, it seems, honeycombs Jefferson's writings.

Contra Brodie and Gordon-Reed, Burstein argues that the relationship between Jefferson and Hemings was based not on mutual love but on "sex and class privilege."[33] Hemings could not have been a "substitute wife" because of her custodial role at Monticello and because of Hemings's blackness. Burstein writes, "The best available evidence suggests two things: If Jefferson was having sexual relations with his servant, they were undertaken to satisfy his personal appetite and, as a result of his medical conditioning, to preserve his health." It is unclear why Burstein chooses a conditional construction here, since elsewhere in the book he is not shy about his commitment to the existence of a liaison. Nevertheless, the first conjunct of the consequent of the conditional claim (the *then* part) —namely, *Sexual relations were undertaken to satisfy his personal appetite*—is not too unreasonable, on assumption of the truth of the antecedent (the *if* part); the second—*Sexual relations were undertaken to preserve his health*—is absurd.

Though a relationship existed, Burstein continues, "There was no place for [Sally Hemings] in the Monticello economy other than as maid-servant."[34] There is no evidence of any displays of warmth to Hemings. He adds, "He evidently got what he wanted at little cost to his comfort when he 'negotiated' with James and Sally in Paris—he retained their continued services." With Sally Hemings, Jefferson got more. Burstein says, "It is critical to remember that the 'treaty' of Paris . . . was a treaty of sexual commerce: Jefferson promised lenient, indulgent treatment in return for sexual favors."

It is absurd to think that there was such a "treaty of Paris." First, all of the Hemingses, prior to the trip to Paris, were given special treatment and Sally, even after her return to Virginia, was treated no better than other Hemingses.[35] Jefferson's codicil (see Appendix C) indicates that his slaves Burwell Colbert, John Hemings (Sally's younger brother), and Joe Fosset were singled out for special favors more than Sally's sons, Madison and Eston. On Jefferson's death, each was to be given their freedom one year after Jefferson's passing, an acre, a log house to be built on it, and "all the tools of their respective shops or callings."[36] Madison and Eston were to be given their freedom, upon reaching age twenty-one, but to be apprenticed under John Hemings until then. Therefore, if Jefferson promised special treatment, he did not much deliver on the promise. Second, recall the treaty, as published by Wentworth, entailed freedom for all of Sally Hemings's children, upon twenty-one years of age. Historian Cynthia Burton addresses the Paris "treaty" fully in *Jefferson Vindicated*: "Imagine an immature slave girl probably insecure and possibly pregnant with her first child wanting to stay behind alone in France in the midst of a Revolution, rather than return to Virginia where her friends and family lived and where she knew she would receive good care."[37] She concludes, "It's difficult to envision this teenage girl confronting the American Minister to France (her master) and demanding a 'treaty' to guarantee freedom to children that were not to be conceived for more than five years." It is best to conclude that the "Treaty of Paris" is a fiction of Madison Hemings or of the newspaper editor of his story.

There remains the curiosity of Jefferson's lack of feeling for his black family in Madison's published story. Burstein explicates that historically, "we must explain his relative lack of affection for the Hemingses according to cultural assumptions as unfamiliar to us as his recurrence to a vocabulary drawn from eighteenth-century neurophysiology."[38] He provided discreetly for Sally and her children, but remained overall unfeeling toward her. Sally to Jefferson was nothing more than a sexual outlet. That Jefferson could have maintained a sexual relationship—an affair of convenience—with Sally Hemings and shown no feelings toward her or her children for thirty-eight years is incredible—too incredible. Yet incredibility nowise fazes Burstein. He merely glosses, "If we judge by the anecdotal evidence presented by those who knew him, no man was more discreet in his behavior."[39] The relationship between antecedent and consequent in that conditional claim is bogus. First, what exactly is the anecdotal evidence to which he refers? To what testimony is he referring? Second, that the anecdotal evidence shows Jefferson to be more discrete than any other human is hyperbolic hogwash. Let us again make use of Occam's razor: Lack of feeling for his "black children" is best explained by Jefferson not having any "black children."

What of the family, by whom Jefferson was habitually surrounded? All, except his daughter Martha, who was too close to him not to know, were blind to Jefferson's lascivious follies. Martha was in on the lie. "They kept their Jefferson on his godlike pedestal," Burstein says.[40] "Yet the DNA findings have led us to draw a different conclusion: Grandpapa lied to them."

The DNA evidence, as I show in chapter 5, does not lead any rational person to any *definite* conclusions. Burstein, here, takes inconclusive evidence and unqualifiedly uses it to incriminate Jefferson. Such a practice is shiftless and scholarly irresponsible.

Burstein next turns to the morality of such an affair. He claims that Jefferson found prostitution unethical and flaunted extramarital sex as unethical, but thought that extramarital sex with discretion—sex kept a secret—was not immoral. Burstein offers no evidence for that claim other than the nonexistence in Jefferson's "ample correspondence" of remarks against discreet liaisons.[41] In a weak effort to make the claim plausible, he turns to Jefferson's love of Greek authors—the topic of the following section.

Against Burstein, Jefferson did look down on sexual promiscuity, as evidenced, for example, in a letter to George Washington (December 4, 1788). Noting his abhorrence of sexual promiscuity, scholar Bernard Bailyn labels the former president a "Puritan revolutionary,"[42] yet that, I acknowledge, is taking matters too far.

Moreover, as I have shown above, Jefferson unequivocally believed that morality was both a public and a private affair.[43] He did not believe that discretion had any influence on culpability. In his writings with moral content, Jefferson is clear that morally incorrect action is morally incorrect action, irrespective of its outcome. Dissimulation, in an effort not to hurt others, was not an option to preserve moral purity or integrity. In that, Jefferson was not a consequentialist, as many have incorrectly asserted,[44] but was following the Stoic Panaetius as well as the empiricists such as Francis Hutcheson.[45]

## JEFFERSON THE GREEK

Burstein also gives Jefferson's Grecophilia as evidence of a liaison between Jefferson and Sally Hemings. Jefferson loved the classical authors, the Greeks especially, so it is reasonable to assume that he would, to some extent, have integrated their mores into his views on sex. "It is not unthinkable," writes Burstein with caution, "that the Greeks gave some shape to his unrevealed sexual views."[46]

Drawing from Karl Lehmann's *Thomas Jefferson: American Humanist*, Burstein offers a succinct account of the ancient Greek view of women:

"In ancient Greece, what apparently intrigued men of ordinary privilege was not so much the thought of a wife's propriety and virtue but the vision of an available sex object, sitting at the spinning wheel. In search of gratification and amusement, they wandered across class lines."[47]

He adds that Greek women were not the moral equals of males, as they were thought to be ruled by desire, but were seen as a "kind of property"—"a transfer of goods from one family to another."[48] And so, "Female infanticide was not unknown."

The account is thin, bereft of substance, and unfocused. Moreover, it does not much follow Lehmann's lead.

First, Burstein refers to "Greek culture" in a homogenous way. Jefferson's Greek books, beginning in the early eighth century BCE with Homer, roughly spanned a millennium. There is no Greek way of life that typified the manner of living of all Greeks of that span.

Moreover, the Greek way of life in any city-state at any particular period was remarkably idiosyncratic. Each city-state was an independent political unit. Fourth-century Athens was a participatory democracy. Fourth-century Sparta and Corinth were oligarchies, different in significant ways from each other. All city-states were held together loosely in that they shared a common language and common gods, though the importance of gods differed from city-state to city-state as did in some regard the manner of worship. Overall the manner of living in fourth-century Athens was remarkably different from fourth-century Sparta and Corinth. Thus, as it makes no sense to speak of a Greek nation, it makes no sense to speak of a Greek approach to sexuality.

Second, the account of women in Greek society as fundamentally ruled by passions is skewed. Women in Greek literature were linked with *ekstasis* (ecstasy, literally a standing outside of oneself) and *enthusiasmos* ("god-inspired," literally having a god inside) in orgiastic cults, so there is a literary link of femininity and irrationality. Yet Aristotle, perhaps the foremost authority on the subtleties of Greek culture in his day, says that women have a fully developed rational faculty, but not one that is manly (*andreios*)—that is, suitable for ruling or governing, hence the political inactivity of Athenian women.[49]

Women in Aristotle's Athens were second-rate citizens only insofar as they were politically inactive due to their unmanly rationality. Though politically inactive, they were every bit as socially significant as were men and were not thought of as mere "sex object[s], sitting at the spinning wheel." Unlike slaves, women were free and, though they had a social presence less than male slaves, they were not considered, like slaves, as property.

Women had an especially important domestic role—household management (*oikonomia*) as it related to production of goods in a household. All things worn and eaten were produced at home. Thus, an Athenian woman, within the sphere of activity within the household, was like the foreman of a small factory.[50] Writes Aristotle, "Household management differs for the two of them, for [a man's] task is to acquire property and [a woman's] to preserve it."[51] Thus, following Aristotle, the nature and social role of women complemented that of men.

In Sparta, women enjoyed relative equality with men—social liberty that Athenian women did not have. Women had to manage the estates when the men were away at war, and soldiering was a man's sole function. Girls were educated like boys to encourage stoutness of body as well as mind. The function of a woman was to bear healthy offspring; of a boy, to grow to manhood and be a courageous soldier; and of a girl, to grow to womanhood and bear stout children.

The relatively equal social significance of women in Greek culture is indicated by the vast number of statues of women or female goddesses, the role of goddesses in Greek mythology, and the large number of temples in honor of a goddess. The importance of honoring goddesses as well as gods shows Greeks were abundantly aware that women contributed to social stability as much as men did. Recall Aristotle's statement on the complementary function of men and women in household management.

Third, if Jefferson looked to the Greeks for a model of his own sexual practices, like Burstein suggests, why did he not direct his sexual urges to young Virginian males or male slaves, instead of a female slave? Homoeroticism was seen by many Greeks in the Classical Era (500–336 BCE)—for example, the Athenian gentry of Plato's and Aristotle's day—as a more exalted form of sexual activity. In *Phaedrus*, for instance, Plato tells us that many Greek men went bankrupt in trying to win the affection of a handsome young man.[52] The early speeches of Plato's *Symposium* are straightforward paeans to male homoeroticism. Pausanius's speech contrasts "celestial love," between males, with "common love," between a male and female, and eulogizes only the former. Common love is base and vulgar.[53]

Finally, to the comment that female infanticide was not unknown, I add merely that male infanticide was not unknown, either.

Burstein also speaks of the Greek mode of concubinage. He offers the example of Aristotle (who was not a Greek) and his concubine Herpyllis: "Among the Greeks, a concubine who was kept for the production of free children was thought to be assuming a positive social role."[54] Jefferson, Burstein adds, might have done the same. Then again, I add, he might not have done the same.

Yet Jefferson seldom refers to Aristotle when he speaks of the Greeks. His collection of Aristotle's works was likely more for reference than for reading. As historian Karl Lehmann correctly notes, Jefferson avoided Aristotle, Plato, and other such philosophers because of his abhorrence of metaphysical dogmatism—that is, Jefferson was an empiricist, not a rationalist.[55]

Burstein quickly enough turns to the Greek philosopher Epicurus and his effect on Jefferson. "The principle appeal of Epicureanism was . . . the ennobling of sensual pleasures, of right passions, and the notion that inner peace was attained through enjoyment of the world rather than an ascetic withdrawal from it."[56] Burstein's characterization of Epicureanism suggests that his grasp of it is dilettantish. Epicurus advocated a life directed toward *ataraxia* or mental equanimity as the chief means of promoting inner peace. *Ataraxia* was achieved by dispelling false notions—that is, that the gods intervene in human affairs, that there exists a life after death, and that there is no limit to human passions. To eliminate the inner disturbances caused by hunger and thirst, bread and water were preferable to extravagant foods and wine, which would create disturbances greater than they were aiming to quell. Most significantly, Epicurus's view of sex was hostile. Sexual desire he acknowledged to be natural, though it was unneeded and an impediment to a tranquil life.[57] Thus, if Jefferson was taking Epicurus as a model for good living, "the Greek option" of "procreative sex with [an] attractive servant" *would have been anathema*—that is, counterproductive to *ataraxia*.[58]

Burstein next turns to the Greek poet Theognis, who comes up in Jefferson's correspondence with John Adams (October 28, 1813) on the nature of the natural *aristoi* (Greek masculine, nominative, plural for "best"). Adams quotes Theognis, who writes of breeding animals for betterment of offspring. When applied to humans, being well-born, Adams says, amounts to wealth, beauty, and good birth. Jefferson replies:

> The passage you quote from Theognis, I think has an ethical rather than a political object. The whole piece is a moral exhortation, . . . a reproof to man, who, while with his domestic animals he is curious to improve the race by employing always the finest male, pays no attention to the improvement of his own race, but intermarries with the vicious, the ugly, or the old, for considerations of wealth or ambition.

Burstein then notes that Jefferson says procreation ought to be done for offspring, not for pleasure. Burstein writes, "*Was the desire to procreate how he characterized his own intent in having sex with his concubine?*"[59] Jefferson acknowledges that humans, by nature, tend to procreate for pleasure, not for offspring, because pleasure could provide more securely for the preservation of the species. Burstein concludes, "*Lustful sex, he is saying, rules human behavior whether we like it or not.*"[60] In other words, neither health nor virtue matters. "And so, Jefferson concludes, it is necessary to 'continue acquiescence' to the degeneration of the race that so long ago troubled Theognis, 'and to content ourselves with the accidental aristoi produced by the fortuitous concourse of breeders.'" Overall, because Theognis's ideal cannot be realized, Burstein says, "Jefferson was 'content' with the 'fortuitous' results of his private sexual behavior."

Burstein gives a serious misreading of Jefferson's reply to Adams. I quote the relevant bit of text:

> For experience proves that the moral and physical qualities of man, whether good or evil, are transmissible in a certain degree from father to son. But I suspect that the equal rights of men will rise up against this

privileged Solomon, and oblige us to continue acquiescence under 'the degeneration of the race of men' which Theognis complains of, and to content ourselves with the accidental aristoi produced by the fortuitous concourse of breeders.

Jefferson is acknowledging that breeding for virtue and talent will probably never happen because the common people will revolt against the Platonic notion of breeding for betterment. Jefferson, however, is not in line with public revulsion on selective breeding. The passage suggests strongly that, were Jefferson to engage in procreative behavior, he would likely be careful to secure a partner of suitable character, fitness, and intelligence to have offspring that are virtuous, physically fit, and intelligent. Burstein instead takes this passage as a rationalization of Jefferson's own lust for Sally Hemings, as he implicitly advocates the following syllogism:

(1) Everyone lusts.
(2) No one can do anything about it.
(3) So there is nothing wrong with sex with Hemings (1 and 2).

The syllogism Jefferson is actually putting forth is this:

(1) Selective breeding for moral and physical traits works.
(2) The masses will never allow selective breeding as public policy.
(3) So selective breeding will never be made public policy (1 and 2).

Jefferson's syllogism gives him no moral warrant for caving into any lusts he might have harbored.

## THE GENITAL-LIQUOR ARGUMENT

Why did Jefferson allegedly have an unfeeling relationship with Hemings? Burstein gives Jefferson's biggest rationalization—his liaison was the result of his interest in maintaining his own physical health.

Jefferson had in possession a large number of books on medicine, among them, Samuel Auguste André David Tissot's *De la santé des gens de lettres*. In the section on onanism (masturbation), Tissot addressed the passionate scholar, whose exertions were coming at expense of his physical well-being. Burstein writes in "Jefferson's Rationalizations" (italics added):

> The doctor recommended that sufferers practice, as Jefferson did, clean outdoor living, gardening, and frequent physical exercise, while following a semivegetarian diet. Tissot's ideal scholar maintained a cheerful disposition; he lived long by remaining coolheaded and self-controlled. (Tissot affirmed that this activity was inseparable from moral self-regard.) It would seem hardly a coincidence that Tissot's and Jefferson's prescriptions for a man of learning to maintain his health are *identical*.
>
> Jefferson made rhetorical gestures to (if not genuinely possessing) monastic tendencies. *It is not incomprehensible that*, for self-protection, he convinced himself that this sexual as well as social activity, whatever it was, would have to comport with his closely monitored diet and exercise routine [italics added]. The theory of onanism condemned 'the heinous sin of self-pollution' . . . , exhorting men not to waste their intellectual energy through masturbation but to find release, as nature intended, with a healthy, fruitful female.[61]

In *Jefferson's Secrets*, years later, he adds what might be dubbed the no-strings clause. "*It seems entirely possible that* Jefferson was a man increasingly fixed in his habits who found self sufficiency [*sic*] preferable to having a partner whom he would feel obliged to consult" (italics added). From here, it is a short leap to his liaison with Hemings, for Sally was just such a partner. He could be sexually active and autonomous with her.[62]

Let us cash out what we might call, following Tissot,[63] Burstein's genital-liquor argument, stripped of the modality of possibility, as follows.

(1) Tissot and Jefferson recommended that to sustain health a "sufferer" should practice clean outdoor living, gardening, and frequent physical exercise; follow a semivegetarian diet; maintain a cheerful disposition; and remain coolheaded and self-controlled.

(2) So Jefferson's and Tissot's prescriptions for health were identical (1).

(3) Tissot also recommended regular sexual outlet without masturbating.

(4) So Jefferson recommended (for himself) regular sexual outlet without masturbating (2 and 3).

(5) Sally Hemings afforded Jefferson the possibility of regular sexual outlet, without strings (no-strings clause).

(6) So Jefferson had an affair with Hemings for the sake of his health (4 and 5).

I have several things to say about this compound argument.

First, claim 2 plainly does not follow from claim 1. Burstein lists some seven commonalities between Tissot's and Jefferson's prescriptions for healthy living. To argue from seven commonalities to the claim that their prescriptions were *identical* is untoward, even foolhardy, but Burstein does just that. In the instantiation of such generalities, Jefferson does not follow Tissot to the letter in matters of health. Tissot mentions following nature and eschewing nocturnal studying, rubbing the stomach with a piece of flannel to aid digestion and the whole body to facilitate circulation of blood, taking in only the tender meats of young animals, and exercises beyond walking such as tennis, shuttlecock, or quick hunting (in preference to leisurely hunting) to "put the whole body in motion," among other things,[64] none of which Jefferson incorporated (or, if he did, he did not incorporate with any consistency). Yet if we allow for the identity of their prescriptions, then claim 4 is uncontroversial: It follows deductively from claims 2 and 3. Nonetheless, identity is uncalled for.

A more sensible route would have been to give claims 1 and 2 as evidence for claim 4, which would be to propose an analogical argument. Here Burstein could have argued that the strength and relevance of the seven commonalities *make it probable* that Jefferson too advocated regular sexual activity, without masturbation—that is, that he read Tissot and followed him in as many suggestions as he could. Yet as with any analogical argument, there are always reasons for regarding the comparison as faulty—that is, the existence of troublesome and many dissimilarities—if one digs deeply enough. That is why analogical arguments seldom make for strong arguments.[65]

Last, the inference from claims 4 and 5 to claim 6 is likely invalid, even if we assume the truth of claim 4. That Hemings was a possible outlet for Jefferson seems plain because she had children by a white father. Yet her accessibility does not mean Jefferson was interested. Even if he was seeking sexual outlet, a man of Jefferson's wealth and esteem would have had the interest of numerous available women, were there interest on his part. That he would have chosen a slave is doubtful. His choice of a slave, however handsome, would only make sense if his sexual needs were a loose cannon and if he were a highly irresponsible father and grandfather. Both are unlikely.

Could not Jefferson simply have remarried and kept himself and his family free of the abuses of a hostile press? Burstein adduces three reasons for Jefferson not remarrying.

First, according to family tradition, there is Jefferson's promise to his wife, on her deathbed, that he would not remarry. By not remarrying and, instead, merely having sex with a slave, he presumably would not be a promise breaker. Burstein seems not to give this argument much weight. He should not. One given to lifelong deceit, as Burstein thinks Jefferson was, would think nothing of breaking promises.

Second, Jefferson, Burstein states, liked his self-sufficiency. With Sally, he could have sex without strings, which for Jefferson was preferable to a sexual relationship within the confines of marriage. Just how Jefferson's marriage to Martha confined his lifestyle, Burstein does not say. His excessive grieving on her death suggests he lost considerably and gained little with her passing.

Finally, Burstein states the loss of Jefferson's daughter Maria proved a crushing below. By having sex with Sally and not remarrying, Jefferson could forefend the pain associated with her untimely death. Here Sally's status as slave would prove a plus.[66]

The last argument is the most puzzleheaded. Maria died in 1804, and Jefferson presumably began his relationship with Sally, according to

Burstein, sometime prior to 1789. Burstein does not explain how one event . (Maria's death) that happened some fifteen years ahead of another event (Jefferson's choice of a sexual relationship with Sally Hemings) could be its cause.

Let us sum by stating the genital-liquor argument is unpersuasive and stringy. Concludes lawyer William G. Hyland Jr., "Jefferson owned [Tissot's *Treatise upon the Disorders Produced by Masturbation*], among his collection of nine thousand books over his life time. . . . [Burstein] selects this *single* book to ascribe all its medicinal cures to Jefferson, including the far-fetched theory on masturbation as it relates to Sally."[67] Hyland's summation is spot-on.

In the main, Jefferson's view of the medicine of his time was unfavorable. Only with great reservation did he buy into the medicine of his day, which was beginning to move from the shadows of the Hippocratics. For instance, he had himself, those persons close to him, and even several members of Indian tribes inoculated to guard against smallpox.[68] Nonetheless, Jefferson was distrustful of physicians. He tells James Madison about the course of yellow fever and of physicians' incapacity to stop it running its course: "They agree that it is a nondescript disease," he adds, "and no two agree in any one part of their process of cure" (September 8, 1793). He writes to Dr. Caspar Wistar (June 21, 1807) of his advice to his grandson not to study medicine in Philadelphia. Nature, Jefferson says, restores better than any physician, for physicians work from a dizzying array of metempirical presuppositions. "In [a] disordered state, we observe nature providing for the re-establishment of order, by exciting some salutary evacuation of the morbific matter, or by some other operation which escapes our imperfect senses and researches. She brings on a crisis, by stools, vomiting, sweat, urine, expectoration, bleeding, &c., which, for the most part, ends in the restoration of healthy action." He does acknowledge some advances in medicine that aid nature. There are also certain substances, applied to the body, that expedite crisis and nature's slower healing touch through evacuation and movement. He lists diseases of the bowels and emetics, inflammation and bleeding, intermittents and Peruvian bark, syphilis and mercury, and watchfulness and opium. He does not speak of the need for intermittent release through onanism. To John Adams, late in life (December 18, 1825), Jefferson writes of the catastrophic results of his following the medical advice of convalescing in hot springs. "They destroyed in a great degree, my internal organism, and I have never since had a moment of perfect health."

## UPSHOT

"We can try to make Thomas Jefferson make sense; but in suiting our needs, we may unknowingly detour from historical truth," says Burstein.[69] What is implicit in these strange claims is that sensible explanations for Jefferson's behavior run great risk of falsehood. To get at the truth, are we to presume that nonsense is the most appropriate etiological path?

Burstein's *Jefferson's Secrets* as it relates to Jefferson and Hemings is not nonsense, but it is not in the least convincing. He is correct to note that if Jefferson had a relationship with Sally Hemings, the relationship was likely one of convenience, not mutual fulfillment. That would best explain his coolness toward Sally and their children. In that, his work is less wildcat than that of Brodie and Gordon-Reed.

Of course, there is another, more reasonable explanation for Jefferson's coolness toward his "black family." He did not have a black family.

Overall, Burstein makes too much of the DNA evidence, which is inconclusive, and the published account of Madison Hemings, which is inaccurate in many details. In his haste to correct the flaws of Brodie and Gordon-Reed, he fails to deal satisfactorily with disconfirmatory evidence—for example, the lack of letters between Jefferson and Hemings, the testimony of family and friends vis-à-vis Jefferson's character, the dearth of even one fond recollection of intimacy or friendliness between Madison's mother and Jefferson, and the fact that no one observed anything untoward between Jefferson and Hemings in thirty-eight years. Jefferson, it seems, could keep his private life perfectly secret, and Hemings was a tight-lipped lover.

Burstein writes that the recent DNA findings, which show that *a*

Jefferson fathered Eston Hemings, and "mounting circumstantial evidence"—whatever that is supposed to mean, for circumstantial evidence cannot mount—have shifted the burden of proof to those persons intent on defending the character of Jefferson.[70] The statement is incautious, if only because there is much on the line. Incontrovertible evidence of a sexual relationship, sustained after Callender's slanderous accusations, would show Jefferson to be a self-indulgent rogue, for whom sexual outlet was more important than the reputation of his family. It would also show him to be a deep-dyed hypocrite.

It is beyond question that Jefferson devoted numerous years of his life in the service of his neighbors, state, country, and fellow man in an effort to promote human flourishing. In doing so, he often neglected his family and his personal affairs. His published defense of the American continent in his *Notes on the State of Virginia* in light of French naturalist Georges Louis Leclerc Buffon's speculative criticisms, his lifelong patronage of science, his tenure as president, his lifelong political struggle for government by the people, his ardent fight for educational reform to instantiate true participatory republicanism, his work on revising the laws of Virginia, and his bill for religious freedom along with the numerous other bills he drafted throughout his life are just a few of numerous examples. Such services testify not only to a remarkable American, but a remarkable human being, whom Karl Lehmann called "one of the greatest humanists of all time," because of his "concrete grasp of human experience, in the records and works of the ancient world, in its integration in individual, progressive personalities who are aware of their duties toward the human society of their time."[71] I certainly agree. Jefferson throughout his life was, like a Stoic, fully involved in the affairs of humans.

The radical statement that Thomas Jefferson had a lasting sexual relationship with Sally Hemings, if true, would have radical, normative implications: It would show Jefferson to be a hypocrite and a scoundrel. Yet radical claims need an abundance of evidence, for, if true, they mark a radical shift in the literature—a shift that blights the character of another human being. For better or worse, Jefferson is not just another human being. He is one of the few acknowledged American heroes. Yet Burstein, like

Brodie and Gordon-Reed, has given readers no sound evidence—nothing upon which readers can hang a hat—to demonstrate that Jefferson's deeds matched his words, that he was authentic and not Janus-faced.

That scholars like Burstein can be so cocksure of Jefferson's duplicity on gauzy, circumstantial evidence is to me the great mystery that requires explication. Without compelling evidence for Jefferson's duplicity, one can only conclude that the reason for Burstein's about-face shift on the issue of Jefferson's avowed relationship with Hemings is psychologically based—perhaps rationalizations for his all-too-hasty assessment of the DNA evidence and his all-too-hasty concordance with the conclusions of the Thomas Jefferson Memorial Foundation on Jefferson's paternity, the topic of chapter 5.

# PART 2

# UNFRAMING THE LEGEND

# CHAPTER 4

# THE "TIRESOME" ARGUMENT FROM CHARACTER

## A Defense of Moral Impossibility

> I do not know myself under the pens of my friends
> or foes. It is unfortunate for our peace, that unmer-
> ited abuse wounds, while unmerited praise has not the
> power to heal.
>
> —TJ TO EDWARD RUTLEDGE, DECEMBER 27, 1796[1]

*I*n an e-mail correspondence with a Jefferson scholar who is agnostic on the issue of the Jefferson-Hemings relationship, my correspondent indicated that he merely encouraged interested persons to read Annette Gordon-Reed's *The Hemingses of Monticello* and William G. Hyland's *In Defense of Thomas Jefferson* and make up their own minds on the plausibility of Jefferson's paternity. He indicated plainly to me that he had an open mind on the matter, but considered the argument-from-character defense of Jefferson to be "tiresome."

I was intrigued by my correspondent's choice of words. The sense of the missive was the argument from character was unpersuasive because it was tiresome—that is, overwrought or overused through the years or long since out of season—not that it was tiresome because it was unpersuasive. In evaluating any non-demonstrative argument, non-deductive arguments are to be dismissed when they are evidentially unpersuasive—that is, invalid—but I have never heard an argument being dismissed because it was "tiresome." One might find, for instance, the argument for evolutionary biology tiresome, but that does not make the evidence on its behalf unpersuasive. It is wholly persuasive.

This chapter concerns the argument from character, which deserves its own chapter, if only because it is so tiresome. In it, I examine revisionists' arguments against the argument from character. Though there is an abundance of literature from which I could draw, I focus on the same trio of revisionists—Fawn Brodie, Annette Gordon-Reed, and Andrew Burstein—to which I have devoted the first part of the book.

## BRODIE'S TWO JEFFERSONS

In *Thomas Jefferson: An Intimate History*, Fawn Brodie makes the case that Jefferson was the seducer of Sally Hemings. She shows him to be a highly sexual man who had an especial attraction for forbidden women. His sexual needs were so great that he undertook a secretive relationship with his handsome slave that lasted thirty-eight years and resulted in as many as seven children, of whom only four survived.

Notwithstanding Jefferson's prodigious sexual appetite, much of her book concerns Jefferson's equanimity. Brodie maintains that Jefferson was a pacific person both in public and in private. She writes, "The necessity for peace dominated his public life, as the necessity for tranquillity [*sic*] ruled his private life."[2] As president, he had a "genius for peace" and prided himself on deflecting the passions of an angry nation to avert war with England during his second term as president, by opting for an embargo. He avoided direct confrontation with "fiery zealots" in his personal life, for, as he wrote to his grandson Thomas Jefferson Randolph (November 24, 1808), "it is not for a man of sense to dispute the road with [angry bulls]." He also avoided a duel with friend and neighbor John Walker over the presumed affair with his wife. With others, Jefferson was always polite. Advice to his daughters, son-in-law, grandchildren, and other family members, Brodie concedes, was always conciliatory. "None of this would have been possible had Jefferson not been at peace with himself both as president and as a man."

It is bizarre that this person, "at peace with himself both as president and as a man," could have been so driven by passion that he would have sought out in-chambers sex with one of his slaves and one who was inordinately young. For Brodie, Jefferson's tranquility and kindness is explicable by reference to his own guilt concerning his hidden secret—his love of Sally Hemings.[3] Might not it merely be that Jefferson was tranquil and kind because he was a tranquil and kind person? Might it not be, as Jefferson himself asserts, that at some point early in his life he came as it were to a fork in the road of life and decided, as did Hercules, on virtue over pleasure? I give Jefferson's own account of his early-life dilemma in a letter to his eponymous grandson, Thomas Jefferson Randolph (November 24, 1808).

> When I recollect that at fourteen years of age, the whole care and direction of myself was thrown on myself entirely [upon the death of my father], without a relation or friend qualified to advise or guide me, and recollect the various sorts of bad company with which I associated from time to time, I am astonished I did not turn off with some of them, and become as worthless to society as they were. I had the good fortune to become acquainted very early with some characters of very high standing, and to feel the incessant wish that I could ever become what they were. Under temptations and difficulties, I would ask myself what would Dr. Small, Mr. Wythe, Peyton Randolph do in this situation? What course in it will insure me their approbation? I am certain that this mode of deciding on my conduct, tended more to correctness than any reasoning powers I possessed. Knowing the even and dignified line they pursued, I could never doubt for a moment which of two courses would be in character for them. Whereas, seeking the same object through a process of moral reasoning, and with the jaundiced eye of youth, I should often have erred. From the circumstances of my position, I was often thrown into the society of horse racers, card players, fox hunters, scientific and professional men, and of dignified men; and many a time have I asked myself, in the enthusiastic moment of the death of a fox, the victory of a favorite horse, the issue of a question eloquently argued at the bar, or in the great council of the nation, well, which of these kinds of reputation should I prefer? That of a horse jockey? a fox hunter? an orator? or the honest advocate of my country's rights? Be assured, my dear Jefferson, that these little returns into ourselves, this self-catechising habit, is not trifling nor useless, but leads to the prudent selection and steady pursuits of what is right.

According to Jefferson, attempts to reason out the correct path in life would have certainly led him astray had he not had the right sort of moral exemplars from whom he could pattern his behavior. Yet Brodie is unmoved. Such a person is inconceivable for her, because psychoanalytic explanation, as I have noted in chapter 1, makes no room for moral uprightness as a genuine feature of a person's character. Behind the façade of tranquility and kindness, there lies the latent jumble of sexual and aggressive impulses, needing discharge. Kindness is a mask for perfidy. Kindness needs to be explained; it cannot be taken at face value.

There are, however, two difficulties for Brodie within the confines of psychoanalytic explanation. First, why is it that Jefferson's pacific nature points plainly to guilt, instead of, say, the calm generated by regular release of sexual impulses through sublimation? Second, given that Freudian psychoanalysis[4] makes use of sexual *and* destructive impulses, why does Brodie try to explicate Jefferson's behavior only by reference to his sexual impulses?

Because evidence of a high-sexed Jefferson is thin, Brodie must manufacture a Janus-faced Jefferson in order to make plausible the contentious part of her book—the love affair between Jefferson and Hemings. In the end, it is much simpler to cast aside the Janus-faced Jefferson—a person who acts one way in public and lives otherwise in private—for the picture of the Jefferson that I maintain is correct—one whose private life and public life are relatively consonant. As Jefferson wrote in a letter to James Madison (August 28, 1789): "I know but one code of morality for men whether acting singly or collectively. He who says I will be a rogue when I act in company with a hundred others, but an honest man when I act alone, will be believed in the former assertion, but not in the latter."[5] Historian Joseph Ellis, whose depiction of Jefferson is anything but roseate, concurred (at least prior to the DNA study): "His psychological dexterity depended upon the manipulation of interior images and personae; he was not that adroit at the kind of overt deviousness required to sustain an alleged thirty-eight-year affair in the very center of his domestic haven. . . . His most sensual statements were aimed at beautiful buildings rather than beautiful women."[6]

Consistency between public and private activity was a staple of much of ancient Greek and Roman ethical thinking (e.g., Plato, Aristotle, Epicurus, and the Greek and Roman Stoics) and Jefferson's cosmology, epistemology, and ethics owe a considerable debt to the ancients—especially the Stoics.[7] I add cosmology and epistemology to ethics here, because, for the ancients, virtue (*aretē*) or, for Epicurus, equanimity (*ataraxia*), could not be attained without a truthful approach to reality and without some sense of integration in the cosmos. Jefferson's ethical thinking also integrated cosmology and epistemology.[8] Against historian Adrienne Koch,[9] Jefferson was not a utilitarian for whom morality encompassed only such actions that affected others. Utilitarianism allows for a Jekyll-and-Hyde approach to behavior, so long as Jekyll never goes out and "mingles" with others. For Jefferson, there was no distinction to be made between public and private realms of morally correct action. One who harbored malicious thoughts but failed to act on them was equally as culpable as another who harbored malicious thoughts and acted on them. Drawing plentifully from Stoic thinking as well as the moral-sense philosophy of his day (e.g., Francis Hutcheson, Lord Kames, Lord Bolingbroke, and even David Hume), Jefferson had demanding moral ideals, as did those he read, and he read often Cicero's moral treatises, the Stoics, the Bible or his Jefferson Bible, and Laurence Sterne, whose works are fraught with moral content.[10]

. That Jefferson had demanding moral ideals, which drew no line between private and public, is a point of extraordinary significance in examining Jefferson's character. It is also a point not readily recognized in Jeffersonian scholarship. It is certainly pretermitted by Brodie and Gordon-Reed, who do not address the philosophical dimension of Jefferson's thinking. It is also missed by Burstein, who attempts to address the ethical dimension of Jefferson in chapter 9 of *Jefferson's Secrets* and whose grasp of the influence of Greek and Roman philosophy on Jefferson is too skewed and unsubtle and, thus, misses the mark. In assessment of Jefferson's character, one must assess the whole man, not just the perceived results of his actions. What is more, in assessing Jefferson's character, one must not attribute deeds to him on mere circumstantial evidence.

Jefferson's rigorous moral ideals make unlikely the possibility of an affair with a slave to slake his own sexual appetite. In contrast to Brodie's depiction of a man driven by libido, Jefferson the man was constrained, both in thought and in action, by his high ethical ideals. Advice to his daughters and grandchildren is filled with reference to virtuous activity. He writes to Martha (April 7, 1787), for example: "Whenever you are to do a thing, though it can never be known but to yourself, ask yourself how you would act were all the world looking at you, and act accordingly. Encourage all your virtuous dispositions, and exercise them whenever an opportunity arises; being assured that they will gain strength by exercise, as a limb of the body does, and that exercise will make them habitual. From the practice of the purest virtue, you may be assured you will derive the most sublime comforts in every moment of life, and in the moment of death."[11] Political addresses and letters to political correspondents often note that correct political action is correct moral action. For illustration, to physician and politician George Logan, Jefferson writes of political expediency: "My principle is to do whatever is right, and leave consequences to Him who has the disposal of them" (October 3, 1813).[12] Moreover, in a letter to his physician Dr. Vine Utley (March 21, 1817) concerning his physical health, Jefferson feels the need to write that he seldom goes to sleep each night without first reading something ethically poignant upon which he can "ruminate in the intervals of sleep." Thus, if it should turn out that Jefferson did carry out an in-chamber, thirty-eight-year relationship with Sally Hemings, then there would be nothing more to say than he was a liar (he expressly denied any wrongdoing other than making a pass at Betsy Walker in his 1805 letter to Robert Smith[13]), an uncaring father (he would have placed his libidinal outlet ahead of concern for his family), and a hypocrite (he would not have lived up to the ideals he embraced)— that is, Jefferson, by his own canons of morally upright activity, would be a moral reprobate. One cannot, as Brodie aims to do, exonerate Jefferson by saying, in effect, that he, in love with Sally and having no recourse other than a furtive relationship, was a victim of his times.

Jennifer Jensen Wallach in "The Vindication of Fawn Brodie"— covered in chapter 1—offers a post-DNA assessment of the merit of Brodie's work that has a bearing on Jefferson's character. She suggests that a conspiracy is afoot. On the issue of character, she says, "As Brodie shrewdly observed, Jefferson scholars committed to the 'canonization' of a singular heroic vision of Jefferson had ultimately dispensed with any ability to search for historical truth." She quotes Brodie: "The unanimity with which Jefferson male biographers—and she mentions Dumas Malone, John C. Miller, Douglass Adair, and Douglas Wilson—deny him even one richly intimate love affair after his wife's death suggests that something is at work here that has little to do with scholarship, especially since they are so gifted in writing about every other aspect of his life."[14] The unanimity of those "male scholars" on the nonexistence of a relationship between Jefferson and Hemings is here taken as evidence of some sort of collusion. That is bunkum. There is unanimity of opinion among biologists on the truth of evolutionary biology too. There is unanimity of opinion among physicists that space and time are relative, not absolute. There is unanimity of opinion among psychologists that nature and nurture are not independent variables, as they were once thought to be. Are these too instances of collusion? All things considered, unanimity of opinion among experts on some claim—when the research behind the claim is thorough, dispassionate, and exhaustive—is always a good reason to believe that that claim is true.

## "NONE OF THIS FOLLOWS"

In *Thomas Jefferson and Sally Hemings*, Annette Gordon-Reed addresses and dismisses the argument from character. She begins her argument by, once again, an appeal to the skewed scholarship of dissenters, without naming persons.

> For some scholars Jefferson's fastidiousness, his attachment to reason and rationality, his zeal for exactitude, his obsession with orderliness, all signal that he was without a real capacity for romantic involvement or sexual passion. What one makes of the fact that an individual possesses some or all of these characteristics is a function of one's own values and experiences and, of course, one's personal view of what it takes to be sexual or romantic. People who are compulsive about making lists have

no interests in sex or romance. People who hold their emotions severely in check have no interest in sex or romance. People who are extremely clean have no interest in sex or romance. None of this follows. It is not even remotely a fact [*sic*] that a person who possesses all of these traits—even in abundance—is without sexual passion or romantic yearnings.[15]

For Gordon-Reed, no psychological evidence is reliable in assessing historical figures. There are not even remote facts, whatever remote facts are supposed to be. The reason is that there are no psychological generalizations, other than the generalization that there are no psychological generalizations. How she is in the privileged position to know that, she never discloses.

In effect, Gordon-Reed tries to block any argument of the following form.

All persons that exhibit features α, β, and γ are π.
Person *p* exhibits features α, β, and γ.
So person *p* is π.

If we instantiate the terms Gordon-Reed uses, we get something like this, though there are numerous ways of formulating the argument:

All persons who are rational, exact, and orderly are asexual.
Jefferson was rational, exact, and orderly.
So Jefferson was asexual.

"None of this follows," we are told categorically.

That is a clever move by Gordon-Reed, because, if it goes unchallenged, one can merely cast aside as fallacious any argument that concludes *Jefferson did not have a relationship with Sally Hemings* on the basis of Jefferson's psychological or moral makeup—namely, she disallows the argument from character. Moreover, by blocking the argument from character, Gordon-Reed has indefinite plasticity for her own outlandish claims concerning Jefferson's lascivious, backstairs lifestyle.

There are, as usual, difficulties. The psychological literature on such issues does not, because it cannot, show that *every* person with attributes α, β, and γ will exhibit the (presumed pathological) behavior pattern π. It merely attempts to establish correlations between personality traits and behaviors, and the correlations are then tested for causal efficacy. That in itself is not trifling. It is, to the extent that the psychological literature is persuasive, extraordinarily helpful. One cannot and ought not to say that Jefferson, for instance, could not have been sexual, because of α, β, and γ. However, one can say that it is unlikely, or even highly unlikely, that he was sexual because of α, β, and γ. That conclusion, being inductively generated, is fallible, but that need not mean it is unsupported. In short, because she cannot, Gordon-Reed has not blocked arguments of the following form:

> Most persons who exhibit features α, β, and γ are π.
> Person *p* exhibits features α, β, and γ.
> So person *p* is π.

The conclusion here, *Person* p *is* π, is sustainable because it is given a reasonable degree of support—for there is more reason to believe the conclusion to be true than to be false, given the truth of the premises. That it is sustainable does not mean it is infallible. Such arguments, however, are best framed not by a professor of law, but by a competent behavioral psychologist.

Thus, what Gordon-Reed argues for, in effect, is the rather mundane claim that there are no psychological laws—that is, that all psychological generalizations admit of exceptions. She says enigmatically, "One could just as easily look to other aspects of Jefferson's activities and tastes to come to an opposite conclusion." She adds, "He was physical man, riding horses some great number of miles a day, laboring with his slave artisans to make furniture and metal tools, pitting himself against much younger men in competitions designed to test strength and winning."[16] Again, it seems, anything goes: One can argue any one thing as well as any other thing because one can find anything one wants to find in the historical evidence as regards Jefferson. Bedlam reigns.

Jefferson's father might have been herculean—he is said to have been able to stand up two hogsheads, each weighing one thousand pounds, at the same time (a ridiculous claim!)[17]—but there is no evidence that Jefferson himself displayed the physical stoutness of this father. He is always described as tall and lean, never stout. Moreover, what such "competitions" are, Gordon-Reed, as is her wont, fails to say, but she is probably retelling a story, rehashed by Brodie[18] and originally given by overseer Edmund Bacon,[19] about Jefferson's acquisition of a machine for measuring strength and his often-victorious contests with younger men on the machine. That story is hardly evidence of uncommon strength.

Jefferson was lanky, not herculean. Concerning manual labor, Jefferson labored more with his pen than with any tools. He was wont to delegate authority to others for physical labor. Historian Silvio Bedini, specializing in the study of scientific instruments, writes, "Although he owned an elaborate chest of hand tools and always intended to use his own hands to fabricate his devices, he never found time to do so."[20] Dumas Malone, whose scholarly knowledge of Jefferson perhaps surpasses all others, describes the youthful Jefferson thus: "He visited homes, made wagers with girls, gossiped about love affairs, served at weddings. Tall, loose-jointed, sandy-haired, and freckled, he was not prepossessing in appearance, but he was a skilled horseman, played on the violin, and seems to have been a gay companion."[21] Malone is, unfortunately, silent about Jefferson's prodigious strength and virulence. Jeffersonian scholar Gilbert Chinard states that Jefferson "had never engaged in back-breaking tasks of felling trees or of splitting rails" and likely never "put his hand to the plow except as an experiment."[22] Emeritus professor of politics Robert Johnstone says, "Despite a height of six feet, two inches, he was physically unimposing, lanky and raw-boned rather than stately in bearing."[23] He too says nothing about Jefferson's virulence. Jefferson also says nothing of those features in his so-called *Autobiography*—though his autobiography, I admit, is not very revelatory, as autobiographies go. Episodes like his injuring his wrist while with Cosway give evidence of clumsiness, not adroitness. Madison Hemings too, in his testimony about "his father," mentions nothing of his strength. "His general temperament was smooth and even; he was very undemonstrative."[24]

Strangely, this depiction of a virulent Jefferson is somewhat at odds with the epicene depiction of Jefferson in Gordon-Reed's *The Hemingses of Monticello*.

Jefferson possessed a curious and, in the end, enormously creative and effective combination of stereotypically masculine and feminine traits. . . . Men of his class often disdained anything that suggested physical labor. But he actually loved the sensation of working with his hands—on his own terms, of course—much like his mother and sisters, who sewed for their own recreation, but were not serious providers of services to their nuclear family or slaves. He made keys, kept his own set of carpenter tools, and occasionally tried his hand at making furniture.[25]

Citing his quasi hermaphroditism, she then again goes on to speak of his virulence—namely, his physicality and inordinate strength (before or after he injured his wrist in 1786?)—without citing any specific instances.

To Peter Carr (August 19, 1785), Jefferson advised long walks as exercise, but that was as much an escape from thinking as it was to make the body fit. "The object of walking," he tells Carr, "is to relax the mind." To soon-to-be son-in-law Thomas Mann Randolph Jr. (August 27, 1786), he writes, "It is of little consequence to store the mind with science if the body be permitted to become debilitated." Again, he advocates walking. One who never walked three miles can readily learn to walk fifteen or twenty miles. Mohandas Gandhi too was an avid walker. That scarcely is a signal of virulence.

Late in *Thomas Jefferson and Sally Hemings*, Gordon-Reed returns to the argument from character and succinctly pummels it in one sentence. "The argument that it would be impossible or even highly unlikely for a man to perform some action because he had written letters highly critical of that action has little or no resonance with anyone living in the modern world."[26] What was presumed to be a meaty argument—the argument from character—now seems to be mincemeat.

Yet there are problems with her statement. First, Gordon-Reed seems to have established herself as an expert in psychological issues. She says that no one can draw any reliable conclusions about the behavior of another by perusal of that other's written works. Note, however, that she addresses only cases of impossibility and high improbability. That leaves untouched the case of probability and the claim *One who is highly critical of some action is unlikely to perform that action*. Second, her sentence, if taken as a broad descriptive statement of universal scope, is simply false; if taken as nearly universal, it is very likely false. She herself has expressly admitted that Jefferson biographer Malone thought a liaison highly improbable because of Jefferson's character. There are, of course, numerous others who think a liaison highly improbable. I too think it is highly unlikely that Jefferson had a liaison with Hemings, and I draw prominently from the "tiresome" argument from character. Yet Malone and I are, by Gordon-Reed's decree, not living in the modern world. Finally, Gordon-Reed's statement exhibits rodomontade. She deems herself an expert on rationality and a suitable spokesperson for all persons in the modern world. As I have argued in chapter 2, she is at best a questionable spokesperson for human rationality, since in her writings, she sidesteps the canons of good reasoning when it suits her purposes. The highly misleading implication of Gordon-Reed's disavowal of the argument from character is this: Jefferson was a passionate man with a clamant need to express that passion. Yet out of *thousands* of his writings, she adduces no direct evidence of such passion. The conclusion is supported wholly on surmise.

Almost everything Jefferson wrote speaks of a sort of asexuality. In a letter to lifelong friend John Banister (October 15, 1785), Jefferson writes of the corrosive effects of Europe and its educational system. After listing numerous European corruptions—"to enumerate them all would require a volume"—he speaks of its greatest defect: indulgence of one's sexual passions. He states that one educated in Europe

> is led by the strongest of all the human passions, into a spirit for female intrigue, destructive of his own and others' happiness, or a passion for whores, destructive of his health, and, in both cases, learns to consider fidelity to the marriage bed as an ungentlemanly practice, and inconsistent with happiness; he recollects the voluptuary dress and arts of the European women, and pities and despises the chaste affections and simplicity of those of his own country.

The simplest explanation for Jefferson's express condemnation of sexual passion to Banister is that he has no qualms about being judged by the standard he expresses. It also shows Andrew Burstein's claim that Jefferson undertook a sexual relationship with his slave for reasons of health to be fatuous. If highly sexual, Jefferson sublimated his sexuality.

Even Jefferson's impassioned letter to Maria Cosway (October 12, 1786), written under smite of love, is framed in the form of a dialog between Head and Heart. That suggests strongly a great discomfort with erotic passion, as even under smite of love, passion must fight it out with reason. Taken as a whole and contrary to Brodie, his "love letters" to Cosway are largely unimaginative, unimpassioned, and often distant, as if to protect himself from rejection—once again (recall his clumsiness apropos of his youthful crush on Rebecca Burwell). After his Head-and-Heart letter, Cosway often complains of the curtness of Jefferson's letters. At one point, she states roundly that the Head-and-Heart letter has made her an *enfant gâtée* ("spoiled child").[27]

Gordon-Reed, however, is reluctant to draw anything definitive from Jefferson's Head-and-Heart letter to Cosway. The Head/Heart is an effective "literary device," she maintains, but it does no more than reveal something about Jefferson at the time of his writing of the letter. The literary device is no more than "a prism"—in effect, "a prison," she writes puckishly. "What matters are of 'the head,' and what matters are of 'the heart'? Who decides? The historian? Jefferson? Are the head and heart always in opposition to one another? Don't they, in fact, usually work together in some combination?"[28] That barrage of questions is, I suspect, a boorish rhetorical device, employed by Gordon-Reed, with the effect of benumbing and addling her readers so that they will defer to her authority on the issue of a liaison.

There are answers to Gordon-Reed's questions. As I have shown in *Dutiful Correspondent: Philosophical Essays on Thomas Jefferson*, Head and Heart do not usually work together in some combination.[29] Influence of Head on matters of Heart (morality) tends to lead to morally wrong action. "Morals were too essential to the happiness of man to be risked on the incertain [*sic*] combinations of the head," says Heart to Head in his letter to Cosway. "She laid their foundation therefore in sentiment, not in science" (October 12, 1786). "The practice of morality being necessary for the well-being of society, [deity] has taken care to impress it's precepts so indelibly on our hearts that they shall not be effaced by the subtleties of our brain," Jefferson states to fellow Albemarle County resident James Fishback (September 27, 1809). To Thomas Law, son of the bishop of Carlisle (June 13, 1814), Jefferson states that the care of the Creator was necessary in making the moral sense "so much a part of our constitution as that no errors of reasoning or of speculation might lead us astray from it's observance in practice." The judgments of the moral sense, then, are spontaneous and relatively independent of the rational faculty.

Gordon-Reed also refers to the argument from character in a 2000 publication, "Engaging Jefferson." She writes, with again a tedious focus on race:

> It is not enough to deny that Jefferson was the father, it had to be made plain that the men chosen to be the fathers were bad people [Samuel and Peter Carr]. Historians picked up on this refrain when they offered their version of Jefferson's character as a defense to the story, presenting the public with the following syllogism: No decent white person could be involved in an affair with a black slave. Jefferson was a decent white person. Therefore, Jefferson could not have been involved with a black slave.[30]

Gordon-Reed would, I presume, expressly deny the first premise, though it is not plain that she considers Jefferson a decent white person and, I presume, she would deny the second, given that she is openly critical of Jefferson's plain disregard of his family by not dealing straightforwardly with his mounting debt. Her misgivings notwithstanding, the syllogism is sound, if relativized to Jefferson's person, station, time, and place—namely, if the first premise is understood as *No decent white person of Jefferson's day and given the mores of the South at that time could be involved in an affair with a black slave.* Gordon-Reed's failure to relativize (i.e., her judging Jefferson from present standards instead of those standards of his time and place) is once again another instance of the fallacy of historical anachronism.

At day's end, it is evident why Gordon-Reed dismisses the argument from character. Jefferson was much maligned during his life because of his political and ethical views, and because he was an easy target, for he flatly refused to address calumny. Yet the persons who best knew him paint a consistent portrait of a shy but venerable man who loved his family, friends, and science; and who, even in retirement, was intimately connected not only to his fellow Virginians and fellow Americans, but also to the world around him. Recall his chastisement of his daughter Maria (March 3, 1802) for wishing to withdraw from social affairs:

> I think I discover in you a willingness to withdraw from society more than is prudent. I am convinced our own happiness requires that we should continue to mix with the world, and to keep pace with it as it goes; and that every person who retires from free communication with it is severely punished afterwards by the state of mind into which he gets, and which can only be prevented by feeding our social principles. I can speak from experience on this subject. From 1793 to 1797 I remained closely at home, saw none but those who came there, and at length became sensible of the ill effect it had on my mind, and of its direct and irresistible tendency to render me unfit for society and uneasy when necessarily engaged in it. I felt enough of the effect of withdrawing from the world than to see that it led to an antisocial and misanthropic state of mind, which severely punishes him who gives in to it; and it will be a lesson I never shall forget as to myself.

Jefferson believed each person had a moral duty to benefit his fellow man and work toward social betterment. That is the same portrait that scholars who scrutinize Jefferson's corpus, without selecting this and overlooking that, get. "In a virtuous government," he writes to politician Henry Lee, "and more especially in times like these, public offices are, what they should be, burthens to those appointed to them, which it would be wrong to decline, though foreseen to bring with them intense labour, and great private loss" (June 17, 1779). "I acknolege [*sic*] that such a debt [of public service] exists, that a tour of duty, in whatever line he can be most useful to his country, is due from every individual," Jefferson writes to James Madison (June 9, 1793). "Some men are born for the public," he writes to James Monroe. "Nature by fitting them for the service of the human race on a broad scale, has stamped with the evidences of her destination and their duty" (January 13, 1803). That is the same portrait that scholars who study his actions upon retirement get. He undertook the drudgery of writing letters because he believed in a duty to help his fellow men. "From sunrise to one or two o'clock, and often from dinner to dark," he writes to John Adams (January 11, 1817), "I am drudging at the writing table. And all this to answer letters into which neither interest nor inclination on my part enters; and often from persons whose names I have never before heard. Yet, writing civilly, it is hard to refuse them civil answers. This is the burthen of my life, a very grievous one indeed." Though here and in numerous other letters he expressed a wish to discontinue such drudgery, he always wrote when his health allowed him to write. Civility required an answer. Finally, his work on the University of Virginia was not merely a matter of giving him something to do in his final years. "I shall feel, too, the want of your counsel and approbation in what we are doing and have yet to do in our University, the last of my mortal cares, and the last service I can render my country," he writes near the end of his life to Portuguese politician José Francisco Correia da Serra (October 24, 1820).

Gordon-Reed, however, largely ignores Jefferson's writings because to her they offer no clue to the person behind the pen. To rule out *thousands* of pieces of evidence apropos of a person's character by dismissing the possibility that those writings, or any parcels among them, are evidence of the man behind the writer is outrageous. Yet Gordon-Reed seems to have preference for what is possible instead of what is factual.


## DOCTOR'S ORDERS

As we have seen in the previous chapter, in *The Inner Jefferson*, Andrew Burstein's picture of Jefferson is that of a morally focused person whose devotion to his family and friends is unwavering and incontestable. He judges himself and others by temper. Inner softness, introspection, sympathy with the sentiments of others, and nobility of taste characterize Jefferson's normative ideals.[31]

In his first book, Burstein spends little time on the Sally Hemings scandal. He briefly weighs the testimonies on behalf of Jefferson against that of Madison Hemings and comes down, though not securely, on the side of Jefferson on account of his character. What tilts the balance in favor of Jefferson is that Madison and Eston Hemings were born after Callender's accusation, and Burstein finds it implausible that Jefferson would have been smug enough to continue a sexual relationship once it was publicly disclosed in 1802. That said, it is highly improbable, he thinks, that Jefferson fathered any of Hemings's children.

In the PBS interview of him after publication of *The Inner Jefferson*, Burstein's admiration for Jefferson is evident, as he talks in a profoundly moving way about Jefferson's reaction to the loss of his wife:

> Thomas and Patty Jefferson [Jefferson's wife] had read Laurence Sterne's novel *Tristram Shandy*. This was a novel about the workings of the human heart. And Jefferson had recorded in his commonplace book, a book of quotations, a section of one of the last scenes in *Tristram Shandy*. And as Patty Jefferson lay dying in September of 1782, the two Jeffersons sat at her bed and they wrote out together this quotation from the commonplace book. And it started out in Patty Jefferson's handwriting, a little four-by-four inch piece of paper. And on the scrip of paper, Patty Jefferson began, "Time wastes too fast, Every letter I trace tells me with what rapidity life follows my pen, The days and hours of it pass over our heads like clouds of a windy day never to return more, Everything presses on." At this moment, orchestrating it as a deathbed adieu of two lovers about to part, Jefferson picks up his own pen and continues the quote, "And every time I kiss thy hand to bid adieu and every absence which follows is a prelude to that eternal separation we are shortly to make." Jefferson kept this little piece of paper in the most private drawer in a secret compartment of the drawer beside his bed. And it was folded and unfolded countless times over the years and in it was a lock of his late wife's hair and a lock of the hair of one of their infant children who had died. And this was the real Thomas Jefferson, the man of sentiment who loved deeply, who felt deeply.[32]

The interview shows intense feelings for Jefferson by Burstein. Nonetheless, years later in *Jefferson's Secrets*, Burstein does an about-face. The DNA tests, he asserts, are a major factor for his reversal. It has shown that Peter Carr, whom he presumably thought was the most likely father of Sally's children, is no longer a candidate as the father of Eston Hemings.[33] Furthermore, attempts to implicate Randolph Jefferson, Burstein thinks, are ad hoc—made only to save Jefferson's reputation. Moreover, Madison Hemings's testimony now seems to have a grip on him that it did not have before. Finally, there is the work of law professor Gordon-Reed, whose testimony has for Burstein enormous weight. Burstein believes that those arguments, taken together, make it highly unlikely that anyone but Jefferson was the father of Sally Hemings's children. Yet, as I have noted in the prior chapter, each argument is independent of the others, and each must be evaluated independently of the others. They cannot be taken together. Moreover, each argument is weak.

To illustrate, let us consider three independent arguments—$A_1$, $A_2$, and $A_3$—on behalf of some claim $c$. Consider further that each argument is given a probability value—that is, an assessment of the probable truth of claim $c$, given the truth of the premises—such that $p(A_1) = 0.2$, $p(A_2) = 0.3$, and $p(A_3) = 0.27$. The arguments cannot be lumped together so that $c$, given the truth of the premises of all three arguments, now has a probability of 0.77. The most that can be said is that the "strongest" of the inductive arguments is the second, with a probability value of 0.3, which is deplorably weak. An analogy is aidful. Imagine a weakly constructed chain that one attempts to strengthen by adding to it ends two other weakly constructed chains. The new chain is nowise strengthened. By adding together his three weak arguments, Burstein has constructed just such a chain. Marveling at its length, he has nowise considered its capacity for work.

Given what he perceives to be the high likelihood of a relationship—he often tends to treat it as factual—Burstein argues that the relationship could have been only sexual because of the unequal standing of the two and because of Jefferson's views on black inferiority. Why, then, did he begin a thirty-eight-year sexual relationship with her and not with a white woman?

Burstein maintains that Jefferson was intimately familiar with the medical work of noted Swiss physician Dr. Samuel Auguste André David Tissot. Tissot argued that regular seminal release through intercourse with an attractive female was needed to maintain optimal health. Jefferson chose Hemings because she was comely and a no-strings-attached option.

It is a defect of character, his tendency to rationalize, that ultimately led Jefferson to Hemings, claims Burstein. In his interview with historian Rick Shankman, Burstein we recall (see chapter 3) says of Jefferson's sexual relationship, "Jefferson could rationalize his behavior to himself on the basis of the medical authority of his age, which literally recommended for a widower like himself occasional sex with a young, healthy, fruitful, attractive female, in order to preserve his own mental and physical health."[34] Yet if Jefferson followed Tissot's advice and took a concubine for the sake of optimal health—as he presumably did with his semivegetarianism, long walks, cheerful disposition, coolheadedness, and self-control—how was that rationalization? If Jefferson took long walks, he did so because they were believed by leading medical authorities, and by him, to optimize health. Likewise if Jefferson took Hemings as a concubine, he did so because it was believed by leading medical authorities, and by him, to optimize health. Following the advice of a leading medical authority is not rationalizing. Rationalizing occurs when one imputes as a cause of one's action something that merely seems reasonable but is unrelated to the actual causes of one's behavior. For Jefferson to have rationalized, he would have had to act on powerful sexual impulses directed toward Hemings and then "justify" such actions to himself later by recourse to Tissot's work.

The medical thesis, as it relates to "confirmation" of a sexual relationship with Hemings, is explanatorily empty. That is strange, since Burstein in an early paper, "The Problem of Jefferson Biography," is highly critical of the Jeffersonian psycho-biographical literature, much of which is "bloated with irresponsible guesswork."[35] There he singles out Fawn Brodie's *Thomas Jefferson* and, more recently, books by historian Alf Mapp Jr. and biographer Willard Sterne Randall. Brodie, he says, has a "tin ear for language" and uses "currently fashionable psychological explanations." Of Mapp's and Randall's books, Burstein says, "they are far from adequate treatments and serve only to give the popular audience what it wants—simple formulas and, where possible, titillating copy." He also castigates bedroom scholars for wishing "to enter the bedroom" because that obscures the historical Jefferson.

What follows in the paper is mostly a critical commentary on how to write good biography—that is, how to bring to life a character while remaining true to the facts of his life and remaining in the context of the character's life. Judged from his own parameters of evaluation, Burstein has brought to life Jefferson in the paper and, in doing so, has remained in the context of Jefferson's era.

Yet in *The Inner Jefferson*, Burstein has no qualms about giving the public "what it wants"—that is, "titillating copy"—by entering Jefferson's bedroom and doing so on gauzy evidence. Led astray by hasty judgments of the DNA data, he has leapt upon the Gordon-Reed bandwagon, where "irresponsible guesswork" takes the place of evidence-based, rational analysis of relevant data, and he seems to have no regrets for having done so.

## JEFFERSON'S CHARACTER

Jeffersonian biographer Dumas Malone dismissed the notion of an affair with Sally Hemings, as it would not have been in keeping with Jefferson's character.

> [The charges] are distinctly out of character, being virtually unthinkable in a man of Jefferson's moral standards and habitual conduct. To say this is not to claim that he was a plaster saint and incapable of moral lapses. But his major weaknesses were not of this sort; and while he might have occasionally fallen from grace, as so many men have done so often, it is virtually inconceivable that this fastidious gentleman whose devotion to his dead wife's memory and to the happiness of his daughters and grandchildren bordered on the excessive could have carried on through a period of years a vulgar liaison which his own family could not have failed to detect. It would be as absurd as to charge this consistently temperate man with being, through a period, a secret drunkard.[36]

Malone's words should resonate with readers. Malone was an impeccable scholar who had an intimate grasp of the nature of Jefferson through some forty years of studying the person and his writings. Given that track record, it is astonishing that Burstein or anyone would count Gordon-Reed's work, as slipshod as it is, as authoritative and decisive and castigate Malone for defending Jefferson.

Merrill Peterson, another of the great Jeffersonian scholars, also defends Jefferson's character in challenging the calumniators:

> Like most legends this one was not created out of the whole cloth.[37] The evidence, highly circumstantial, is far from conclusive, however, and unless Jefferson was capable of slipping badly out of character in hidden moments at Monticello, it is difficult to imagine him caught up in a miscegenous relationship. Such a mixture of the races, such a ruthless exploitation of the master-slave relationship, revolted his whole being.[38]

Historian John C. Miller also takes the argument from character as inductively strong. He focuses on Jefferson's avowed neglect of his own black children.

> The Sally Hemings story can be made credible only by a major suspension of disbelief. Jefferson was reported to have seduced Sally in Paris when she was fifteen years old, under the promise that any children she might bear him would be freed when they reached maturity. In accord with this agreement she produced five children, four of whom survived infancy. Jefferson took no interest in the upbringing of these children; he made no effort to educate them—Sally herself was apparently illiterate—but he did give them their freedom even though they were wholly unprepared for it. Such indifference to the welfare of his own children is incomprehensible in a man who, like Jefferson, took such joy in family life and who was so vitally concerned with education.[39]

There are, of course, numerous detractors. One of the most outspoken is Conor Cruise O'Brien, author and diplomat, whose fame with respect to Jefferson has come in arguing several outrageous claims concerning Jefferson's purchase of "liberty."

O'Brien assaults the conventional wisdom of such traditional Jeffersonian scholars. He is unafraid of being categorized as one of the "wanton men" or one of the "biographers in quest of 'titillation.'" On assumption that Sally Hemings was the half sister of Jefferson's wife Martha—both were presumably fathered by John Wayles—he adds that Sally was an accepted member of Jefferson's household. "From the fact that Sally Hemings was acceptable as a member of his household, we have to infer that he felt no horror at the idea of miscegenation between white masters and black female slaves. So if he felt comfortable with what John Wayles had done, with his female property, why should he not do the equivalent himself, and sleep with Sally Hemings?"[40] We arrive at the following argument.

(1) Sally Hemings was fathered by miscegenator John Wayles.
(2) Sally Hemings was an accepted member of Jefferson's household.
(3) So Jefferson was not horrified by miscegenation (1 and 2, independently).
(4) So Jefferson was comfortable with miscegenation (3).
(5) So Jefferson had sex with Sally Hemings (4).

Thus, a sexual relationship with Sally Hemings, in disagreement with Malone and others, was not out of character for Jefferson.

There are several problems. First, we cannot merely assume claim 1 is factual. It is not known that Sally Hemings was fathered by John Wayles.[41] Second, given the truth of claim 2—that Sally Hemings was an "accepted member of Jefferson's household"—why is it that "we have to infer" that he was not horrified by white male–black female miscegenation (claim 3)? I concede that claim 3 is strongly supported by claim 2, but the statement that it necessarily follows—namely, "we have to infer that . . ."—is sophistic. Third, not being horrified by something (claim 3) is not equivalent to being comfortable with it (claim 4). Thus, claim 4 is a non sequitur—that is, it does not follow. Finally, claim 5 is also a non sequitur. One can be comfortable with another doing something—say, deciding on a career in business or joining the US Marines—without oneself being comfortable doing the same thing.

As Malone, Peterson, and Miller state, character is not a nonissue that makes for a "tiresome" argument. My own research on Jefferson focuses on a mostly ignored and massively underappreciated dimension of Jefferson's writings—his philosophical thinking. Perusal of his writings indicates that Jefferson was a person with a keen and lifelong interest in philosophy; that his political and educational thinking was fundamentally value-driven; that he generally thought people were good, at least that each was born with a functioning moral-sense faculty; that humans as a whole were progressive; and that he prized highly morally correct action—his own, above all.[42] "To do wrong is a melancholy resourse [*sic*], even when retaliation renders it indispensably necessary. . . . I have ever deemed it more honorable and more profitable, too, to set a good example than to follow a bad one," he writes to José Francisco Correia da Serra (December 27, 1814). To Louis Hue Girardin, educator and writer (March 12, 1815), he says that he wishes to be viewed by historians, writing of him while he lives, as a dead subject—that is, with strictest impartiality and sobriety: "The only exact testimony of a man is his actions, leaving the reader to pronounce on them his own judgment. In anticipating this, too little is safer than too much." That is not to say that intention is nothing for Jefferson. Intention is equally as important as action. It is, however, inaccessible to others than oneself.

As evidence of Jefferson's stalwart character, I offer the following.

First, Jefferson had high expectations of his own moral behavior and that of his family and associates. He wrote often to his daughters, grandchildren, and Peter Carr of his expectations of their moral behavior. Recall that he told his physician Vine Utley (March 21, 1819) that he seldom went to bed without first having read something morally uplifting. He expressed in several letters his opinion that Jesus Christ was a paragon of moral perfection, insofar as any human being could approximate moral perfection, and that motivated him to make his own version of the Bible by cutting out the influence of supernature in Christ's words and deeds.[43] He stated with great candor to General Henry Knox and the nation's first secretary of war (April 8, 1800) that he never deserted a friend due to differences of opinion in politics, religion, or physics, though numerous friends had deserted him for such differences. Granddaughter Ellen Wayles Randolph Coolidge describes Jefferson's interaction with his grandchildren as "delightful." He was spontaneous, affectionate, pleasant, instructive of manners, and tolerant of their ignorance and foibles.[44] Granddaughter Virginia J. Trist says that Jefferson freely corresponded with all grandchildren who could write and would teach the children fanciful games, which he would then play with them.[45] To Dugald Stewart, Scottish philosopher and mathematician, he writes that anyone considered for a professorship at University of Virginia must meet these qualifications: "Besides the first degree of eminence in science, he must be of sober and correct morals and habits, having a talent of communicating his knowledge with facility, and of an accommodating and peaceable temper. The latter is all-important for the harmony of the institution."[46]

Second, there are Jefferson's express role models—for example, William Small, George Wythe, and Governor Francis Fauquier—mentioned in his unfinished *Autobiography*. Of these figures, Small and Wythe had the most influence. Small was Jefferson's teacher at the College of William and Mary and instilled in him a passion for learning—especially, natural philosophy. More important, Jefferson esteemed and tried to emulate Small's "even and dignified line of conduct."[47] Wythe was Jefferson's tutor in law and inspiration for enjoyment of classical literature in the Greek and Latin languages. Jefferson says of his mentor in his *Autobiography*, "Mr. Wythe continued to be my faithful and beloved mentor in youth, and my most affectionate friend through life."[48] In a letter to lawyer John Saunderson (August 31, 1820), Jefferson states of his departed mentor and friend:

> The exalted virtue of the man will . . . be a polar star to guide you in all matters which may touch that element of his character. But on that you will receive imputation from no man; for, as far as I know, he never had an enemy. Little as I am able to contribute to the just reputation of this excellent man, it is the act of my life most gratifying to my heart: and leaves me only to regret that a waning memory can do no more.

That Jefferson modeled his life after such personages—as well as such historical figures as the moralists Epicurus and Jesus and the "scientists" Bacon, Locke, and Newton—speaks volumes for the sort of person he was.

Against Brodie, nowhere does he mention any influence of John Wayles, who likely had very little effect on the development of Jefferson's character.

Third, the later letters exchanged between Jefferson and John Adams, former political adversaries, show Adams to have had a need to correspond with Jefferson and a profound respect for the person as a moral figure. Upon renewal of their friendship in 1812 and until their deaths in 1826, Adams wrote Jefferson 109 times, while Jefferson wrote Adams 49 times. Adams himself excuses Jefferson from fault for the asymmetry of the correspondence. "If I write four Letters to your one; your one is worth more than my four" (July 15, 1813). Lester Cappon, former senior research fellow at the Institute of Early American History, explains the asymmetry by the "wider range of Jefferson's intellectual interests, his political connections as first head of the Republican party, and the rigid self-discipline he imposed on his time throughout most of a busy life."[49] Adams often lauds Jefferson's character. For illustration, in an 1817 letter to Jefferson (February 2), Adams relates the manner he has dealt historically with excess of letters received. Adams either had neglected to reply to a correspondent or he had given "gruff, short, unintelligible, misterious [*sic*], enigmatical, or pedantic Answers." What he adds thereafter speaks volumes about Jefferson's character: "This resource is out of your power, because it is not your nature to avail Yourself to it."

Fourth, there is Jefferson's obsessive attraction to order, recording, calculation, efficiency, and symmetry—an attraction duly noted by Brodie[50]—which was a consequence of his view of nature as a *kosmos* (Greek for "something ordered"). That was evident in everything Jefferson did—for example, his "compulsion to make a meticulous record of data" (including records of his slaves),[51] his scrupulously ordered garden, his nearly mulish interest in employing octagons in architecture, his continual rebuilding of Monticello, his overseeing of almost all aspects of the planning and building of the University of Virginia, his punctilious and painstaking recordings of meteorological phenomena almost every day for over fifty years, his passion for invention, his nearly obsessive attraction to economy in all activities, his six-plot and seven-plot arrangements of his fields for farming, his attachment to intellectual and moral advance, and his dutiful letter writing, among numerous other things. Historian James Bear writes that Jefferson habitually woke always before the rise of the sun and patterned similarly each day: "Thomas Jefferson was a man of habit, and despite visitors or other circumstances, nothing seriously disrupted his daily routine."[52] Jefferson's obsession with order, recording, calculation, efficiency, and symmetry neither can be dismissed flippantly as Gordon-Reed does when she asserts "none of this follows," nor can it be preter-mitted as Burstein tends to do. An obsession with order and symmetry does not characterize a man driven to seek outlets for passion. Passion needs spontaneity. An obsessional person does not make allowances for sponta-neous erotic escapades when the urge surfaces. An obsessional person acts in ways that betray a lifelong interest in taming one's passions—a debt Jefferson owed to the ancient eudaemonists, to friends like Wythe, and to Jesus—or, in Freudian language, excessive sublimation.

Fifth, there are the reports of others on Jefferson's character. Brodie herself notes the impression Jefferson made on Margaret Smith, wife of Samuel Harrison Smith and publisher of the *Washington National Intelligencer*, when Jefferson called on her husband on election day. Mrs. Smith met the stranger at the door. "I know not how it was, but there was something in his manner, his countenance and voice that at once unlocked my heart."[53] So overwhelmed was she, upon learning that the man was Jefferson, that she could not utter a word in his presence. It was inconceiv-able to her that this man "with a voice so soft and low, with a countenance so benignant and intelligent," could be "that disturber of the peace, that enemy of all rank and order." Even Brodie agrees: "Those who loved and served him," writes Brodie of a kind and mild temperament, "so admired his amiability and control that they did him the further honor of imitating him."[54] "The leadership he sought was one of sympathy and love, not of command," writes historian Henry Adams.[55] Jefferson disdained power and thought lust for power an indication of vice. "I know that I have never been so well pleased, as when I could shift power from my own, on the shoulders of others; nor have I ever been able to conceive how any rational being could propose happiness to himself from the exercise of power over others," writes Jefferson to political philosopher Antoine Louis Claude

Destutt de Tracy (January 26, 1811). Virginia J. Trist, granddaughter of the former president, says: "These remembrances [of Grandfather] are precious to me, because they are of *him*. . . . Cheerfulness, love, benevolence, wisdom, seemed to animate his whole form. . . . He would gather fruit for us, seek out the ripest figs, or bring down the cherries from on high above our heads with a long stick."[56] Writes granddaughter Ellen Wayles Randolph Coolidge: "I have never known anywhere, under any circumstances, so good a domestic character as my grandfather Jefferson. . . . As a child, girl and woman, I loved and honoured him above all earthly beings. . . . My Bible came from him, my Shakespere, my first writing-table, my first handsome writing-desk, my first leghorn hat, my first silk dress."[57] Monticello's overseer, Edmund Bacon, mentions that Jefferson was "always very kind and indulgent to his servants."[58] Even Madison Hemings's controversial account in the *Pike County Republican* in 1873 mentions Jefferson as "universally kind to all about him."[59] Ellen Wayles Randolph Coolidge summarizes grandiloquently in a letter to husband Joseph Coolidge her grandfather's character: "I ask is it likely that so fond, so anxious a father . . . [would] have selected the female attendant of his own pure children to become his paramour! The thing will not bear telling. There are things, after all, as moral impossibilities."[60] Finally, there is the account of William DuVal, a neighbor of George Wythe. DuVal writes to Jefferson of Wythe's death and Wythe's love of Jefferson: "I believe that the great & good Mr. Wythe loved you as sincerely as if you had been his Son; his attachment was founded on his thorough knowledge of you, personally. Some years ago he mentioned that if there was an honest man in America, T.J. was that person" (June 29, 1806).

Sixth, there is Jefferson's commitment to occupation, which went hand-in-glove with his remarkably broad range of interests. "Mr. Jefferson was the most industrious person I ever saw in my life," Edmund Bacon said. He was always "reading, writing, talking, working upon some model, or doing something else."[61] Only twice does his overseer mention seeing Jefferson unoccupied—once when he had neuralgia and once when he had a toothache. Jeffersonian scholar Julian Boyd adds that Jefferson was amazingly connected to the world around him:

There was . . . the astonishing range of the man. His view swept an arc of
the intellectual horizon wider even than that of Franklin. From architecture to zoology Jefferson probed, reflected, and adapted his findings to
the society in which he lived. His insatiable inquiries fathered versatility.
Even before he drafted the Declaration of Independence at thirty-three he
could "calculate an eclipse, survey an estate, tie an artery, plan an edifice,
try a cause, break a horse, dance a minuet, and play the violin," to say
nothing of being an informed parliamentarian, a collector of manuscript
laws, an author of a revolutionary tract, a craftsman in metal, a creative
pioneer in archeology, and an organizer of plans for improving the navigation of a river.[62]

That does not speak to the sort of person who would have involved himself
in the vagaries of a lengthy, furtive liaison.

Seventh, Jefferson in his *Notes on the State of Virginia* strongly
objected to the admixture of white and black blood.[63] There is little to
suggest a change of mind in his lifetime. Over twenty years later, he writes
to politician and antislavery advocate Edward Coles (August 25, 1814),
"The amalgamation with the other color produces a degradation to which
no lover of his country, no lover of excellence in the human character can
innocently consent." Consequently, Jefferson would have found sexual
release with a black or mulatto too degrading for its practice. (I cover the
issue of Jefferson's "racism" in chapter 6.) To say Jefferson could "rationalize" his behavior, as does Burstein, is unavailing.

Eighth, there was Jefferson's love of his children. He showed remarkable concern for the well-being of his two daughters in his correspondence
with them. It is difficult to imagine that he would have embarked on a relationship with a slave at the risk of shaming his daughters. Moreover, it is
almost inconceivable that he would have continued that relationship, once
"revealed" by Callender in 1802, and exposed his daughters to potential
for greater scandal. In addition, given his manifest concern for Martha and
Maria, it is too much to believe that he would have fathered children with
Sally and then completely ignored the children, as Madison Hemings said
Jefferson did. Jefferson was a greatly responsible person.[64] "Such callous-
ness," writes lawyer William G. Hyland Jr., "was an atypical character

trait of Jefferson's. If Madison and Eston were indeed his own, Jefferson should have displayed some consideration, if not affection, which there is no recorded evidence to support."[65] Dumas Malone artfully and accurately uses Monticello as a metaphor for Jefferson's passion for lifelong learning as well as domesticity:

> The building of the mansion at Monticello in its historic form proved to be little short of a lifetime's work. Nothing else that he ever did was more characteristic of him as a person and a mind. In spirit he was pre-eminently constructive, and he could not think of himself or of his house or of human society as finished. But he was not merely creating an architectural or intellectual monument; he was a deeply domestic being, making a home. Throughout his maturity his spirit ceaselessly roamed the universe, searching out the good things in it, but his heart was on his mountaintop, and if his ghost now walks it is surely there.[66]

Finally, there is Jefferson's obsession concerning science, in the broad eighteenth-century sense, that virtually goes unmentioned by proponents of a liaison. For instance, so narrow is Gordon-Reed's focus on the sexual dimension of Jefferson's personality that she in *The Hemingses of Monticello* astonishingly does not even have a listing for *science*, whether by itself or under *Jefferson*, in her index. Jefferson woke daily to take meteorological measurements at 4 a.m. Mrs. Samuel Harrison Smith said that the president would often walk the Potomac or its hills or woods to observe plants. "Not a plant from the lowliest weed to the loftiest tree escaped his notice," she stated.[67] He would get off his horse and then "climb rocks, or wade through swamps" for a plant he desired and generally returned with a variety of specimens. The East Room of the White House contained a large fossil collection from the Big Bone Lick. Jefferson was keenly interested in astronomy, horticulture, invention, surveying, philology, paleontology, chemistry, classical literature, weights and measures, coinage, and medicine, among other things. Historian Karl Lehmann adds that he was no dilettante. He shows a "record of contributions to human civilization, knowledge, and outlook which made this life more valuable to his contemporaries and to posterity than that of most other men."[68] A polymath such as he would have had little interest in the cheap, fleeting enjoyment that a liaison with Hemings or any other woman would have afforded him. Fondness for sensual attachment does not easily admit of routine and, because of that, it does not readily escape detection—especially over a thirty-eight-year span. It is not sufficient for scholars like Burstein to note Jefferson was highly secretive and masterfully deceptive. The keen interest that he presumably had in Hemings would have come at expense of his daily scientific "experiments" and his letter writing, as well as time with his family and friends and his nocturnal indulgence in classical literature. Also, a liaison would not have gone unnoticed over thirty-eight years.

It follows that Thomas Jefferson was very likely a man of steadfast character, and that makes it highly improbable that he would have had a liaison with Hemings. It is inexplicable that so many "disinterested" scholars can be so irrevocably convinced by tenuous, gossamery "evidence." That is the real phenomenon worth investigating, and I can only explain it by assuming their interest is not disinterested. Jefferson-bashing is in vogue and it sells books.

It is sometimes said that Jefferson's refusal to answer any of the countless defamations of his person is proof sufficient that he had something to hide. The charge is ridiculous. It is clear that people who are smeared are sometimes silent, though guilty. Yet silence is no verification of the smear, as certain revisionists have taken it to be. As Jefferson explains simply to Samuel Smith (August 22, 1798), responding to any particular criticism would have been like cutting off one of the heads of the Lernaean Hydra:

> At a very early period of my life, I determined never to put a sentence into any newspaper. I have religiously adhered to the resolution through my life, and have great reason to be contented with it. Were I to undertake to answer the calumnies of the newspapers, it would be more than all my own time, & that of 20. aids could effect. For while I should be answering one, twenty new ones would be invented. I have thought it better to trust to the justice of my countrymen, that they would judge me by what they *see* of my conduct on the stage where they have placed me, & what they knew of me *before* the epoch since which a particular party has supposed it might answer some view of theirs to vilify me in the public eye.

If there is evidence that any of the numerous accusations significantly bothered him—and Jefferson was no pachyderm—it is that of misrepresentation of his religiosity—that is, the brand "atheist"—not his putative liaison. "As to the calumny of Atheism," he writes to James Monroe, "I am so broken to calumnies of every kind, from every department of government, Executive, Legislative, & Judiciary, & from every minion of theirs holding office or seeking it, that I entirely disregard it. . . . It has been so impossible to contradict all their lies, that I have determined to contradict none; for while I should be engaged with one, they would publish twenty new ones. Thirty years of public life have enabled most of those who read newspapers to judge of one for themselves" (May 26, 1800).[69]

## UPSHOT

For Plato, Aristotle, Epicurus, and the Greek and Roman Stoics, truth and truth-telling were part and parcel of human thriving. An honest approach to everyday life was needed for happiness, for happiness entailed immersion in reality and blue-penciling all false notions. It was inconceivable for such philosophers that one could live in cloud-cuckoo-land and be happy.[70]

Jefferson made purchase of the ancient coupling of happiness and truth.[71] Lying and dissembling were, as John Adams noted, not "in [his] power." That is not to say that Jefferson never lied and never dissembled, only that it was his moral aim always to avoid both, and evidence suggests that, though he was no plaster saint, he generally did a good job at both.

Scholars who wish to implicate Jefferson in a lengthy sexual relationship with Sally Hemings know plainly, even if they expressly deny it, that in accusing Jefferson of a liaison they are at once accusing Jefferson of insidiousness, hypocrisy, and dishonesty. Yet Jefferson's character—the testimony of others and his writings show—was very likely foursquare. Thus, the revisionists must amass "anecdotal evidence" and, of course, ignore any evidence inconsistent with their dreamed-up crotchets. However, numerous bad inductive arguments will not amount to one strong one any more than numerous baseballs hit long but foul will add up to one home run.

Attacking a person's character on insufficient evidence is not only illustrative of bad scholarship, but also of insidiousness, hypocrisy, and dishonesty—that is, the sort of moral depravity of which Jefferson today is commonly accused. Jefferson devoted much of his life to serving his fellow human beings in the capacities of statesman, inventor, farmer, scientist, patron of the sciences, benefactor, father, grandfather, friend, letter writer, and so forth. Those things we do know. There is no firm evidence to indicate that he did have a relationship with Sally Hemings. When evidence is wanting, guardedness is needed, even if it does not sell books.

Yet scholars such as Brodie, Gordon-Reed, and Burstein treat Jefferson's relationship with Hemings as fact, or nearly so. So influential has been their assault that many introductory-level history books treat the relationship as factual. My wife's sister, for instance, was astonished to hear from me that we do not know whether Jefferson had sex with Sally Hemings and that I thought it very unlikely. She was taught otherwise in high school. She learned from a text that stated the liaison as fact and from a teacher who regurgitated that "fact." In my classes on philosophy, more of my students know Jefferson as the president who had a sexual affair with his slave than they know him as the person who wrote the Declaration of Independence. Something is horridly skewed.

Character is an important issue, not a tiresome argument. To counter the boldness of such imaginative revisionists, I wish to turn the tables on them. I maintain it is not so much Jefferson's character that is in question but that of any scholar who reduces himself to use of unfounded vilification to sell books, gain fame, or win favor *ad captandum vulgus*—to please an uninformed audience. That is manifestly unethical. Yet many of today's historians are quite unlike the historians of yesterday like Gilbert Chinard, Adrienne Koch, Merrill Peterson, and especially Dumas Malone. That is most unfortunate.

CHAPTER 5

# HIGH PRIESTS OF THE MORAL TEMPLE

## Shifty Science and "Aesopian History"

> Truth will do well enough if left to shift for herself. She
> seldom has received much aid from the power of great
> men to whom she is rarely known and seldom welcome.
> She has no need of force to procure entrance into the
> minds of men.
>
> —THOMAS JEFFERSON, "NOTES ON RELIGION," 1776

*W*hen I first turned to the historical literature on Jefferson, I was astonished by its unevenness. While many scholars contented themselves with modest and measured assertions from a careful scrutiny of the literature—historians Dumas Malone, Merrill Peterson, and Adrienne Koch come readily to mind—others took the liberties of speculating, often wildly from scant evidence, and of ignoring the work of other historians whose theses were inconsistent with theirs.

The most popular books, like the ones I have thus far considered, were those that focused exclusively on Jefferson's private life. They aimed to show, against the celebrated Jeffersonian scholars, that the persona one gets from examination of the thousands of writings Jefferson has left behind differs significantly from the real Jefferson. The real Jefferson was no plaster saint but a Janus-faced master of secrecy and duplicity—the consummate hypocrite. So skilled was he at leading a clandestine double life that he kept a lengthy sexual relationship from his associates, friends, and even his family for thirty-eight years.

To show Jefferson was Janus-faced, such scholars have taken great license with the canons of sound historical scholarship. Many, like Fawn Brodie and Annette Gordon-Reed, seem to think a tendentious approach to history is acceptable—that it is appropriate to begin with the conclusion for which one wishes to argue and then seek out evidence in support of it. Inconsistent evidence, gleaned along the way, is merely ignored. Andrew Burstein, in arguing that Jefferson's sexual relationship with Hemings came at the advice of Samuel Auguste André David Tissot (author of *De la santé des gens de lettres*), seems to think nothing of hasty, shoddy induction—that is gilding an inordinately weak argument to give it the look of plausibility.

There are also abuses of science. Those scientists involved in the DNA study thought nothing of leaping to the conclusion, in spite of the inconclusiveness of the study, that Thomas Jefferson was the most probable father not only of Eston Hemings but also of all six of Sally Hemings's children. The Thomas Jefferson Memorial Foundation (TJMF) followed their lead in confirming their quick conclusions. Soon, Fraser Neiman, one of the members of the TJMF's committee, thought up a clever "proof," involving Bayes's theorem and Monte-Carlo statistical methods, to show Jefferson must have fathered all six children. The proof showed, at least in Neiman's eyes, that it was nearly impossible for anyone other than Jefferson to be the father of all of Hemings's children. Likewise, historian Alan Golden and professor of rhetoric James Golden, following a Toulminian model of argument assessment, used the data of historians and scientists to show Jefferson was likely the father of all of Sally Hemings's children.

What is most disheartening is that Jeffersonian psychobiographical history and the science behind it are generally replete with normative judgments: Jefferson was racist, Jefferson was a hypocrite, or Jefferson was a rogue. Just when did history and science become a normative and moralistic, not descriptive, discipline—namely, when did history and science become "Aesopian"? What gives certain scholars the right to assume a normative perch and pass moral judgment on Jefferson?

In this chapter, I begin by analyzing the appeals to science to indict Jefferson of paternity: the results of the DNA analysis, their interpretation by the TJMF, Fraser Neiman's Bayesian argument, and a Toulminian analysis of the scientific data. I end with a critique of the methodological abuses of some Jeffersonian scholars in their attempt, come what may, to indict Jefferson.

The shoddiness of the arguments used by scientists and by historical scholars today to show that Jefferson had a relationship with Hemings or to explicate the nature of that relationship indicates that either sound reasoning is not in vogue or there is a witch hunt. Those two alternatives, as we shall see, need not be exclusive.

## APPEALS TO SCIENCE

### The DNA Evidence

In November 1998, a DNA study was published in the prominent weekly publication *Nature*. What precisely did the DNA study show? DNA samples were taken from the descendants of five men: Field Jefferson (Jefferson's uncle), Eston Hemings (last son of Sally Hemings), Peter Carr (nephew of Jefferson), Samuel Carr (nephew of Jefferson and brother of Peter), and Thomas Woodson (who claimed to be the famous missing first son of Jefferson and Sally Hemings). The scientists who studied the DNA material agreed to the misleading title "Jefferson Fathered Slave's Last Child," which strongly suggests that it is Thomas Jefferson and not *a* Jefferson—someone in Jefferson's bloodline, including Thomas Jefferson—who fathered Eston Hemings. The abstract, summarizing the findings, reads:

> There is a long-standing historical controversy over the question of U.S. President Thomas Jefferson's paternity of the children of Sally Hemings, one of his slaves. To throw some scientific light on the dispute, we have compared Y-chromosomal DNA haplotypes from male-line descendants of Field Jefferson, a paternal uncle of Thomas Jefferson, with those of male-line descendants of Thomas Woodson, Sally Hemings' putative first son, and of Eston Hemings Jefferson, her last son. The molecular

findings fail to support the belief that Thomas Jefferson was Thomas Woodson's father, but provide evidence that he was the biological father of Eston Hemings Jefferson.[1]

What was the evidence that Jefferson was the biological father of Eston? The findings showed that Jefferson could not be ruled out as the father of Eston Hemings—namely, that Eston was descended from a male in Jefferson's bloodline, which ruled out nephews Peter and Samuel Carr. The findings also showed that Jefferson was not the father of Thomas Woodson, the alleged missing first child of Thomas Jefferson and Sally Hemings. The scientists—comprising three geneticists, a pathologist, a statistician, and a biochemist—argued that the evidence, coupled with historical circumstances, made Jefferson the most likely candidate for paternity. In their own words:

> The simplest and most probable explanations for our molecular findings are that Thomas Jefferson, rather than one of the Carr brothers, was the father of Eston Hemings Jefferson, and that Thomas Woodson was not Thomas Jefferson's son. . . . We cannot completely rule out other explanations of our findings based on the illegitimacy in various lines of descent. For example, a male-line descendant of Field Jefferson could possibly [*sic*] have illegitimately fathered an ancestor of the presumed male-line descendant of Eston. But in the absence of historical evidence to support such possibilities, we consider them to be unlikely.[2]

What is strange is that this group of scientists would consider themselves qualified to pronounce it to be "simplest and most probable" that Jefferson fathered Eston when the DNA study left open so many possibilities in keeping with known historical evidence. With what notions of "simplest" and "most probable" were the scientists working?

When many causal claims—say claims $c_\alpha, \ldots, c_\varepsilon$—are put forth to address an etiological issue, such as the paternity of Sally Hemings's children, to say *Claim* $c_\delta$ *is the simplest claim* in an Occamistic sense is to say *Claim* $c_\delta$ *explains the explanandum (i.e., what is to be explained) with the fewest assumptions or explanatory principles* and *Claim* $c_\delta$ *accommodates the known relevant facts better than claims* $c_\alpha$, $c_\beta$, $c_\gamma$, *or* $c_\varepsilon$. Yet what compelling *biological* evidence is there that Thomas Jefferson and not some other Jeffersonian fathered Eston? There is none. The biological evidence shows only that someone in Jefferson's bloodline was the father, not that that someone could only have been Thomas Jefferson or that that someone was more likely to be Thomas Jefferson than to be the offspring of any other person. In ruling out the Carrs in the paternity of Eston, one cannot simply implicate Jefferson. That is not giving the simplest explanation but rather the most convenient explanation. For instance, any of the following, along with Thomas Jefferson, are possible fathers of Eston. (The list covers Y-chromosome-carrying Jeffersons being neither too young nor too old to be a plausible father and living within a reasonable distance from Thomas Jefferson):

- Thomas Jefferson's brother, Randolph Jefferson;
- Thomas Jefferson Jr., son of Randolph Jefferson;
- Randolph "Isham" Jefferson Jr., son of Randolph Jefferson;
- Peter "Field" Jefferson Sr., son of Randolph Jefferson;
- Robert "Lewis" Jefferson, son of Randolph Jefferson;
- John Jefferson Sr., son of Thomas Jefferson's uncle (Field Jefferson) and Jefferson's first cousin;
- George Jefferson Jr., son of George Jefferson Sr. (son of Field Jefferson and brother of John Jefferson Sr.) and grandson of Field Jefferson;
- John "Garland" Jefferson, son of George Jefferson Sr. and brother of George Jefferson Jr.; and
- John Jefferson Jr., son of John Jefferson Sr., as well as his sons.

Each of these Jeffersons was around Monticello some or much of the time.

It seems clear that the scientists are working on some non-Occamistic notion of "simplicity." I suspect convenience and expeditiousness are driving forces, not disambiguation and etiological accuracy, given the lack of historical knowledge of other potential candidates at the time of the publication in *Nature*. For geneticists, a pathologist, a statistician, and a biochemist to declare that lack of historical evidence for the paternity of any other Jefferson in conjunction with the DNA findings makes Thomas Jefferson the most likely father of Eston Hemings is unconscionable. Yet that is precisely what they did in the published study.

Dr. Eugene Foster, who spearheaded the study, knew that the study was inconclusive, yet seems not to have kicked up much of a fuss over the misleading title, which implicated Thomas Jefferson in the paternity of Eston Hemings. However, Foster is reported by Jefferson family historian Herbert Barger to have said, "Since I am not a professional historian I don't have the training and skills needed to evaluate one item of historical evidence in the context of other evidence. So, I will continue to leave that to the historian and will read their opinion and conclusions with interest."[3] Yet what of the absence of historical evidence showing that Jefferson was intimate or even friendly with Sally Hemings? Foster, it seems, was working from the following argument:

(1) The DNA evidence is consistent with Jefferson as well as numerous other Jefferson males being the father of Eston Hemings.
(2) There is no historical evidence to date that any of the other Jefferson males were intimate with Sally Hemings.
(3) Therefore, it is likely that Thomas Jefferson was intimate with Sally Hemings.

This argument is compelling only if an additional premise, something like *There is noncircumstantial evidence that Thomas Jefferson was intimate with Sally Hemings*, is included. Otherwise, absence of evidence shows nothing. Without noncircumstantial evidence, one could just as easily plug in for premise 2 *There is no historical evidence to date showing that Thomas Jefferson was intimate with Sally Hemings* and derive *Therefore, it is likely that some other Jefferson was intimate with Sally Hemings*.

One must ask, What prompted the DNA study? The DNA study was originally designed to be included in a book by Winifred Bennett, a friend of Foster. Bennett approached Foster about spearheading the DNA study. Foster agreed. Excited by the results of the study, however, Foster contravened his verbal agreement with Bennett not to publish his data independently of her proposed book. The data was appropriated by Foster and published in *Nature* without Bennett's consent. According to Barger, Foster was aware that publication in *Nature* would mean quick fame, and quick fame was a larger enticement for Foster than being true to his promise to Bennett.[4]

## Thomas Jefferson Memorial Foundation Report

Aware that the findings only showed definitively that Jefferson was not the father of Thomas Woodson and that the Carrs could not be implicated in the paternity of Eston Hemings, President Daniel Jordan of the Thomas Jefferson Memorial Foundation, now simply the Thomas Jefferson Foundation, formed a committee to investigate the role of Jefferson in the paternity of Eston Hemings and perhaps of the other children of Sally Hemings. Members of the committee were the following:

> Chair: Dianne Swann-Wright, Director of Special Programs
> Whitney Espich, Communications Officer
> Fraser Neiman, Director of Archaeology
> Anne Porter, Education Instructor
> David Ronka, Interpreter
> Lucia Stanton, Shannon Senior Research Historian
> Elizabeth Dowling Taylor, Head Guide
> White McKenzie Wallenborn, Associate Interpreter
> Camille Wells, Director of Research

The report of the committee, published in January 2000, is titled "Report of the Research Committee on Thomas Jefferson and Sally Hemings." Members met ten times from December 1998 to April 1999 to discuss the scientific data and relevant historical evidence. They formed subcommittees and consulted with experts from other committees.

After combing through the available DNA and historical evidence, the research committee came to the following four conclusions.

(1) Dr. Foster's DNA study was conducted in a manner that meets the standards of the scientific community, and its scientific results are valid.

(2) The DNA study, combined with multiple strands of currently available documentary and statistical evidence, indicates a high probability that Thomas Jefferson fathered Eston Hemings, and that he most likely was the father of the five other of Sally Hemings's children appearing in Jefferson's records: Harriet; Beverly; an unnamed daughter who died in infancy; a second Harriet; and Madison.

(3) Many aspects of this likely relationship between Sally Hemings and Thomas Jefferson are, and may remain, unclear, such as the nature of the relationship, the existence and longevity of Sally Hemings's first child, and the identity of Thomas Woodson.

(4) The implications of the relationship between Sally Hemings and Thomas Jefferson should be explored and used to enrich the understanding and interpretation of Jefferson and the entire Monticello community.

The first conclusion is uncontroversial, with one exception. Researchers examined six Thomas Woodson descendants, but only a single descendant of Eston Hemings. Testing for six Thomas Woodson descendants makes it relatively certain that any error in testing will come to the fore—namely, a mistake would show up as an inconsistency, which could be rectified through retesting. Why there was not a greater effort to locate and test another Eston Hemings descendant to guard against the possibility of contaminated evidence is unclear. Writes Eyler Robert Coates Sr., "Dr. Foster reported that there were other Eston descendants, but he did not bother to test them, since the first one yielded the results he was looking for."[5] In other words, the first test was consistent with Jefferson's paternity, so he did not wish to waste time testing another descendant in the event that the second test might give him an inconsistent result. That strongly suggests scientific bias.

The second conclusion is outlandish. The DNA results in conjunction with "multiple strands of currently available documentary and statistical evidence" yield neither high probability of paternity nor probability of paternity. The notion that he was "most likely . . . the father of all six" children works on assumption of Sally Hemings's lack of promiscuity and is, at best, poppycock. The research committee drew much on oral traditions for their historical evidence, though they seemed to be unfazed both (a) that the strongest oral tradition, that of Tom Woodson, who was said to be the missing first child of Sally Hemings, had proven worthless and (b) that evidence of oral traditions is insubstantial. Conclusion 2 also gives short shrift to inconsistent evidence. Madison Hemings's account, flaws notwithstanding, is allowed to trump any testimonies of others, who flatly deny any involvement of Jefferson with Hemings—for example, Edmund Bacon (overseer of Monticello), Thomas Jefferson Randolph (Jefferson's grandson), Martha Jefferson Randolph (Jefferson's daughter), and even Jefferson himself in his letter to secretary of navy Robert Smith. What is worse, Madison Hemings's testimony cannot be other than hearsay, as he was born many years after the birth of his putative brother Tom and was not privy to many of the "recollections" expressed in his testimony, while the testimonies of Bacon, Thomas Jefferson Randolph, and Martha Jefferson Randolph are those of persons who lived and interacted with Jefferson. Overall, the weight of the historical evidence tends to support Jefferson's noninvolvement with Hemings, though nothing is known to decide the issue. With the paucity of evidence to implicate Jefferson, agnosticism is the only plausible stance.

The third conclusion, on assumption of a liaison, is obvious. Yet notice that the mystery enveloping the nature—the nature of the relationship, the existence and longevity of Sally Hemings's first child, and the identity of Thomas Woodson—is obliterated, once the assumption of a liaison is not presumed.

The fourth conclusion is overstated. The committee moves from a "likely relationship" in conclusion 3 to a relationship, presumed factual, in conclusion 4. That is the move that both Brodie and Gordon-Reed make with the tomfool narratives they weave.

More needs to be said about conclusion 4, which I repeat here: "The implications of the relationship between Sally Hemings and Thomas Jefferson should be explored and used to enrich the understanding and interpretation of Jefferson and the entire Monticello community." This seems to be something very reasonable *once it is known to be the case that Thomas Jefferson did have a relationship with Sally Hemings.* Without such certainty, historians are off in cloud-cuckoo-land.

Thus, the TJMF's report needs to be called into question.

Note the TJMF is now called the Thomas Jefferson Foundation (TJF). Why has the term *memorial* been eliminated? Here I can only speculate, but speculation might prove profitable for understanding.

Foundations are established for several reasons: a foundation can be supported by endowment with the aim to assist certain charities, it can be a charter that establishes and regulates an institution, or it can be, as is the case with the TJF, an institution established to honor the legacy of a personage. Yet the mission statement of the TJF says merely this: "Today, the Thomas Jefferson Foundation remains committed to a twofold mission: 1. preservation—to conserve, protect, and maintain Monticello in a manner which leaves it enhanced and unimpaired for future generations—and 2. education—to interpret and present Thomas Jefferson to the widest possible audiences, including scholars and the general public."[6] The first aim of the mission is to preserve Monticello, not Jefferson's legacy. The second aim is interpreting and presenting Jefferson "to the widest possible audience." Interpreting and presenting to reach the widest possible audience allows neatly for fabrication at the expense of fact. Analogously, *The Jerry Springer Show* had a much greater viewing audience than does *Charlie Rose* today. I am greatly bothered by this mission statement, as it seems to pretermit truth.

Overall, the effect of the article in *Nature*, given sanction by TJMF's skewed report, convinced historians of Jefferson's role as father of Hemings's children. They hopped on the Jefferson-did-it bandwagon in droves. It is as if they were working from a narrow syllogistic window: *Peter Carr, Samuel Carr, or Thomas Jefferson must be the father of each of Sally's children; neither Peter Carr nor Samuel Carr is the father of Eston Hemings; so, Thomas Jefferson must be the father of each of Sally's chil-*

*dren.* The difficulty with the syllogism, of course, is that the first premise is needlessly restrictive.

Imagine a scenario where Lord B's wife, Lady B, has been murdered. On account of his character, Lord B is never suspected of the murder, because it has long been suspected on circumstantial evidence that friends of the Bs, Mr. and Mrs. M, are the murderers. After many years, incontrovertible evidence surfaces to clear Mr. and Mrs. M and to implicate either Lord B or numerous other members of the household staff at the time of the murder. No other candidates are possible. That evidence does not single out Lord B however, any more than it does any other of the members of the household at the time of the murder. It is eventually accepted that Lord B is the murderer in spite of the ambiguity of the evidence. It is, in some sense, the simplest and most plausible explanatory scenario, because Lord B was, as her husband, closest to her. Those who aim to defend Lord B—and many of his closest friends attest to his spotless character—and to entertain any of the other possibilities, at least until they can be ruled out, are merely ignored. Lord B is implicated, tried on thin and uncertain evidence, and thereafter executed.

Any sober person, on reading the account of the murder, trial, and execution, would be beside himself. It was, after all, a man's life that was at stake. How could a jury implicate Lord B on flimsy circumstantial evidence for such a serious crime—especially without having ruled out any of the other possible candidates as perpetrators?

The scenario with Jefferson is much the same. He has been implicated, tried, sentenced, and found guilty, although evidence is ambiguous and wanting.

One must admit that scholars had been working from a narrow syllogistic window in which the Carr brothers were chiefly suspected and Jefferson only secondarily. That candidates other than the Carrs were not seriously considered prior to the DNA study is irrelevant. The window needs to be widened. All other possible candidates need to be explored and ruled out by eliminative reasoning before Jefferson can be implicated as the father of Eston. Moreover, ruling out the Carrs as candidates of Eston's paternity does not rule them out as candidates of Eston's siblings. As founding fathers historian Lance Banning states: "Although they implicate a Jefferson, not a Carr, as Eston Hemings' father, the DNA results cannot exclude the Carrs as possible fathers of Sally Hemings' earlier children. Neither can they show . . . that Thomas Jefferson was any more likely to have been Eston's father than any of Thomas's male-line relatives who might have had relations with Sally Hemings at the relevant times."[7] A man's legacy is at stake and tainting a legacy on gossamer evidence is unconscionable. So too, I dare add, is the integrity of the discipline of history on trial.

## The Neglected Minority Report

Members of the committee, however, were not of one voice. Dr. White McKenzie "Ken" Wallenborn was distressed about the anti-Jefferson sentiments expressed openly by the other members of the committee prior to evaluation of the data, about dismissal or mitigation by members of the committee of evidence that tended to exonerate Jefferson of paternity, and about the often sheer hatred of Jefferson incautiously expressed by experts consulted by the committee. He writes, "I was right when I reported to Dan Jordan in early March that the committee had reached their decision long before all of the information had been studied, and that sure enough, all of the evidence that would have exonerated Mr. Jefferson had been discarded."[8] He thus prepared his "Minority Report to the DNA Study Report," which he sent to Dianne Swann-Wright, chair of the DNA Study Commission, and gave personally to Jordan, president of the foundation.[9] Neither Swann-Wright nor Jordan shared the dissenting report with any other committee members. Wallenborn began to circulate copies of his report to committee members and was eventually called into Jordan's office to discuss his furtive activities. Jordan was ultimately persuaded to attach Wallenborn's "Minority Report" to the Research Committee Report and make it available to all committee members.

In his report, Wallenborn addressed flaws in the historical scholarship that putatively implicated Jefferson. The historical evidence, seen with unjaundiced eyes, showed nothing at all. He concludes:

There is historical evidence of more or less equal statue on both sides of this issue that prevent a definitive answer as to Thomas Jefferson's paternity of Sally Hemings' son Eston Hemings or for that matter the other four of her children. In fairness to the descendants of Sally Hemings and the descendants of Thomas Jefferson and Martha Wayles Jefferson, the Thomas Jefferson Foundation should continue to encourage in-depth historical research in hopes that accurate answers to very sensitive questions may be found.

In regards to the historical interpretation of Thomas Jefferson and his family, Monticello, and slavery at Monticello, The Thomas Jefferson Foundation should continue to present a properly weighted historical interpretation to visitors. As new historical evidence is found, it should continue to be incorporated into interpretive presentations. However, historical accuracy should never be overwhelmed by political correctness, for if it is, history becomes meaningless. Construction of historically inaccurate buildings on the mountaintop at Monticello would detract from the historically accurate picture that the Thomas Jefferson Foundation is trying to portray.

This is a sober assessment of the relevant data regarding Jefferson's paternity. It enjoins not exoneration of Jefferson, but merely that scholars ought to seek the truth and admit agnosticism when evidence is wanting.

## Neiman's Monte-Carlo Data

In *White over Black*, historian Winthrop Jordan noted that Jefferson was at Monticello nine months prior to the birth of each of Sally Hemings's children and there was no evidence of any other one person being present nine months prior to the birth of each child. Fraser Neiman, director of archaeology at Monticello, argues in "Coincidence or Causal Connection" that "until now, the significance of this finding has rested on personal intuition."[10] The coincidences bespeak a causal connection, and Neiman brashly "outlines a quantitative means of combining that estimate with other evidence to produce an overall assessment of the probability that Jefferson fathered all of Hemings' children." He attempts to oppugn those remaining doubters and convince them by dint of unassailable statistical reasoning.

For Neiman, the question is this: If someone other than Jefferson was the father, what is the probability of each of Hemings's conception dates being within a period when Jefferson was at Monticello, not elsewhere?

Because Jefferson was home roughly 50 percent of the time since Sally's first and last pregnancy, the scenario is not unlike flipping a fair coin. However, flips of a fair coin are independent events. That is neither the case with Jefferson's stays at Monticello, which were not random (being at Monticello on a given day makes the likelihood of being there the next day greater), nor the case with Hemings's conception dates (getting pregnant one day makes it impossible to get pregnant the next).[11]

In an effort to get a better handle on the slippery data, Neiman opts for the Monte-Carlo statistical method—a method of simulation-based inference, usually used for highly complex systems (e.g., physical systems) for which deterministic algorithms are unsuited because there is considerable uncertainty about the inputs. The method, in essence, uses the relative-frequency, not the a priori approach, of probability. Repeated random samplings take the place of a priori calculation. Computers are generally employed to expedite the number of random tries.

Consider a noncomplex example—one who wants to figure out the probability of "six" occurring in one roll of a die. According to the a priori approach, on assumption of all outcomes being equiprobable, one merely places the expected outcome over all possible outcomes to arrive at the probability assessment of 1/6 or 0.167. Yet what if one has good reason to believe that the die is loaded, but has no means to ascertain just how? One then might approach the problem by rolling the die a large number of times—say, one thousand—and simply gauging the probability by the frequency of successful outcomes over possible outcomes. That will give some indication of the bias of the die—the more rolls, the better the indication. The Monte-Carlo method is similar, only that the rolls of the die (or whatever outcome for which one desires a probability assessment) are done by a computer in an effort to generate quickly large amounts of data.

Neiman does something similar with the probability of Jefferson being the father of any or all of Hemings's children. He constructs four models, with slightly different parameters, and comes up with the following distribution schemes, given the record of Jefferson's stays at Monticello and the birthdays of Hemings's children. The table he titles "Relative Frequency Distributions for the Number of Conceptions That Fall during or Three Days before a Jefferson Visit, for the Four Monte Carlo Models."

Table 5.1. The Four Monte Carlo Models

| | 0 | 1 | 2 | 3 | 4 | 5 | 6 |
|---|---|---|---|---|---|---|---|
| Model 1 | 0.0 | 3.6 | 19.1 | 37.3 | 29.2 | 9.7 | 1.2 |
| Model 2 | 0.0 | 0.0 | 13.8 | 37.7 | 34.3 | 12.7 | 1.5 |
| Model 3 | 0.1 | 6.3 | 24.6 | 36.8 | 24.2 | 7.2 | 0.8 |
| Model 4 | 0.0 | 4.3 | 18.3 | 34.3 | 30.6 | 11.1 | 1.3 |

Given these distribution schemes, Neiman then uses Bayes's theorem to derive a probability assessment for Jefferson being the father of all six children.

$$p(\text{J/e}) = \frac{p\,(\text{J}) \times p\,(\text{e/J})}{p\,(\text{J}) \times p\,(\text{e/J}) + p\,(\sim\!\text{J}) \times p\,(\text{e/}\!\sim\!\text{J})}$$

Given an extremely low a priori probability of 0.05 that Jefferson was the father of all six children [(J), assumed arbitrarily, just to get the ball rolling] and given a probability of 0.012 that Jefferson was not the father of all six children though he was present each time at conception (e/~J), Neiman arrives at an 84 percent a posteriori likelihood that Jefferson was the father of all six—a probability that increases commensurate with an increase in the a priori probability (e.g., an a priori probability of 0.10 generates an a posteriori probability of 92 percent and an a priori probability of 0.50 generates near certainty). On assumption of a very low prior probability of Jefferson being the father of all six children, we ultimately arrive at an extremely high probability that he was, given the coincidence of him being present at Monticello nine months prior to the birth of each child. (Note how that coincidence drives the argument.) Moreover, the low a priori probability of Jefferson being the father of all six children that was given at the start does not take into consideration any other evidence that might also implicate Jefferson—for example, DNA evidence. Factoring that evidence, the prior probability increases commensurately. At some point, it becomes ridiculous to consider Jefferson's stays at Monticello and Hemings's conception dates as independent. Coincidence is best explicated by causal relationship. Jefferson fathered all six children. QED.[12]

It is a clever argument, but ultimately unavailing. First, even if Jefferson was at Monticello nine months prior to the birth of each child, as others have pointed out, one gets the high degree of coincidence only if Sally Hemings was at Monticello every time she became pregnant.[13] We know nothing of her whereabouts each time, and one cannot just assume she was at Monticello on all such occasions. In addition, the birth dates are taken from Jefferson's *Farm Book*, yet little is known about the precise time each birth was noted, because Jefferson was not present for all the births and, thus, likely obtained that information from overseer Edmund Bacon or Sally Hemings. Much rides on that, since conception dates by Jordan were ascertained by working backward from the birth dates in the *Farm Book*.[14] Furthermore, the argument says nothing about the sixteen times Jefferson was at Monticello between the conceptions of the first and last child and Hemings did not get pregnant. Moreover, the argument merely takes for granted that other possible Jefferson-chromosome paternity candidates were not present at each conception. Finally, and this point attends on the last, Neiman's argument works on assumption of there being one and only one father for all of Hemings's children. That is gratuitous.

Lawyer William G. Hyland Jr., for instance, notes some perplexing coincidences between the activities of Jefferson's brother Randolph and Sally Hemings that Neiman does not accommodate. Sally quit having children after having had Eston in August 1807. Jefferson returned from the presidency in 1809. Jefferson's brother, Randolph, was widowed around 1796 and remarried in late 1808 or early in 1809. Randolph's son, Thomas Jefferson Jr., married on October 3, 1808. Those coincidences suggest that Randolph or Thomas Jefferson Jr. might have been the father of Eston or all of Sally's children. Hyland does not rush to vindicate Jefferson but merely writes, "Neiman's statistics cry out for valid comparative studies of the other Jefferson males who might have fathered Eston and in the absence of these comparisons, the results are inconclusive."[15]

Science writer Steven Corneliussen's "Sally Hemings, Thomas Jefferson, and the Authority of Science" is one of the few attempts to address Neiman's paper. He begins with a caveat. He notes a basic tenet of statistics: Association does not imply causation, no matter how strong the correlation might prove to be.[16]

Corneliussen's caveat does little to vitiate Neiman's argument. Correlational associations in scientific studies are undertaken only to disclose potential causal relationships. If at day's end the most one could say is that two events are strongly correlated, the information is unavailing. Noting a strong correlation between smoking and lung cancer, for instance, does not compel one to quit smoking. It could, after all, be that persons who have the early stages of lung cancer crave cigarettes and take up smoking or, if smokers already, tend to smoke more heavily. At some point, strong correlations point to a causal relationship of some sort. If not, there would be no point to suggesting that people who smoke should quit. Thus, to say that two events, $\alpha$ and $\omega$, are strongly correlated is to say that $\alpha$ is a cause of $\omega$ or $\omega$ is a cause of $\alpha$, or that there is some third thing, $\mu$, as a common cause, that is, the cause of both.[17] Lung cancer and smoking are strongly correlated, just because smoking causes lung cancer.

Following the criticisms of statisticians, Corneliussen notes that the use of Bayes's theorem is question-begging—the "paternity argument's nonstatistical thread . . . validates the simulation results."[18] He also notes that one cannot merely arrive at probable conception dates by counting backward from date of births. Each birth requires a probability distribution for the variable length of human gestation—that is, that uncertainty must be measured and factored into the equation. In addition, he shows that there is a problem with the probability distribution of Beverly's conception. That would give a less than 50 percent likelihood of Jefferson having been at Monticello and would challenge the conclusion that Jefferson was at Monticello for all six conceptions and is, thus, very likely the father of all six children.

Neiman ends his paper with unwarranted boastfulness. "Serious doubt about the existence and duration of the relationship and about Jefferson's paternity of Hemings's six children can no longer be reasonably sustained."[19] That statement is humbug. Neiman has shown it highly unlikely that anyone other than Jefferson was the father of all six of Sally's children by stacking the deck—that is, not vetting his data for accuracy and not considering all the relevant data.

Statistical arguments are only as good as the data that go into them. Let us go back to the loaded-die illustration of the Monte-Carlo method. One cannot run, with any assurance of legitimate results, a large number of random computerized rolls of that die to get information on just how that die is loaded unless first a sufficient amount of accurate data about just how the die is loaded is plugged into the computer. Contaminate the data and one contaminates the results. That is Corneliussen's point of the study begging the question. Neiman has gotten the results he desired to get simply because he plugged in exactly the sort of data that would assure him of those results. Change the data and you change the results.

David Murray is another scholar who has addressed Neiman's argument. He uses an analogy of vases to show the limits of Neiman's reasoning. He considers six vases at Monticello that become broken at different times. Each time, Jefferson is around Monticello. All that is known about the vases is that some Jefferson broke one of them. He asks, "Are we willing, therefore, to subscribe to the conclusion that there is a 99% probability that Thomas Jefferson broke all six vases?"[20]

Difficulties are these. First, Neiman presumes that Sally Hemings was not promiscuous—namely, that all of her children were of the same father. Second, on assumption of the first, Neiman presumes that no other Jefferson was present each time Hemings got pregnant. Finally, Neiman presumes that Hemings was at Monticello each time she got pregnant. Concerning the last presumption, to conclude that Sally Hemings must have been at Monticello when there is no evidence to show she was not is question-begging. Neiman, for instance, acknowledges that his conclusion applies to any other person, a Jefferson doppelgänger, who might have been around Monticello each time Hemings was impregnated. "Because the model outcomes are tabulated against Jefferson's arrival and departure dates, the probabilities that result apply to Jefferson or any other individual with identical arrival and departure dates." He merely adds flippantly, "The chances that such a Jefferson *doppelganger* [*sic*] existed are, to say the least, remote."[21] If we take "the probabilities that result apply to Jefferson or any other individual with identical arrival and departure dates" literally, we could then conclude that, on assumption of a doppelgänger, there is a 99 percent probability that Jefferson fathered all six of Hemings's children *and* a 99 percent probability that a Jefferson doppelgänger fathered all six, which is impossible. Both sets of data would have to be accommodated, and that would diminish the probabilities considerably.

Defects notwithstanding, Neiman's argument is uncritically cited by historians[22] as additional evidence of the scientific sort for a liaison. Historian Jan Lewis, for example, writes, "Fraser D. Neiman's ingenious statistical evaluation of the relationship between the pattern of Jefferson's returns to Monticello and Hemings' conceptions should quiet those who have resisted accepting Jefferson's paternity."[23] At some point, given the deceitful nature of such "scientific" studies, speculation about a witch hunt is not unreasonable.

## The Goldens and the Toulmin Model

In 2002, not long after the published DNA testimonial, James Golden and Alan Golden published a book on Jefferson's use of rhetoric. In the final chapter, they address Jefferson's view of black Americans and examine the Jefferson/Hemings controversy. They analyze the issue through the lens of Stephen Toulmin's informal-reasoning model, which was designed to assess the strength of a nondemonstrative argument. Toulmin uses a basic *data/ qualifier/claim* schema (see below), and he bridges the gap between data and qualifier by *warrant* (for data and qualifier) and *backing* (for warrant)—both of which are in the form of universal hypotheticals—and *reservation*, which contextualizes the *claim* vis-à-vis reasonableness, relevance, soundness, strength, and appropriateness. (I overpass here critical discussion on the significance of the model and the Goldens' reconstruction of it.)

Table 5.2.

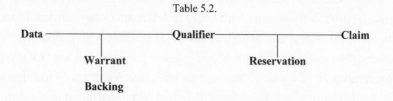

With respect to the putative liaison between Jefferson and Hemings, the Goldens' reconstruction is as follows:

Table 5.3.

| Historical Data | Qualifier | Claim |
|---|---|---|
| 1. Presence of TJ at Monticello nine months before conception of Sally Hemings's children | It is highly probable *or* There is a strong likelihood | That TJ was the father of Eston Hemings |
| 2. Preferential treatment of Hemings's children in TJ's will | *Warrant (Since)* 1. The historical data are based upon documentary sources. | *Reservation (Unless)* 1. Future DNA studies generate results supercede [*sic*] the findings of the Foster report |
| 3. Testimony of Madison | 2. DNA results were developed by accomplished scholars with national and international reputations | 2. Hitherto undiscovered historical data which can alter the claim |
| **Scientific Data** DNA results establishing a 99 percent probability level TJ is father of Eston Hemings | *Backing (Because)* 1. Testimony of Madison Hemings, Foster says, is historically important | 3. Future advances in DNA theory may lead to reevaluation and give different research methods and results |
| | 2. Distinguished experts in genetics have affirmed the reliability of DNA study | |
| | 3. The TJMF Committee supports findings of DNA study | |

The scholars conclude, "Despite the important Reservations we have listed, however, we feel that, given the evidence that is currently available, it is reasonable at this time to assume that Jefferson took part in a sexual relationship with Sally Hemings, culminating in the birth of Eston Hemings and perhaps her other children."[24]

Little, at this point, needs to be said to explicate the flaws of this "gilded" Toulminian examination. From analysis of the historical research upon which the "historical data" are drawn—and the Goldens cull much from Brodie and Gordon-Reed, whose works are called into question in chapters 1 and 2—one can readily see that all the historical evidence they list is severely contaminated, hence whatever follows must be taken with a grain of salt.

A few additional comments are worth making, however. First, they give not the scientific evidence of the 1998 DNA study, but the conclusions of the "researchers" of the study. As we have seen, those conclusions are paralogisms. Concerning *backing*, it is astonishing that anyone would take Foster, who led the study, as a reliable and suitable expert on Madison Hemings's account being "important historical evidence." Foster was a pathologist, not a historian. Furthermore, the DNA evidence is acknowledged to be indeterminate, and the determinations of the DNA experts were decided by historical considerations in conjunction with the indeterminate DNA evidence.[25] That the Thomas Jefferson Memorial Foundation has sided with the DNA experts has all but closed the door on the issue for most scholars. The reason likely has nothing to do with concern for truth. As William G. Hyland Jr. notes, with the "findings" of the experts corroborated by the foundation, public donations to Monticello have more than quadrupled.[26] One grasps plainly why the mission of the TJF is to interpret and present materials concerning Jefferson to the widest possible audience. There is little incentive to search for the truth.

Attending upon their "analysis" and after fifteen chapters of highly laudatory examination of Jefferson's "rhetoric of virtue," the Goldens conclude that the legacy of Jefferson is tainted. "It is quite clear that Jefferson's sexual relationship with Sally Hemings could not possibly [*sic*] conform to his belief that all persons are endowed with a 'moral sense' at birth that helps them to distinguish between right and wrong, and follow a path in life that promotes the 'pursuit of happiness.' Additionally, the role he played in this story was in direct contrast to his conviction that there must be a productive interaction between private and public good."[27] It is strange that their analysis of Jefferson's rhetoric of virtue does not accord with their own adoption of the correct "calculation of probabilities," used throughout the book. Faulting Jefferson often in the final chapter for inferences on insufficient or unvaried evidence and for failure to accept evidence without checking meticulously their sources, they wind up condemning Jefferson on faulty and incorrect calculation of probabilities. Consequently, their assessment of the various other aspects Jefferson's rhetoric of virtue must be judged suspect.

## THE CANONS OF "NORMATIVE HISTORY"

### Why Is Jefferson an Easy Target?

I am certainly not the first scholar to grapple with the issue of the contrarian trend of historical scholarship that concerns Jefferson. Why has Jefferson become an easy target in last fifty years or so?

Jefferson biographer Douglas Wilson writes that oppugnation of Jefferson is in some sense a scholarly reaction to the sage-of-Monticello trend. "What seems to have happened is that a laudably corrective trend has predominated to such an extent that the emphasis seems somehow reversed."[28] The "corrective trend," he adds, is laudable insofar as it brings to light information that has been ignored or suppressed. It is discreditable insofar as it unduly emphasizes what has been ignored or suppressed.

Historian Jeffrey Pasley places Jefferson within the "Founder Studies movement" of the late 1990s—a genteel, latte-sipping, inversionist backlash against the post-1960s rejection of conventional political history: "The Founder Studies approach did not actually reject post-1960s historiography so much as apply some of its worst habits to the 'dead white guys': the automatic privileging of personal life and personal relationships over other matters and a disdain for electoral democracy, political parties, and government policy as worthwhile subjects."[29] Jefferson was their foil—an "inconsistent, elusive, slyly manipulative, and just not a very forthright or likable fellow"—to be contrasted with personally honest and politically prescient Federalists like Adams and Hamilton—the true heroes of the revolutionary period. He adds:

> "Conservative" may or may not be the proper adjective, but the celebrated figures were those who resisted many of the socially and politically democratizing trends of their day in favor of policies that may have increased national security and pushed toward a modern economy but that also served the interests and protected the prerogatives of early America's established social, economic, and political elites.[30]

According to Founder-Studies scholars, Jefferson turns out to be a false friend of liberty, democracy, and equality. Adams and, especially, Hamilton —who championed upward mobility of wealth, child labor, and military repression of dissent, among other things and who was both dueler and adulterer—are the true heroes.[31]

Law and history professor David Mayer explains the assault on Jefferson through a sexual link with Sally Hemings as the result of laxity of the standards of historical scholarship due to political correctness, multiculturalism, and postmodernism. Political correctness, the anthem of conservatives at college and university campuses, seeks to protect all persons from leftist harangues—especially those harangues with sexual or racial undertones. Multiculturalism, a movement directed toward increasing diversity, has morphed into particularism, a movement that rejects any consideration of group identity. Postmodernism, a movement that tries to deconstruct the subjectivity and underlying uncertainty of all things known, has targeted objectivity and convinced many historians that there is no right reconstruction of events—that is, anything goes. These three movements have had a corruptive influence on the practice of history. "Sadly, the historical profession today has lost much of the standards by which evidence can be objectively weighed and evaluated in the search for historical truth. History, in effect, has become politicized in America today, as illustrated by the widespread acceptance of the Jefferson-Hemings myth as historical fact."[32] There is pressure in the academic community to take the Jefferson-Hemings myth as fact or be branded "racist" for not accepting the Hemings's oral tradition. "Among many proponents of the Jefferson paternity claim there has emerged a truly disturbing McCarthyist-like inquisition that has cast its pall over Jefferson scholarship today."

David Murray says that the issue is cultural and race is at the forefront. "It is hard to escape the concern that Thomas Jefferson has been enlisted, on the losing side, in a battle of cultural symbolism, where the sexual and racial elements of the story have been allowed to predominate, turning a quest for evidence into a moral referendum on the evils of slavery."[33] This "morality play," however, has come at expense of facts and has functioned to "cow critics into silence," for to defend Jefferson, in effect, is to defend racism. He concludes: "When we are forced to accept an 'official story' by means of a process more political than scientific, driven by a well-meaning desire to mythologize, we do so at the expense of the unfettered search for truth. As for whites and African Americans, once we as a united people with a shared landscape and mutual past hook our mythologized desires to contingent scientific outcomes, we thereby put both in jeopardy."

Wilson, Pasley, Mayer, and Murray offer compatible explanations, which taken together go far in completing the etiological puzzle concerning widespread acceptance on gossamer evidence of the putative liaison between Jefferson and Hemings. They also give an explanation for the normative turn in history—the in-vogue tendency to pass moral judgment of historical figures.

To those explanations, one can add two more, consistent with the others: political orientation and Jefferson's refusal to respond to scurrilous accusations.

First, political orientation of critics is surely a factor. Jefferson's republicanized views will certainly offend today both extreme conservatives and extreme liberals. Political conservatives who advocate a strong presidency, for instance, ultra-conservatives, will be put off by Jefferson's strict constructionism, his championing of small government, and his appeal to the interests of the majority as means of curbing political power. Political liberals who champion equal rights for all will be taken aback by the fact that Jefferson pushed to eliminate the institution of slavery but did not free his own slaves, that he believed women were to have nothing more than a domestic role, and that he recognized the teachings of Jesus to be the purest moral teachings while he lived in some respects very much unlike Jesus.

Second, Jefferson, as we have already seen,[34] had a habit of not replying to scurrilous accusations, though he certainly had no objection to others replying on his behalf and sometimes prompted others to do so. The political slander leading up to the elections in Jefferson's two terms as president, for example, was customarily brutal. Consider the Federalist party line for Jefferson's first term: "THE GRAND QUESTION STATED: At the present solemn and momentous epoch, the only question to be asked by every American, laying his hand on his heart, is 'Shall I continue in allegiance to GOD—AND A RELIGIOUS PRESIDENT; or impiously declare for Jefferson—and no god!!!'"[35] In spite of the accusation of atheism, Jefferson won the election. Jefferson's campaigners, in turn, branded Adams a British-sympathizing Presbyterian and earned the sympathy of non-Presbyterian sects. Adams later reflected that Baptists, Quakers, Methodists, Moravians, Lutherans, and Calvinists—so dissatisfied with Presbyterianism—voted in droves for Jefferson.

An overreaching corrective trend in the literature; the Founder-Studies movement; political correctness, multiculturalism, and postmodernism; political extremism; a morality play; and Jefferson's sheepishness concerning slander are all reasons why he is today an easy target. None of them, however, is a good reason.

## Aesopian History and How It Is Done

In his *Literary Commonplace Book*, Jefferson commonplaces a passage by Archbishop John Tillotson on how history ought to be done. Tillotson argues that proper history (1) must be written by a contemporary author or one with contemporary materials, (2) must be published by persons who are capable judges of the abilities of the author and the evidence, (3) must not contain anything repugnant to the "universal experience of mankind," and (4) must at least have its principal facts corroborated by collateral, disinterested testimony.[36]

After a brief critique of British history in a letter to newspaper editor John Norvell (June 14, 1807), President Jefferson turns to a related issue—newspaper reporting. Newspapers are most useful, he begins, when stories are restrained by "true facts & sound principles only." Such a publication, he acknowledges, would likely sell little. Thus, the papers of his day have prostituted themselves to falsehood—especially in the guise of defamation—in an effort to cater to the wants of the public, at expense of the truth. "Defamation is becoming a necessary of life; insomuch, that a dish of tea in the morning or evening cannot be digested without this stimulant," Jefferson laments. The accounts a person reads are "just as true a history of any other period of the world as of the present, except that the real names of the day are affixed to their fables."

Plato in *Phaedrus* argues that a writer or presenter of speeches—whether a rhapsode, poet, or politician—cannot claim to be a *technikos* (skilled speaker[37]) unless what he writes or recites is truthful or aims to be so.[38] Socrates says, "There is no genuine art of speaking without a grasp of truth, and there never will be" (260E). And later, "The art of a speaker who doesn't know the truth and chases opinions instead is likely to be a ridiculous thing—not an art at all" (262C). A poet or politician, and we might add here historian, who speaks or writes about what seems reasonable (*to eikos*), instead of what is the case, is merely pandering to the crowd—giving an audience what they wish to hear, not what is true (273A).

The scenario is very similar in much of the Jeffersonian scholarship today. It has become "Aesopian"—that is, it deals with fables and there is a moral at the end of each fable—and many "historians," in *Jerry Springer Show* fashion, cater to or feed off of the uninformed. One cannot take Jefferson at his word. One must look for euphemism, innuendo, and metaphor. The best researcher is the one who reads between the lines, as it were—in the language of hermeneutics, one who deconstructs—and deconstruction has as its sole aim criticism. In consequence, fable takes the place of truth. Evidence is not vetted. Baseless speculation masquerades as fact. At the end of the day, there is a subtle, latent moral for patient readers—one that shows Jefferson was no American patriot or hero, but a scurrilous rogue, a racist, an egoistic hedonist. There seems to be a contest to see who can throw the most stones, to see who can really maim Jefferson. History for many Jeffersonian scholars has become slapdash.

These are not merely my own botherations, but, as I have already shown, genuine concerns of numerous scholars. The liberties taken with Jeffersonian scholarship are setting a disturbing methodological trend for historians for whom rationality, evidence, and integrity are prized. Normative assessment, following the *Jerry Springer Show*–like pattern of titillation, has become vogue, as if historical scholarship should admit of vogue. Selection of evidence has become acceptable. The canons of rationality are shelved or ignored. Speculation, masquerading as fact, is admissible, when fact is wanting.

I offer below a rough, eight-step sketch that characterizes much of the Aesopian scholarship of certain of the ultraist Jeffersonian "revisionists."

(1) One begins by selecting from topics related to Jefferson's personal life—the more personal, the better.

(2) One forms a general conclusion prior to research or while research is in its infancy and that conclusion, assumed true, drives research forward.

(3) One selects only historical materials in keeping with one's preconceived conclusion—that is, inconsistent materials are ignored or downplayed.

(4) When constructing arguments to support one's preconceived conclusion, strength of those arguments is not a desideratum.

(5) When desperate, lack of evidence for some claim can be taken as positive evidence for its contradictory.

(6) If there is a significant gap in one's explanatory account and no evidence can be found to help one fill that explanatory gap, then one is justified in making up a story, in keeping with one's overall conclusion, to fill that gap.

(7) Historical assessment must include moral judgments, which are to be made from the safe moral perch of contemporary standards to ensure condemnation.

(8) If possible, "gild" one's account with paternalistic prosaisms.

## (1) Do Psychobiography

This first step needs scant articulation. *The Jerry Springer Show*, I have mentioned already, has had a larger audience and better ratings than has *Charlie Rose*. As Brodie's *Thomas Jefferson* has shown, history gone wild sells. As Gordon-Reed's *The Hemingses of Monticello* has shown, history gone wild can earn one numerous awards—even a Pulitzer Prize. Perhaps that is why Burstein, who formerly chided scholars for their in-chambers scholarship, has recently gone that route.

## (2) Begin with the Conclusion

History is traditionally done much like philosophy. One picks an area of study, does research in that area, and perusal of the research itself dictates the conclusions that can be drawn. That, of course, requires open-mindedness.

That is not true of normative, Aesopian history. Here one begins by assuming as true what ought to be shown true. Gordon-Reed, taking Madison Hemings's account as unshakeable, elaborates imaginatively on the details of Jefferson's seduction of Sally Hemings in *The Hemingses of Monticello*. Burstein, taking Gordon-Reed's research as pioneering but correctable, expatiates in *Jefferson's Secrets* on how Jefferson likely conducted a sex-only relationship with Hemings for thirty-eight years without detection.

## (3) Select the Evidence

Since one begins research with a preconceived conclusion, there is no constraint to temper one's conclusions to the strength of the evidence. Instead, evidence is culled to fit the conclusion.

Beginning with *Jefferson and Hemings had a thirty-eight-year liaison*, one merely looks for confirmatory evidence—Madison's "testimony," DNA evidence, and so forth—to settle skeptical readers, before moving on to the particulars of that liaison. Since there is no conclusive evidence for a liaison, the aim is to pile up circumstantial evidence. The hope is to swamp undiscerning readers with bad arguments and, eventually, force capitulation. When circumstantial evidence is wanting, it is allowable to take evidence that is not inconsistent with one's hypothesis and use it as confirmatory evidence of it. I use two illustrations from Brodie. First:

(1) While traveling through Europe in 1788, Jefferson used *mulatto* eight times in twenty-five pages of his travel journal.
(2) Therefore, Jefferson was sexually preoccupied with Sally Hemings (1).

Next:

(1) Jefferson's letters to his daughters exhibited great tenderness.
(2) Therefore, Jefferson used tenderness as a means of sexually seducing his daughters (1).

Moreover, as the conclusion is preconceived, there is no need to address inconsistent data or to address authors with inconsistent views. Gordon-Reed, for instance, strongly suggests that historians have passed over the account of Madison Hemings, from which she reconstructs her history, because of racism. In doing so, she can ignore all testimonies—and there are many—that contradict Madison's. "In the process," writes Mayer, "she breaks down most accepted standards for weighting evidence, particularly for weighing oral tradition evidence, creating a new double standard which gives preference to the oral tradition supporting the Jefferson paternity thesis."[39] I add that that standard is racistist: The hearsay account of one black person, even when there are incontestable difficulties with that account, trumps the testimonies of all white persons. Yet blackness and whiteness are not on trial. Human rationality, history, and Jefferson's legacy are.

## (4) Ignore Canons of Inductive Strength

Normative historians focus on the inner dimension of Jefferson—his private life. It is acknowledged to be extraordinarily difficult to ferret out and assess Jefferson's inner life. That is not the case for the revisionists, however. For instance, Jefferson's coolness to his mulatto children can be readily explained by his thirty-eight-year relationship with Hemings being sex-only, Burstein states. What would have driven such a "principled" person to seek out sex with his slave? Burstein notes that Jefferson had a medical book of Tissot in his library. Tissot's regimen for a healthy life, which avowedly fit Jefferson to a T, included occasional sexual release through sexual intercourse with an attractive partner.

However, Jefferson had thousands of books in his remarkable library. Many of the books, like Johann Jakob Brucker's *History of Philosophy* or the works of Plato and Aristotle, were reference-only books, or mostly so. It is likely that Jefferson's books on medicine were also reference-only—that is, books to which he had recourse in times of crisis or for research in replying to a letter. Burstein's argument that he followed Tissot's regimen to a T uses poor analogical reasoning, as I have shown in chapter 3. Lacking any other evidence, to say that Jefferson would have undertaken a lengthy and extraordinarily risky liaison with a slave for seminal release is absurd. Were Tissot to have had such a remarkable influence on Jefferson concerning regimen for health, that would have leaked out somewhere in his large correspondence. It has not. Much more evidence is needed. Burstein's hypothesis is weakly supported.

## (5) Be Merciless

In philosophy, there is something called the principle of charity. It states that if there is any uncertainty, due to ambiguity or vagueness, concerning how to take something that another has said or written—especially when it has a bearing on an argument one is intending to evaluate—then it is proper to clean up the uncertainty in the manner that allows for the strongest possible argument for that other. The principle of charity, in effect, enjoins critics never to build a straw man—an argument shoddily constructed in order to be easily refuted.

Aesopian historians, however, are anything but charitable, when it comes to historical reconstruction. So wildcat are they that they will put forth with contemptuous ease the zaniest, most ruthless claims, irrespective of evidence.

## (6) Use No Evidence as Evidence

When circumstantial evidence is wanting, one must be bold enough to argue ex silentio—namely, to use lack of evidence as evidence. For instance, Brodie maintains that the lack of evidence of a correspondence can only be taken as evidence that the letters between Jefferson and Hemings were destroyed.

(1) There is no evidence of letters between Jefferson and Hemings.

(2) Therefore, the letters must have been destroyed (1).

Again, Gordon-Reed acknowledges that nothing is known about Sally's whereabouts while in France. Still, she concludes conveniently that Hemings must have stayed with Jefferson.

(1) We know nothing about Sally Hemings's whereabouts while in France.

(2) Therefore, it is reasonable to conclude she stayed in Jefferson's four-room apartment, where there were some opportunities for the two to consummate a sexual affair (1).

Moreover, Burstein concedes Madison Hemings's claim that Jefferson ignored his black family. Yet, instead of taking it as evidence of no relationship between Jefferson and Sally Hemings, he takes it as evidence for a sex-only relationship with Sally Hemings.

(1) Madison Hemings stated that Jefferson ignored him and his siblings over the years.

(2) Therefore, Jefferson's relationship with Sally Hemings was merely sexually fulfilling, not emotionally binding (1).

Those are the sorts of corners into which one can readily get painted, when one begins by assuming what ought to be demonstrated—here, the existence of a liaison.

## (6) Fill in Gaps with Baseless Speculation

Where large evidentiary gaps appear in one's overall historical account, nothing rules out freest use of one's imagination to fill in the gaps in a manner that offers confirmatory evidence of one's preset conclusion. History is, after all, a highly imaginative enterprise. It is aidful, however, to preface one's speculations with *In light of evidence to the contrary . . . , One must assume that . . . , It is not unthinkable that . . . , There is nothing to show it is impossible that . . .* , or something similar. That, we have abundantly seen, is the modus operandi of Brodie, Gordon-Reed, and Burstein. Here I invite readers to read their reconstructions and highlight the number of times claims are prefaced by such phrases.

For instance, given that we know Jefferson and Hemings had a lengthy sexual relationship (that is, Madison Hemings's account is unshakable), one can conclude that the liaison was very likely mutually fulfilling, Hemings, who was fourteen when she came to France, was not only handsome, but also highly intelligent.

(1)  Jefferson and Sally Hemings had a thirty-eight-year liaison.
(2)  Hemings was a handsome woman.
(3)  Jefferson was a highly intelligent man.
(4)  No highly intelligent man would have had a lengthy relationship with a slave, however attractive, who was not highly intelligent.
(5)  Therefore, (in light of evidence to the contrary) Hemings was not only handsome, but highly intelligent (1–4).
(6)  Therefore, Hemings's liaison with Jefferson was mutually fulfilling (5).

There is evidence of Hemings's attractiveness, but *nothing* is known of her intelligence. We do not know whether she could read or write. That she was given the role of Maria's companion is suggestive, in spite of Abigail Adams's comments to the contrary, of some amount of maturity and trust in her youthful judgment. Yet that she would have had the wherewithal and pluck to bargain with Jefferson while in Paris at the age of sixteen, as stated by Madison Hemings', is incredible. Overall, there is no evidence of high intelligence. The argument flounders.

## (7) Conclude with a Subtle Moral Condemnation

History, like newspaper reporting, is supposed to be a descriptive discipline. Given Aesopian historians' tendency to probe into the personal lives of political figures and draw psychological inferences and to moralize, revisionists have turned history into a normative discipline. Jeffrey Pasley asserts: "History would become an almost religious enterprise if its mission were really to compare the weights of various worthies on some cosmic scale. One hopes that most present-day historians did not sign on to become high priests of a moral temple."[40] They have, it seems. Normative Jeffersonian historians have forsaken empirical science for Aesopian history. Such historians have become high priests of the moral temple. That they can be so cocksure of their conclusions with such lack of evidence must be taken as incontrovertible evidence that those who slander and vilify are themselves morally irreproachable.

Nonetheless, one could argue that Jefferson himself preferred Aesopian, not descriptive history, as his fondness for the Roman writer Tacitus shows. Jefferson writes to granddaughter Anne Randolph Bankhead (December 8, 1808): "Tacitus I consider as the first writer in the world without a single exception. His book is a compound of history and morality of which we have no other example." That Jefferson shows a preference for reading history with moral content does not show that he thought all history should have moral content. Consider, for illustration, his subtle chastisement of biographer and statesman William Wirt (November 12, 1816) on the latter's account of the life of founding father Patrick Henry. "You have certainly practiced vigorously [in *The Life of Patrick Henry*] the precept of 'de mortius nil nisi bonum' ["About the dead, write nothing but what is good"]. This presents a very difficult question,—whether one only or both sides of the medal shall be presented. It constitutes, perhaps, the distinction between panegyric and history." The suggestion strongly is that selective history is panegyric, not history.

Nonetheless, Jefferson's preference for history that morally elevates is not a preference for Aesopian history. Aesopian history embraces fabulizing, which has little regard for accuracy.

Overall, history should not be Aesopian. It should neither be normative nor be based on innuendo or fiction.

## (8) Gild with Paternalistic Prosaisms

Finally, Aesopian history can be gilded, as it were, by needless, paternalistic prosaisms. What is the potential payoff? The paternalistic manner in which such commonplace insights are given might give a revisionist a sense of wisdom that readers lack and create a sense of distance between themselves and readers. I offer a sample of prosaisms from Gordon-Reed's works.

- "Of course one cannot put in everything [in a historical reconstruction], but why shouldn't the record of a person's life include that person's characteristic and uncharacteristic actions; all individuals are the sum total of both."[41]
- "The people and places [Sally Hemings] encountered gave her multiple personal contexts."[42]
- "Like all families, each had its own unique characteristics: some couples may have loved each other more or less than other couples, they may have had ways of dealing with their children different from those of other parents, or the children in one household may have been better behaved or kinder to one another than children in other families."[43]
- "Seeing the face and figure of one's father or mother is important for many reasons."[44]
- "Contingencies drive the making of history on scales large and small. To speak of the inevitability of any historical event or outcome is to ignore this salient fact."[45]

## ENOUGH, ONUF!

At this juncture, readers might object that I have willingly engaged in hyperbole in my criticism of revisionist history apropos of Jefferson. I admit that there is something to the objection, but only if one takes me to be saying that all revisionists are committed to each step of the eight-step process I have delineated. That however would be to overstate my case.

The problem is disregard of objective standards of historical rigor that are applicable to historians across the globe. Following Mayer's objections and related to Jeffersonian scholars, revisionist historians take history to be a highly, if not exclusively, constructive discipline. With objectivity in disrepute, anything goes.

In "Thomas Jefferson's Lives: Learning from History," philosopher David Schrader comments on the 2012 Sons of the American Revolution annual conference, held in Charlottesville.[46] The conference, titled "Thomas Jefferson's Lives: Biography as a Construction of History"—and note here the preference for *lives* and not *life*—was held in honor of Peter J. Onuf. "The basic premise of the conference," writes Schrader, "was that biographies of major historical figures construct images of history." Another substratal premise was the influence of the civil rights movement on Jeffersonian scholarship. Schrader then mentions that Onuf, as the Thomas Jefferson Foundation Professorship in History at University of Virginia, has followed in the footsteps of two other distinguished scholars, Dumas Malone and Merrill Peterson, who formerly held the position. The conference, he concludes, was a "feast for the Jefferson scholar."

Much in Schrader's depiction of the conference greatly disturbs me. There is the basic premise of the conference—namely, the construction of history through construction of the biographies of key historical figures. Then, there is the secondary premise—namely, how the civil rights movement is influencing today's Jeffersonian scholars. Finally, there is the implicit assertion, which I shall leave to posterity to decide, of Onuf being a scholar of the same rank as Malone and Peterson.

First, history is not a matter of construction, which implies whim not evidence, but of evidence-driven reconstruction. Evidence drives history;

evidence admits of degrees; and evidence is not indefinitely plastic. Canons of rationality are applicable to historians' research. Without such canons, historians might just as well write poetry.

Second, what precisely does the civil rights movement, a child of the twentieth century, have to do with understanding Jefferson? It is true, as I show in the next chapter, that Jefferson considered blacks intellectually and physically, but not morally, inferior to nonblacks. In that, he was certainly wrong, but so too were the majority of the cognoscenti of his day. To evaluate and denigrate Jefferson in a moral way for incognizance of something of which most intellectuals in his day were unaware is absurd. One might as well castigate him for preferring horse-drawn buggies to automobiles and Newtonian dynamics to the general theory of relativity. In addition, why should revisionists stop with Jefferson? Aristotle thought all non-Greeks were naturally inferior to Greeks because of the advance and greatness of Greek culture, Athens especially, in his day. Aristotle also thought bodies fell in proportion to their weight in a particular medium—whether in air or in water—and, thus, was unaware that weight (in a vacuum) is not a factor in the rate of fall ($d \propto t^2$). In both instances, Aristotle is wrong. Yet there is something wrong about holding historical figures accountable to present-day intellectual standards and mores that were nonextant in their day. It is like a parent castigating his daughter for not having mastered Euclid at the age of three. Jefferson was on top of the science of his day and was a product of the science of his day. To castigate him for being a product of his day is to commit the fallacy of historical anachronism.

Bringing together the two notions—that of history being a matter of construction and that of holding past figures accountable to current mores and standards—we arrive at something outlandish. If accounts of historical figures are constructions—that is, they do not aim at, because they cannot arrive at, even an approximation of the truth—how then can historians normatively evaluate historical figures like Jefferson from current standards, which must themselves be constructions? The real Jefferson must be forever inaccessible because he is accessible only through the lens of modern-day culture. Yet what is inaccessible cannot be held accountable to evaluation and condemnation—especially of the moral sort. The best one can say is that, at a particular time and in a particular culture, scholar A's depiction of Jefferson makes him a scapegrace and scholar B's depiction makes Jefferson a plaster saint, and so on, or that the majority of today's scholars in a particular intellectual climate tend to think Jefferson was a scapegrace. On either account, there is no way of knowing the real Jefferson, if history is constructive. If either scenario is the best we can do, then there is no reason, other than intellectual masturbation, to pursue history. Yet the notion of history being mere construction falls prey to the objection that, if true, it applies to itself and nullifies itself—that is, the claim *History is construction* is a construction and, thus, need not be taken seriously. What, then, is the motivation to write history, when one can grab a pint of cheap scotch, a pocketful of bad cigars, and go fishin'? There is none.

How does this analysis relate to Onuf? In his compilation of essays titled *Jeffersonian Legacies*—note here the preference for *legacies* and not *legacy*—Onuf begins in the opening paragraph of the foreword:

> The fifteen essays in this volume are an outgrowth of a remarkable conference on "Jeffersonian Legacies," held at the University of Virginia in October 1992 as the opening event in the University's commemoration of the 250th anniversary of the birth of its founder, Thomas Jefferson. Revisionist in spirit, innovative in format, the conference sought new perspectives on the Jefferson legacy by measuring Jefferson's life and values against major concerns of the 1990s.

Onuf's opening salvo makes it clear that he is aiming at a break with past scholarship and its canons of historical rigor. No longer will it be a matter of trying to know the real Jefferson through amassing and evaluating evidence, reading and responding to alternative views, and accommodating, altering, or changing one's view in light of newly disclosed evidence, but, as his choice of *legacies* suggests, painting varied pictures of the polymathic statesman, irrespective of canons of history and rationality.[47]

Stephen Conrad in one of the essays included in Onuf's *Jeffersonian Legacies*, writes in a footnote to his essay of a 1992 symposium "Jefferson and Rights" in which philosopher Richard Rorty "eloquently made the case for setting aside questions of historical accuracy and philosophical justification in order to sustain the present-day cause of international human rights, a cause that has lately invoked the Jeffersonian tradition to profound effect."[48] To what is Conrad referring, if not Onuf's agenda?

In both instances, we find evidence of an agenda-driven movement. It is not that the cause of advance of human rights is a poor motive, but to sacrifice truth to do so is a colossal risk. As a realist and not a Rortian, I am inclined to believe that human rights are best advanced by adherence to truth, not fabulation—a very Jeffersonian point. Without truth, whose vision of which rights uniquely and categorically belong to humans are we to adopt? I suppose it will come down to trickery and coercion, but that is just what Jefferson fought so long and hard all of his life to eradicate from governing.

Finally, I turn to what Joyce Appleby writes in the introductory essay of Onuf's *Jeffersonian Legacies*. Noting that today we live in a world of "posts"—postmodernism, poststructuralism, postpositivism, postrealism, and so on—she asks, "Are we now post-Jefferson?" The question, she acknowledges, is not easily answered, but she attempts an answer.

> A telling sign of our postmodernity is that we have difficulty accepting Jefferson's arguments with their scientific gloss of universal truths, first principles, and immutable norms. The words that fill our public debates—*pluralism, diversity, multiculturalism, relativism*—point to different truths about the human experience. Jefferson developed a powerful rationale for his liberal reforms in the idea of a natural social order that reveals itself to scientific inquiry. Success long ago froze that rationale into an American creed. Should we continue to reason with outworn concepts of nature and truth? We can be certain of one thing—Thomas Jefferson would not have.

Appleby's account as a description of what increasingly tends to be occurring among historians today is apple pie. Yet that is only a description of how many of historians, ultraist liberal scholars especially, speak, not how they behave. Science is for us today as important, as truth-generating, and as progressive as it was for Jefferson in his day. Jefferson abandoned timeworn concepts not because of an embrace of relativism, but because they no longer did the work they needed to do—when they failed to accommodate advances in scientific knowledge. He never was and never would have embraced treadmill relativism or any of the "posts" of which Appleby writes in the sense she writes about them. Today's "posts" are what select intellectuals choose to do to mark the passage of time and the changes they have verbally embraced as signifiers of that passage. However, they mark no change-of-life commitments. We trust today's medical doctors not because they are infallible, but because medicine, the product of numerous years of empirical research, has made noticeable advances over time. We trust today's engineers and give little thought to the safety of occupying high-rise buildings. We trust today's astrophysicists when they write of newfound moons of planets in our solar system or newfound planets in other solar systems.

Appleby has relativized Jefferson, and she is dead wrong to think Jefferson would have been comfortable with her relativizing him. Jefferson was never a relativist. He ever thought the human condition was capable of substantial improvement; he was a deep-dyed progressivist and a realist.[49] Wedded to progressivism and realism,[50] progress meant movement, measurable movement, toward some end. That end, for Jefferson, was increased knowledge of man as moral, political, and intellectual agent and of his place in nature.

Thus, to understand Jefferson, we need to return to the language of truth, progress, and realism—Jefferson's language, the language of everyday citizens, and the language relativizing "intellectuals" use when they eschew their intellectualness—and return to the sober Malonian practice of history. Otherwise, history will have proven itself to be effete and, in time, obsolete.

## UPSHOT

Where do we go from here, when the inmates, it seems, have taken control of the prison?

It is a disconcerting question. Novelty in historical scholarship today seems to be the only norm. Critical assessment is seen as rudeness. Today's wolves play with the sheep.

So many historians are dutifully engaged in the project of deconstructing in an effort to expose the underlying subjectivity of things—whatever that is supposed to mean—that there is little room, let alone time, for taking words at face value. That is perhaps why so little attention is paid to what Jefferson has literally written and so much attention is paid to the meaning behind his words—the latent behind the manifest. So long as deconstruction leads "research" and we allow for the infinite plasticity of the meaning of words, then, of course, anything goes. So long as political agendas, not truth, can drive historical research, anything goes. Who dares to criticize wild psychoanalytic speculation, a racistist sociological agenda, or hasty and shoddy induction? Even critical projects, such as this one, can be deconstructed and, if deconstructed thoroughly enough, pulverized. We might as well take seriously the interventions of gods in Homer and Herodotus as well as the miraculous cures in the Aesculapian temples.

I am, however, one of those dinosaurs who think words generally have definite meanings at a particular time in a language and those meanings constrain how we interpret properly formed sentences in a particular language. I am one of those dinosaurs who believe we can learn much about Jefferson through his messages, addresses, proposals, bills, and the thousands of letters he has written. I am one of those dinosaurs who maintain conclusions on a historical figure ought to be evidence-based and ought to follow canons of reason, instead of being products of paralogism. Finally, I am one of those dinosaurs who insist history is not an Aesopian discipline. Let those critics who morally castigate Jefferson first explain to their readers why they are in a fitting position, in the right normative perch, for moral assessment. Let those critics who prefer reading into Jefferson's words first explain to their readers why they are in a fitting position, in the right critical perch, to judge the latent behind the manifest content of Jefferson's words.

# CHAPTER 6

# A "CONVENIENT DEFECT OF VISION"

## Jefferson's View of Blacks

**Time, which outlives all things, will outlive this evil [slavery] also.**

—TJ TO JAMES HEATON, MAY 20, 1826

*T*hroughout his life, Jefferson was clear that he considered the institution of slavery to be a moral abomination. In spite of that, he was a lifelong owner of slaves. For most of the twentieth century, the hypocrisy was generally ignored or sloughed off by recourse to the facts that he tended to treat well his slaves, who in the main very much liked him, and that he was no different from other Southerners of his day.

With the civil rights movement, the 1960s were revolutionary. Scholars returned to a reexamination of Jefferson's writings, especially his *Notes on the State of Virginia*. What they found was both that Jefferson embraced black inferiority in mind and body and that he abhorred the thought of any tainting of white blood with black blood. What they found was that Jefferson, the father of the Declaration of Independence and champion of emancipation, was racist.

Today it is customary for Jeffersonian scholars not only to acknowledge Jefferson's great hypocrisy—what I have elsewhere dubbed his "wide-gap duplicity"[1]—but also to acknowledge other key defects of character. Though a strong advocate of manumission, Jefferson's incapacity or refusal to manumit his slaves shows opportunism, bigotry, monumental confusion, self-absorption, and, especially, racism. Thus, the huge gap between his words and his deeds is sufficient warrant for moral reproof. The sage of Monticello has become the Monticello miscreant.

This final chapter concerns a presumed defect of Jefferson's character—his so-called racism. Was Jefferson racist? If so, why would a racist have taken a black slave as his concubine for thirty-eight years? If not, is that enough to show that he would have been amenable to a liaison with a black slave?

## THE CASE FOR RACISM

Jefferson came under assault in the 1960s through the works of historians Robert McColley, Winthrop Jordan, and William Cohen, among others.

In 1964, Robert McColley published *Slavery and Jeffersonian Virginia*. McColley came to terms with Jefferson's assessment of the inferiority of blacks in *Notes on the State of Virginia* as well as his refusal to manumit his own slaves. Taking an actions-speak-louder-than-words tack, he argued that Jefferson quietly embraced the institution of slavery. Yet in that, McColley acknowledges, Jefferson differed nowise from other Southerners. He was merely a product of his time, not a racist.[2]

The critical work was Winthrop Jordan's *White over Black* in 1968. Jordan stated boldly that Jefferson possessed a hatred of blacks—a hatred based on ambivalence, fueled by "libidinous energy" toward black women. Though Jefferson advocated manumission, his principal reason was not humanitarian. He was not in the least sympathetic with the plight of Americanized blacks. Instead of worrying that slavery dehumanized blacks, Jefferson concerned himself with the degrading effect of the institution on white slave owners, who generally became tyrants when owning slaves. Overall, Jefferson's writings on the institution of slavery betray, at times, "monumental confusion."[3]

In 1969, William Cohen writes in "Thomas Jefferson and the Problem of Slavery": "Jefferson's practical involvement with the system of black bondage indicates that, while his racist beliefs were generally congruent with his actions, his libertarian views about slavery tended to be mere intellectual abstractions. This is particularly true for the years after 1785; and to a somewhat lesser degree, it holds true for the earlier period as well." He concludes that there was a "significant gap between his thought and action with regard to the abolition question."[4] His refusal to manumit his own slaves, in spite of his protestations concerning the evils of slavery, was the result of unwillingness to change his lavish manner of living. Jefferson was crapulous and liked to live sumptuously and large.

The 1960s assault was ammunition for later scholars.

In 1977, John C. Miller published *The Wolf by the Ears: Thomas Jefferson and Slavery*, which many consider to be the most comprehensive study of Jefferson's views of blacks and slavery. Miller writes, "It is as though when Jefferson wrote and spoke about these matters, he experienced a convenient defect of vision which prevented him from seeing black." Jefferson had such an eye for the future, he sometimes wrote about slavery as if it had already been abolished. That, however, was merely rationalization, for envisaging the abolition of the institution enabled him to keep his own slaves and do so without a sense of guilt. It also allowed him sufficient justification for his inaction concerning their emancipation.[5]

Garrett Ward Sheldon, professor of politics, in 1991 stated that Jefferson Epicurean (i.e., egoistic) hedonism was the reason for his declination to manumit his slaves. He says succinctly, "In Jefferson's hierarchy of values, the emancipation of slaves occupied a lower position than either his personal lifestyle or the ideal republic."[6]

In 1994, law professor Paul Finkelman in "Thomas Jefferson and Antislavery" maintained Jefferson's express hatred of slavery was a cover for his "profound racism."[7] Following Jordan, he states Jefferson, in his *Notes on the State of Virginia*, worried about the corruptive effects of slavery on white Americans and about a black uprising that might destroy white America. The overall depiction in the *Notes on the State of Virginia* was racist. He could have carefully studied blacks, as he did fossils, plants, and other animals. He chose otherwise because he was racist.

In the late 1990s, the criticisms turn harsh—even vicious. Scholars had an axe to grind and Jefferson became the grinding stone.

In 1996, author and critic Conor Cruise O'Brien's *The Long Affair* vigorously assaulted Jefferson's liberalism, which O'Brien concluded was inescapably racist. O'Brien added that Jefferson might also be called the father of the KKK. Why? Populist leader Tom Watson of Georgia put out a magazine titled *The Jeffersonian*—a magazine that spread the parochial racism of the South to future generations. "*The Jeffersonian* . . . propagated in crude emotive forms ideas to which the master had given discreet and overtly unemotional expression. And in the southern states in the years after the Civil War the whites who most practiced what *The Jeffersonian* was preaching were members of the Ku Klux Klan."[8] O'Brien concludes: "The Ku Klux Klan was ideologically descended from Thomas Jefferson."

In "Jefferson and Slavery" (1997), historian Howard Temperly states Jefferson, more than any other president, was a hypocrite on slavery, acquisitiveness, and self-sufficiency. Though he advocated liberty and self-sufficiency, his own liberty and self-sufficiency was obtained through the labor of slaves. "The Jefferson whose likeness appears on Mount Rushmore was, at bottom, an opportunist," he writes.[9] "The principle to which he was most committed was his own convenience."

Finally, in 1999, Nicholas Magnis published "Thomas Jefferson and Slavery: An Analysis of His Racist Thinking as Revealed by His Writings and Political Behavior." The title makes a thesis superfluous.[10] One hopes that he wrote his paper prior to thinking up his title.

Of the triad of Jeffersonian revisionists whose works I critically examine in this book, Andrew Burstein and Annette Gordon-Reed are not shy about labeling Jefferson *racist*.

Andrew Burstein in *Jefferson's Secrets* (2005) acknowledges that *racist* is anachronistic. "Can [Jefferson] be called a liberal and a racist at once? Are such terms at all useful to us in chronicling the range of views among his generation? Though they help us to frame his general sentiments, it is best said that there are other, more accurate measures of Jefferson's thought, because the ideology we know as racial tolerance . . . did not exist until the twentieth century."[11] Nonetheless, *in the following paragraph*, Burstein writes, "Thus, class background or regional identity was not the only determinant of Jefferson's racism; his attachment to the books in his library mattered, too." Again, in the second paragraph after his caveat,

Burstein states that Jefferson's racism trumped his liberalism. *Racist* might be an anachronistic term, but Burstein, it seems, cottons to the use of anachronisms when it serves his purposes.

Annette Gordon-Reed makes abundant use of the epithet *racist* to describe Jefferson in her works. In addition, she often suggests that the historians who disacknowledge the liaison are racist. For instance, she begins in the preface of *Thomas Jefferson and Sally Hemings* with the statement "The Sally Hemings story has remained in a curious time warp."[12] It continues to be told in a "'through-the-eyes-of-white-southerners' view." The phrasing is unsubtle and betrays her political and racial agenda. We are presumably not to take seriously scholars like Dumas Malone, who was born in Coldwater, Mississippi, because, being born in the South, he is incapable of objectivity.

The instances, collected above, are sufficient illustrations of the extent of critical condemnation in today's literature and to allow for an examination of the tenability of the thesis that Jefferson was racist.

## WHY JEFFERSON WAS NOT RACIST

Those scholars who label Jefferson *racist* fall upon his notion of black inferiority. Did Jefferson consider blacks naturally inferior? If so, does that warrant the charge of racism?

Critical discussion of Jefferson's view of blacks is a touchy issue. Irrationality often controls the discourse. Anyone who challenges or has an open mind concerning the issue of Jefferson's racism is generally and uncritically called *racist*. I offer one illustration. In a review of Andrew Burstein's early book *Jefferson's Secrets*—recall here Burstein was convinced that Jefferson could not have had an affair with Hemings on account of his character—critic Cynthia Kierner states, "Some attempts [by Burstein] to defend a contextualized Jefferson are eerily reminiscent of white supremacist arguments of the civil rights era."[13] The clear and absurd insinuation is that Burstein's attempt to explain Jefferson's belief in black inferiority by contextualizing Jefferson, by judging Jefferson by the norms of his day—which is what historians ought to be doing—is itself a cover for Burstein's own racism. One sees plainly why many scholars simply avoid the issue.

My reasons for exonerating Jefferson of the charge of racism are two. First, Jefferson's belief that blacks are inferior in body and mind is based on observations, not prejudgments. Like other critical examinations he undertakes in his *Notes on the State of Virginia*—for example, his examinations of seashells in the mountains ("Query VI"), of the mammoth ("Query VI"), of medicinal springs ("Query VI"), of the biota of North America as they compare with biota of Europe ("Query VI"), American-Indian burial mounds ("Query XI"), or even the formation of moisture on the walls of houses with walls of stone or brick ("Query XV")—he approaches the nature of black intelligence, physicality, and morality through collection of data and enumerative induction. His conclusions, founded on observations, are, he consistently maintains like a sound empiricist, always subject to revision. In "Query XIV," as illustration, he writes on the issue of black inferiority, "To justify a general conclusion, requires many observations," and blacks have never been "subjects of natural history"—that is, they have never as a race been studied scientifically. Thus, "I advance it . . . as a suspicion only, that the blacks . . . are inferior to the whites in the endowments both of body and mind."[14] That is what it means to have a scientific attitude toward phenomena in the manner of Francis Bacon or Isaac Newton—and a scientific attitude is not consistent with racism, since racism is judgment based on prejudice and not on an unbiased examination of facts. Second, there are problems with scholars' use of *racism*. Scholarly work by historians is supposed to stay at the descriptive level. Epithets such as *racism* are value judgments, often unceremoniously ascribed to a historical figure, as in the case with Jefferson, without due discernment. Ascription of terms like *racism* makes historians normativists. Moreover, *racism* is an anachronism, which does little to help us to understand Jefferson's ownership of slaves.

### Jefferson's "Observations" of Black Inferiority

Jefferson's most sustained discussion of the issue of blacks is in his *Notes on the State of Virginia*. In "Query XIV," Jefferson considers whether blacks should be retained and incorporated into the new nation. His "political" reasons are chiefly four. "Deep rooted prejudices by the blacks,[15] of the injuries they have sustained; new provocations; the real distinctions which nature has made; and many other circumstances, will divide us into parties, and produce convulsions which will probably never end but in the extermination of one or the other race." Jefferson is often disparaged for not listing injustice among the reasons, but one must grant that he is giving political, not ethical, reasons.

Jefferson also lists several "physical" reasons. Much of what he has to say is aesthetical: The skin color of blacks is a difference due to nature and gives blacks a lesser share of beauty. Furthermore, their form is less symmetrical and elegant than whites and they lack flowing hair. There is also less facial and bodily hair on blacks. They secrete less by their kidneys and more by skin glands than whites and that produces a "very strong and disagreeable odour." They seem to require less sleep than whites, as they will work all day and stay up late. They are more adventuresome and, at least, equally as brave as whites, both of which may be due to lack of forethought. They are more passionate than whites in sex, but less tender. In the main, they are more sensual and less reflective than whites. They are equal in memory to whites, inferior in reasoning, and "dull, tasteless, and anomalous" in imagination. They are the equals of whites in moral discernment.[16]

Jefferson's description of blacks in his *Notes on the State of Virginia* is customarily taken to bespeak his racism. That would be so if his observations were skewed because they were driven by prejudice. Scrutiny of Jefferson's analysis of blacks and his comparison of them with whites in his *Notes on the State of Virginia*, against Finkelman and consistent with his analysis of all undecided issues in that book, do not show prejudice, but instead an effort to examine the issue of racial differences through empirical investigation. Even the issue of inferiority of skin color, an aesthetic judgment, he broaches empirically. It is an issue for the faculty of taste to decide and Jefferson invites readers to look at black skin and judge for themselves, presumably through appeal to the aesthetic sense.[17]

Jefferson then tackles the issue of whether observation of black intellectual and physical inferiority is due to nature or their situation, obviously oppressive.

Here a caveat is in order. One cannot advance the issue of Jefferson's attitude toward blacks if one ignores the extent to which progressivism imbued Jefferson's scientific thinking—science, for Jefferson, included politics and morality as well as what we consider science today. Whatever the pitfalls of European culture—which Jefferson thought was politically and morally degenerate when compared to American culture with its embrace of republican principles—one cannot deny great progress in agriculture, chemistry, geology, natural history, natural philosophy, biology, meteorology, navigation, astronomy, and even music and domestic manufacture in Jefferson's day. There were the discoveries of Harvey concerning the circulation of blood, of Jenner concerning inoculation against smallpox, of Boyle concerning the inverse relationship of pressure and volume of gas in a container, of Kepler concerning the elliptical orbits of the planets and their motions, of Galileo concerning the rate of fall of bodies and projectile motion, and of Newton concerning the laws of bodily motion and the universal law of gravity. There were inventions. Cristofori invented the piano. Fahrenheit invented the mercury thermometer. Kay invented the flying shuttle to improve looming; Hargreaves, the spinning jenny; Crompton, the spinning mule; and Whitney, the cotton gin. Franklin invented the lightning rod and bifocal glasses. Harrison invented a navigational clock for measuring longitude. Priestley invented carbonated water. Bushnell invented the submarine; the Montgolfier brothers, hot-air balloons; and Fitch, the steamboat. Volta invented the battery; and Davy, the electric light. There were the political advances of Locke, Montesquieu, Rousseau, Kames, and Smith that marked progress for Jefferson insofar as they paved the way for government for and by the people. There were the progressive moral insights of Hume, Bolingbroke, Hutcheson, Ferguson, Reid, and Stewart that for Jefferson complemented the equalitarian shift in political thinking.

Scientific discoveries and inventions were commonplace in Jefferson's day, and such advances required more forward-looking moral and political ideologies to accommodate them. For Jefferson, those new political and moral insights were advances every bit as genuine as the scientific discoveries and inventions that accompanied them. Therefore, one must acknowledge that Jefferson, perhaps more than any other prominent political figure of his day except perhaps Franklin, was swept up by the current. Jefferson was a deep-dyed progressivist, whose approach to all matters related to the sciences of his day, broadly construed, was empirical, not metaphysical.[18] Those who approach the issue of Jefferson's attitude toward blacks seem conveniently to forget Jefferson's deep-dyed empiricism and progressivism.

Jefferson saw that most Americanized blacks had been confined to tillage and their own society, but also that many had the fortune of frequent conversations with their masters, many had learned handicraft arts, some had been liberally educated, and all had lived in a country where the arts and sciences had been considerably cultivated. He writes:

> But never could I find that a black had uttered a thought above the level of plain narration; never see even an elementary trait of painting or sculpture. In music they are more generally gifted than the whites with accurate ears for tune and time, and they have been found capable of imagining a small catch. . . . Religion indeed has produced a Phyllis Whately; but it could not produce a poet. The compositions published under her name are below the dignity of criticism.[19]

Those observations of exposure to white culture—here Jefferson has principally in mind Enlightenment science in its varied manifestations—without assimilation of it suggest to him a natural cause of intellectual inferiority.

A comparison with Jefferson's critique of American Indians, who had not had much exposure to white culture, is helpful.

> To judge of the truth of [American Indians' want of genius], to form a just estimate of their genius and mental powers, more facts are wanting,

and great allowance to be made for those circumstances of their situation which call for a display of particular talents only. This done, *we shall probably find* that they are formed in mind as well as in body, on the same module with the "Homo sapiens Europæus."[20](italics added)

Why the difference in assessment of black Americans and American Indians? American Indians have been observed only in their own culture, which places few demands on their talents, and so Jefferson is willing to give them benefit of doubt. In contrast, blacks have been exposed to white culture and have not assimilated it. That, for him, is a critical difference.

Further evidence of a natural cause comes with miscegenation. He writes incautiously, "The improvement of the blacks in body and mind, in the first instance of their mixture with the whites has been observed by every one, and proves that their inferiority is not the effect merely of their condition of life."[21]

Ascription of intellectual and physical deficiencies notwithstanding, Jefferson considers blacks the moral equals of whites—a point missed by nearly all scholars, historian Alf Mapp Jr. being an exception.[22] "Whether further observation will or will not verify the conjecture, that nature has been less bountiful to them in the endowments of the head, I believe that in those of the heart [i.e., morality] she will be found to have done them justice."[23] That is a prodigious observational concession that makes it difficult to maintain Jefferson's views of blacks is prejudicial, because he is clear in several writings that he considers a sound moral faculty more important than a sound rational faculty or even handsomeness of physical body: "An honest heart being the first blessing," he states to nephew Peter Carr (August 19, 1785), "a knowing head is the second." "I think it [the moral sense] the brightest gem with which the human character is studded," he writes to Thomas Law (June 13, 1814), "and the want of it as more degrading than the most hideous of the bodily deformities."[24] Racists are disinclined to make such concessions—especially significant ones.

The tone throughout Jefferson's comparison of blacks with whites is starkly unfavorable and, as we know from our modern perch, untrue. That is so obvious that it scarcely needs stating. Nonetheless, his judgments throughout are decidedly empirical, not prejudicial. There is no prejudging. That is the issue that scholars today do not see—one they do not wish to see—and that is a ponderous issue. Those scholars who have studied thoroughly Jefferson's *Notes on the State of Virginia* are quick to observe the through-and-through empirical bent of the work and the relatively meticulous research—not all of which that has stood the test of time—that went into its composition.[25] However, those scholars who have studied Jefferson's depiction of blacks in the *Notes on the State of Virginia* cite racial prejudice, not observation, as the source of Jefferson's conclusions. Why? I suspect strongly that they have not finecombed the work as a whole, but rather read through only those passages in which Jefferson addresses the issue of blacks, without attention to the empirical bent of those passages and of the rest of the book. Jefferson's comments on blacks in his *Notes on the State of Virginia* cannot be read in isolation to the work as a whole. That is a convenient way to build a straw man.

In a tremendously significant passage that is often ignored or poorly paraphrased, Jefferson writes on the difficulties of assessing black intelligence. I quote it at length.

The opinion, that [blacks] are inferior in the faculties of reason and imagination, must be hazarded with great diffidence. To justify a general conclusion, requires many observations, even where the subject may be submitted to the Anatomical knife, to Optical glasses, to analysis by fire, or by solvents. How much more then were it is a faculty, not a substance, we are examining; where it eludes the research of all the senses; where the conditions of its existence are various and variously combined; where the effects of those which are present or absent bid defiance to calculation; let me add too, as a circumstance of great tenderness, where our conclusion would degrade a whole race of men from the rank in the scale of being which their Creator may perhaps have given them. To our reproach it must be said, that though for a century and a half we have had under our eyes the races of black and of red men, they have never yet been viewed by us as subjects of natural history. I advance it therefore as a suspicion only, that the blacks, whether originally a distinct race, or made distinct by time and circumstances, are inferior to the whites in

the endowments both of body and mind. It is not against experience to
suppose, that different species of the same genus, or varieties of the same
species, may possess different qualifications.

There can be no clearer statement that the issue is as yet undecided and
to be decided empirically, not metempirically or prejudicially. He is clear
to state blacks have been observed, but not *scientifically* observed. His
position is one of flexibility, not inflexibility. In stark contrast to Jefferson's
empirical perspective, prejudice is not sufficiently flexible to accommodate
new evidence. Moreover, prejudice is not indulgent of inconsistent evidence.
In addition, I repeat, prejudice is loath to make concessions.

There is other evidence, consistent with his purchase of empiricism,
that shows Jefferson to have the same open-mindedness and flexibility on
the issue of slavery. While in France, he not only translated, but also took
notes on the Marquis de Condorcet's avant-garde views against slavery.
That suggests minimally an open empirical attitude on the subject. Writing
to General Chastellux (June 7, 1785), he states, "I have supposed the black
man, in his present state might not be in body and mind equal to the white
man; but it would be hazardous to affirm, that, equally cultivated for a
few generations, he would not become so." Six years later, he writes to
Benjamin Banneker (August 30, 1791), a black astronomer and surveyor:

> No body wishes more than I do to see such proofs as you exhibit, that
> nature has given to our black brethren, talents equal to those of the other
> colors of man, and that the appearance of a want of them is owing merely
> to the degraded condition of their existence, both in Africa & America.
> I can add with truth, that no body wishes more ardently to see a good
> system commenced for raising the condition both of their body & mind
> to what it ought to be, as fast as the imbecility of their present existence,
> and other circumstance which cannot be neglected, will admit.

To Condorcet (August 30, 1791), he says: "I shall be delighted to see
these instances of moral eminence so multiplied as to prove that the wont
of talents observed in them, is merely the effect of their degraded condition,
and not proceeding from any difference in the structure of the parts on which

intellect depends." In a letter to Henri Grégoire, bishop in the Roman Catholic Church and advocate of racial equality (February 25, 1809), he adds:

> Be assured that no person living wishes more sincerely than I do, to see a complete refutation of the doubts I have myself entertained and expressed on the grade of understanding allotted to them by nature, and to find that in this respect they are on a par with ourselves. My doubts were the result of personal observation on the limited sphere of my own State, where the opportunities for the development of their genius were not favorable, and those of exercising it still less so. I expressed them therefore with great hesitation; but whatever be their degree of talent it is no measure of their rights.

Intellectual superiority, he goes on to say, grants no one any rights that the intellectually inferior do not have, otherwise Newton would have been lord over all others.[26]

For all the reasons given, it is difficult to charge Jefferson with racism. To be a racist, Jefferson's views must be prejudicial. There must be evidence of prejudging, and the prejudging must be indifferent to evidence to the contrary. Jefferson formed his judgments on race through observing blacks, predominantly in his own state, and through sustained interaction with them. The number of his observations were insufficient—he says so in his *Notes on the State of Virginia*. Moreover, his observations were unvaried—he admits to that in his 1809 letter to Grégoire. Furthermore, he presumes the standards of Western culture are an adequate measuring stick and does not give sufficient weight to environmental factors.[27] Jefferson is guilty not of racism, but of hasty and biased induction—and that is not an anachronistic claim. Yet one must acknowledge that his views were in keeping with most of the scientists of his day and perhaps even most of the blacks of his day. Historian Alf Mapp Jr. writes, "In pronouncing the black intellectually inferior to the white, Jefferson was voicing an opinion with which in that age nearly every white, and probably nearly every black, would have agreed."[28] Abolitionists too often acknowledged black intellectual inferiority, but argued for abolition on moral grounds—that is, that slavery was depraved. That scarcely warrants the label "racist."

There is an additional issue—what Miller called Jefferson's "convenient defect of vision" concerning the plight of American blacks. Miller's choice of words implicates Jefferson on two counts: on treating unfairly the issues of black Americans' intelligence and of their physicality. I focus on the former. To say that Jefferson had a convenient defect of vision is to exaggerate—to grossly overstate the problem—a problem of empathy, not selectivity. Though clearly empathic at times, as his letters to Banneker and Grégoire indicate, Jefferson might reasonably be accused of failing to be *fully* empathic. He goes some ways toward empathizing with individual blacks in certain instances, but never does he seem to be fully empathic. In vitiating situation as a cause of black inferiority, he neglects to consider the stultifying effects of the institution of slavery on the collective will of a people—any people. Jefferson's letters on emancipation and expatriation show an acute grasp both of the moral evils of the institution of slavery and the collective effect of that institution on black Americans, but they seldom show any capacity to empathize with individual blacks. In short, Jefferson tends to speak of the plight of blacks as a race, not of the plight of particular blacks. For him, slavery is as much an intellectual problem that requires a timely solution as it is a moral difficulty.[29]

It is, as Jordan states, that Jefferson is more concerned with solving the problem of whether blacks are different by nature or by environment than he is with helping individual blacks. He has an intellectualist's, not a humanist's, approach to slavery. Yet that is merely Jefferson being Jefferson. Against Temperly, Jefferson was more inquisitive than acquisitive. In that, he was, perhaps following nature—his own natural impulses toward scientific investigation of phenomena. Wrote Seneca, millennia ago, "Nature has bestowed on us an inquisitive disposition and, being aware of her own skill and beauty, it has made us spectators of her mighty display."[30]

Following Douglas Wilson in his excellent paper "Thomas Jefferson and the Character Issue," we might concede that Jefferson did not "make adequate allowance for the conditions in which blacks were forced to live."[31] Yet he did not conclude, as did many others of his day—and this is an especially significant point—that "blacks were fit only for slavery." He consistently championed their emancipation *and* education—a point conveniently overlooked by many who are quick to dub Jefferson "racist."

## THE PROBLEM WITH "RACISM"

My second reason for rejection of the claim *Jefferson was racist* concerns *racism* itself. The difficulties with the word are three. First, it has pejorative emotive content that obscures its cognitive meaning. Second, it is an evaluative (i.e., normative) term and history is not a normative discipline. Finally, it is anachronistic.

First, many commonly used words have pejorative emotive content that blinds persons to their cognitive meaning. Emotive content comprises the feelings a term *evokes* independent of its meaning, which is cognitive, not emotive. Emotive content does not properly belong to a term's meaning, but is somewhat accidentally attached to it through culturally engendered emotively packed use (i.e., literally a misuse) of the term. *Racist* is especially emotion-packed in America. For most of American history, nonblack Americans have treated unfairly blacks due to perceived differences between blacks and nonblacks that presumably warranted treating the former as slaves or, at least, second-class citizens—an attitude that is unfortunately still prevalent in many Southern states. Thus, to say *Person* p *is a racist* is minimally to say *Person* p *discriminates against some race because of ascribed differences that do not exist and a commitment to those differences in spite of evidence to the contrary*, but also suggests, due to its emotive content, something like, *Person* p *is malicious, hateful, and (perhaps even) prone to violence against that race, based on* p*'s misperceptions*. Neither of the two depictions fits Jefferson. His attitude was consistently labile, not prejudicial. His attitude was never hateful, but always scientific. Nonetheless, because of its pejorative emotive content, *racist* has little place in serious scholarship—the exception being clear instances of racism, as in the case of Adolf Hitler.

Second, *racist* is a value judgment, not a descriptive claim. Given that, it seems to be a term that a biographical historian ought to shun, not use. The job of a biographical historian is to unearth facts related to a personage and then offer a plausible and consistent account of that person's life that not only accommodates everything known, but also presents itself as a more plausible account than existing, often-inconsistent accounts of other historians. It is not the job of a biographical historian to evaluate through passing moral judgment on a personage. It was a staple of Stoic ethical thinking, which Jefferson integrated, to avoid judgments of others that went beyond what was readily observable. Why? The best sort of life was deemed one in which one's judgments about things squared neatly with what was the case. Where doubt existed, suspension of judgment was warranted. Hasty judgments beyond what was readily observable were a stairway to vice.[32] Consequently, the statement *Jefferson was racist* has no room in historical scholarship done aright.

Third, *racist* is anachronistic. It is easy to state that Jefferson or even John Adams or James Madison was racist, just because all were Virginia land owners who owned slaves. Yet slavery was an acceptable part of Southern living for most persons during Jefferson's time. Most white property owners who lived in the South and who were among the gentry in Jefferson's day owned black slaves. Moreover, they thought little of the enormity of the institution. Were any of us transplanted to the South in Jefferson's day, we too would likely have owned slaves and thought little of that in the same way that we drive daily our vehicles and think little of the cumulative effects of polluting the air to the detriment of future generations. Thus, someone passing judgment on Jefferson from today's current moral perch is someone who states boldly, though counterfactually, that he would have been an exception to the rule in Jefferson's day, and that seems overstated, if not brash. Historian Leonard W. Levy states, "I have . . . ignored the strain of racism in Jefferson's thought simply because he cannot be held responsible for having been born a white man in eighteenth century Virginia."[33] Moreover, labeling Jefferson *racist* would implicate others, such as Benjamin Franklin, who was a slave trader as a young man, but who founded the first school for blacks in 1758 in Philadelphia and served as president of his regional abolition society.[34] The difficulty is noted by law professor David Mayer, who maintains that much of revisionist history is a result of *presentism*—the tendency to evaluate the past by the standards of the present, to commit what I call the *fallacy of historical anachronism*.[35] Presentism is an obstacle to historical understanding.

Andrew Burstein, who, we have seen in *Jefferson's Secrets*, deems *racism* anachronistic but makes liberal use of the epithet to judge Jefferson, attempts a medial solution in an earlier, 1996 interview with PBS.

> I would describe Jefferson as a scientific racist. What he wrote in the *Notes on Virginia* was a description of what he thought was an objective scientist's appraisal. He did not feel that he was bringing his personal emotion to his statement that African-Americans had offensive body odors, or African-Americans could not aspire to the same degree of rationality as whites. This is unfortunate but Jefferson did not do this with any ill will. He did not write other than what he considered to be the search for objective truth. We don't like it. It doesn't make us happy to think that the man who is heralded for his love of equality and liberty, who believed in the promise of America perhaps more than any of his generation, that within Jeffersonian optimism, there could exist this dark side. We don't like to think of it that way, but Jefferson was not alone. He was merely a conservative, socially a conservative, Virginian.[36]

Burstein's view in this early interview, in spite of the awkwardness of *scientific racist*, is note-perfect. Jefferson approached the issue of race in his *Notes on the State of Virginia* as he did all other issues—completely from an empirical point of view. That his conclusions prove offensive to many persons, if not most persons, today, because they are wrong, is unfortunate. Jefferson's intentions were not malicious. He was in pursuit of truth. No one is offended by Descartes's vortex theory or Priestley's theory of phlogiston, even though both are wrong. Yet it is the job of today's historians and critics to apprehend Jefferson in his day, not in ours. It is distressing that it seems Burstein no longer holds this point of view.

## JEFFERSON'S MORAL PROGRESSIVISM

I have already mentioned in a caveat the importance of non-neglect of Jefferson's purchase of progressivism in assessing his views of blacks. I have mentioned too that he thought humans were progressing politically as well as morally. In what follows, I expand on his moral progressivism.

Jefferson was an essentialist, not an evolutionist—namely, he did not think that human organisms could change substantially over time. What he did believe—and here his thinking squared with Aristotle and the Greek and Roman Stoics of antiquity—was that humans massively underutilized their capacities for intellectual activity and moral discernment.

In that regard, Jefferson was a moral progressivist in two overlapping senses.

First, though he believed all persons equally possessed a moral sense in the manner in which all persons possessed the faculty of sight, he did believe that that moral sensory capacity was communally contaminated, as it were. A comparison with sight is illustrative. In some sense, let us acknowledge that there is nothing as *seeing really*, but merely *seeing as*—that is, how we think about the world determines in some measure what it is we see. By that I do not mean that when one looks out one's window and sees a fully blooming, fully flowering Mimosa tree one is not actually seeing a fully blooming, fully flowering Mimosa tree. I do mean that our grasp of *Mimosa plant* is in effect conditioned by our current scientific understanding of *Mimosa plant*. It is currently known that Mimosas are small- to medium-sized deciduous plants in the family of legumes. With light-brown bark, their leaves, numbering from twenty to sixty per branch, are arranged alternately and appear fernlike. The plants have pink flowers from early to midsummer. Now, say, if a botanist should discover a Mimosa in some remote part of China that is well over one hundred feet tall, has over one hundred leaves on each branch, and has bright yellow flowers, our knowledge of Mimosas would change. Yet such change would not be replacement of one picture of Mimosas with another, radically distinct, but a change in terms of a refined grasp of Mimosas. The change would be progressive. I give another, more personal, illustration. Decades ago, I undertook the study of observational astronomy with the aid of a small telescope, a pair of 20×80 binoculars, and a pair of 10×50 binoculars. To this day, what I see when I look up to the sky is radically different than what I had been seeing prior to study. It is a world of familiar, not foreign, objects.

That is how Jefferson sees morality, and that depiction is mostly Aristotelian or Stoical. Moral discernment, which Jefferson often says occurs spontaneously and without the corruptive effects of reason,[37] is in large part for him determined by the depiction one has of reality. Certain peoples, like Americanized blacks and American Indians, have retrogressive depictions of reality. Certain persons, from undereducated families, have retrogressive depictions of reality. Hence, one cannot expect from them anything like perfect moral discernment. Perfect moral discernment comes only with having perfect understanding of reality—grasped parochially and cosmically. There is nothing all that strange about this claim.

That leads to my second point. Communal contamination implies that societies of people, isolated from advances in knowledge, will be both intellectually and morally retrograde. In that regard, the "right" thing to do in a certain scenario will likely differ for them because the scenario they see, though they are well-intentioned, is warped. That is precisely what Jefferson asserts in letters to Thomas Law and John Adams. To Law, he states. "Men living in different countries, under different circumstances, different habits and regimens, may have different utilities; the same act, therefore, may be useful, and consequently virtuous in one country which is injurious and vicious in another differently circumstanced" (June 13, 1814). To John Adams (October 14, 1816) two years later, he writes:

> The non-existence of justice is not to be inferred from the fact that the same act is deemed virtuous and right in one society, which is held vicious and wrong in another; because as the circumstances and opinions of different societies vary, so the acts which may do them right or wrong must vary also: for virtue does not consist in the act we do, but in the end it is to effect. If it is to effect the happiness of him to whom it is directed, it is virtuous, while in a society under different circumstances and opinions, the same act might produce pain, and would be vicious. The essence of virtue is in doing good to others.

That does not make moral judgments relative or make Jefferson an early Utilitarian, as some scholars mistakenly conclude.[38] Intentionality, I take myself to have shown, factors importantly into right moral judgment as much as outcome. It is not that an outcomes-oriented approach to morality is necessarily irreconcilable with an intentionalist approach. Here

Jefferson's Panaetian Stoicism comes forth. Jefferson had a Panaetian take on morally correct action. What was morally good was useful and what was useful was morally good—namely, moral goodness and utility were mutually entailing. That explains Jefferson's references to utility as the standard of moral goodness, without narrowly painting him a Utilitarian, because for Jefferson, as for Panaetius, moral goodness is also the standard for utility. Intention counts as much as outcome. Note carefully what Jefferson says in the same letter to Law, "Virtue does not consist in the act we do, but in the end it is to effect. If it is to effect the happiness of him to whom it is directed, it is virtuous." Here he does not say virtue is measured by its effect, but by the "end it is to effect." It is, as Lord Kames says, decided by the "end which the actor has in mind," not by the end itself. Intention is critical.[39] "By the [moral sense] certain actions are perceived to be right, and are approved accordingly as virtuous. The most illiterate rustic would [know] that to be honest or to be grateful is right; and there he would stop, never having thought of their useful tendency."

Jefferson's embraces of cultural variation in ethical mores and of progress in all areas of "science" commit him to moral advance toward moral perfection—a limiting ideal toward which human behavior ought to converge, a limiting ideal that has best been actuated in Jefferson's view by Jesus the Nazarene, a personage from the remote past.[40] The notion of moral advance is comparable to and likely derived from Lord Kames's notion of moral refinement.[41] For Kames, as for Jefferson, all persons have a moral sense characterized by desire for benevolent-rooted activity. That sense gets refined over time through progressive cultural conditioning. "The moral sense also, though rooted in the nature of man, admits of great refinements by culture and education. It improves gradually, like our other powers and faculties, till it comes to be productive of the strongest as well as the most delicate feelings."[42] Kames gives the example of a savage, "inured to acts of cruelty," who puts to death an enemy without remorse. To that, he contrasts one of "delicate feelings," who responds with horror to the amputation of another's fractured leg. Such a person will be "shocked to the highest degree" in seeing an enemy killed savagely. Moreover, the laws of nations to regulate affairs between nations, Kames adds, "are no other but gradual refinements of the original law of nature, accommodating itself to the improved state of mankind. The law of nature," he concludes, "which is the law of our nature, cannot be stationary: it must vary with the nature of man, and consequently refine gradually as human nature refines." Jefferson read Kames and expressed agreement on moral refinement in a marginal comment of a copy of Kames's *Essays on Morality and Religion*.[43]

Thus, it is Jefferson's purchase of Kames's moral progressivism that explains why Jefferson acted as he did when it came to slavery. Kames's notion of moral refinements, culturally conditioned, allowed Jefferson to make cross-cultural comparisons and judge one culture's ethical mores to be superior or inferior to another's. It allowed for criticism of King George III's refusal to allow the colonists the rights of those in England. It allowed for criticism of the indulgences of the French and British lifestyles. It allowed for criticism of Federalists' conservatism. Likewise, it allowed for criticism of Americanized blacks.

For Jefferson, it is the key notion of moral refinement that is wanting from African blacks. They are as equipped by nature with a moral sense as are whites, but it is an unrefined, brutish sense because they are culturally retarded. That does not make blacks morally lax. It is just that their moral sense is conditioned to more primitive social conditions. Thus, they are ill-equipped to integrate in European or American culture, as the influence of such an integration could only, in the best scenario, be retrograde and, in the worst scenario, result in civil strife.

Jefferson's embrace of progress, following the measurable advances of the physical sciences of his time, makes it easier to grasp his moral judgments of other peoples and other cultures. He suffered not so much from "Eurocentrism," but from a sort of *philomathēs*—a passion for knowledge or learning that he insisted all persons ought to have. So moved was he by the discoveries and inventions of his day that Jefferson believed himself to be part of a world in which novelty and advance in all sciences, morality and politics included, were the norm. That explains his love of neology in languages, expressed eloquently in letters to lawyer and jurist John Waldo (August 16, 1813) and John Adams (August 15, 1820) as well as his stark ambivalence toward American Indians, due to their embrace of inherited customs in preference to science.[44] Yet with blacks, Jefferson had no such ambivalence. The science of his day and his own observations suggested natural inferiority of body and mind in blacks, and so the most "progressive" solution for Jefferson was emancipation wedded to expatriation, for he feared the retrogressive influence of the taint of white blood by black blood—just another reason why he would have abhorred even the thought of any relationship with Sally Hemings.

## *OU KAIROS*

There is still much grit in the oil. The largest puzzle linked to Jefferson's view of emancipation is his insistence from his *Notes on the State of Virginia* onward that blacks must be expatriated. It is easy to be sympathetic with Jefferson's constant moral indignation concerning slavery and his devotion to emancipation. What is puzzling is that he consistently maintained that the most reasonable and humane option is expatriation, given its sizeable expense and the need and added expense of importing nonblacks to do the labor of the expatriated blacks.[45]

Jefferson's most exhaustive explanation of expatriation, we have seen, is in his *Notes on the State of Virginia.* There he lists, among his political reasons for expatriation, blacks' prejudices, blacks' recollection of injuries, and natural differences.[46] In "Query XVIII," he writes that slavery destroys the morals of the slave owners and makes it impossible for slaves to love their country, hence expatriation.

> And with what execrations should the statesman be loaded, who permitting one half the citizens thus to trample on the rights of the other, transforms those into despots, and these into enemies, destroys the morals of the one part, and the amor patriæ of the other. For if a slave can have a country in this world, it must be any other in preference to that in which he is born to live and labour for another: in which he must lock up the faculties of his nature, contribute as far as depends on his individual endeavours to the evanishment of the human race, or entail his own miserable condition on the endless generations proceeding from him.[47]

Yet there is more to be said. Jefferson's concern is also fear of reprisal. The tension between slaves and slave owners is real and the numbers of whites to blacks in Virginia, we find in "Query VIII," is 296,852 to 270,762—roughly, an 11-to-10 ratio. At the end of "Query VIII," he writes:

> Under the mild treatment our slaves experience, and their wholesome, though coarse, food, this blot in our country increases as fast, or faster, than the whites. During the regal government, we had at one time obtained a law, which imposed such a duty on the importation of slaves, as amounted nearly to a prohibition, when one inconsiderate assembly, placed under a peculiarity of circumstance, repealed the law. . . . In the very first session held under the republican government [with the overthrow of the regal government], the assembly passed a law for the perpetual prohibition of the importation of slaves. This will in some measure stop the increase of this great political and moral evil, while the minds of our citizens may be ripened for a complete emancipation of human nature.[48]

The "blot" to which Jefferson refers is as much the number of slaves as it is slavery. Given that the number of blacks is nearly the same as that of whites and that the black population is increasing at a faster rate, it is only a matter of time before there is a bloody uprising, the consequence of which might be a black takeover of whites' lands. Revolts and revolutions were, so to speak, in the air and Jefferson was especially chary of British enticement of them.[49] He says in "Query XVIII," "The spirit of the master is abating, that of the slave rising from the dust, his condition mollifying, the way I hope preparing, under the auspices of heaven, for a total emancipation, and that this is disposed, in the order of events, to be with the consent of the master, rather than by their extirpation."[50] "If something is not done," he writes years later to professor of law St. George Tucker (August 28, 1797), "and soon done, we shall be the murderers of our own children. . . . [T]he revolutionary storm, now sweeping the globe, will be upon us, and happy if we make timely provision to give it an easy passage over our land."[51] And so, fear of reprisal is in the back of Jefferson's mind. Integration and miscegenation with whites would compromise the offspring and make America inferior to Europe. Expatriation is the only solution.

Jefferson's belief that black inferiority is likely natural also explains the paternalistic manner in which he often speaks of blacks. "To give liberty to, or rather, to abandon persons whose habits have been formed in slavery," he writes to physician Edward Bancroft (January 26, 1789), "is like abandoning children." Twenty-five years later, he says in a letter to young politician and Albemarle native Edward Coles (August 25, 1814), who manumitted his slaves in 1819:

> My opinion has ever been that, until more can be done for them, we should endeavor, with those whom fortune has thrown on our hands, to feed and clothe them well, protect them from all ill usage, require such reasonable labor only as is performed voluntarily by freemen, & be led by no repugnancies to abdicate them, and our duties to them. The laws do not permit us to turn them loose, if that were for their good: and to commute them for other property is to commit them to those whose usage of them we cannot control.

The protean Andrew Burstein, in *Jefferson's Secrets*, argues that Jefferson's "pseudoscience" concerning black inferiority is unpardonable, because Jefferson "did not grow over time."[52] He never changed his view of black inferiority. He never changed his mind about expatriating blacks. He rationalized his inactivity on the issue by noting that the time was not right. It is insufficient to say he preoccupied himself with the University of Virginia in his final years, for Jefferson took up other issues "beyond the university" and left behind slavery. "We should fault him," Burstein adds, "for missing the opportunity to prove—and improve—himself." He "refused to do more to end slavery" and "in aiming to avoid pain, he caused pain." It is as if the offices Jefferson held and the numerous matters Jefferson did see through to completion are not proof sufficient of a life well spent. Like other critical scholars, Burstein never says why he would have been more sensitive to the plight of black Americans had he been in Jefferson's shoes. Burstein never says what he would have done otherwise.

Yet Jefferson's refusal to grapple with the issue of slavery in his later years was not mere rationalization. Jefferson lived by several maxims, one of which was that everything had its right season or right time. Farming is an outstanding example. Crops needed to be planted and reaped at the right times, as each crop had its own critical period.[53] Agricultural innovation—such as inventions, exchange of plants and animals between nations, experiments in crop rotation, and new fertilizing techniques—needed to answer to the problems of the time.[54] Education was much like farming. Subjects needed to be taught during the right period of life. "There is a certain period of life, say from eight to fifteen or sixteen years of age, when the mind, like the body, is not yet firm enough for laborious and close operations."[55] History and the "first elements of morality" can be taught early on. Democratizing too had its proper season. "I am sensible how far I should fall short of effecting all the reformation which reason would suggest," Jefferson, upon assuming the presidency, writes to Dr. Walter Jones (March 31, 1801), "and experience approve, were I free to do whatever I thought best; but when we reflect how difficult it is to move or inflect the great machine of society, how impossible to advance the notions of a whole people suddenly to ideal right, we see the wisdom of Solon's remark, that no more good must be attempted than the nation can bear." Upon acquiring the Louisiana territories, Jefferson quickly recognized, through a letter from Governor Claiborne in 1804 to James Madison (January 2 or January 10), that "the principles of a popular Government are utterly beyond [the inhabitants'] comprehension."[56] He thought the same of the French revolutionists in a letter to James Madison (November 18, 1788). "The misfortune is that they are not yet ripe for receiving the blessings to which they are entitled." Finally, morally correct action was especially time sensitive. An illustration is Jefferson's hesitation to pick up a "poor weathered soldier" at Chickahomony, mentioned in his Head-and-Heart letter to Maria Cosway (October 12 ,1786). Reason led him astray, not moral sensibility. He reasoned that if he should pick up the wounded soldier, all other wounded soldiers would wish to be picked up, and that was impossible. Jefferson drove off, only to be hounded by his moral sense, which told him he had acted immorally. Jefferson turned back the wagon, only to find that the soldier had gone.

The notion of each thing having its right season and each action having its right time was especially Greek—*kairos.*[57] *Kairos* had usage in Ancient

Greek rhetoric, politics, athletics, tragedy, philosophy, and medicine. The Hippocratic author of *Precepts* distinguishes between *chronos*, time considered in its expanse, and *kairos*, time considered as a moment (usually critical), thus: "Time (*chronos*) is that in which opportunity (*kairos*) exists, and opportunity is that in which there is not much time. Healing is a matter of time, but at times also a matter of opportunity."[58] In *Aiax*, Sophocles writes of the right time (*es auton kairon*) for burial of fallen Aiax's corpse.[59] In *Republic*, Plato speaks of the right moments *(tous kairous kalos apergazesthai)* for doing well one's work.[60] Pausanias in *Guide to Greece* tells of the altar and statue of the god *Kairos* (Opportunity) near the gate to the stadium.[61]

Jefferson lived an inordinately, almost pathologically structured life[62] centered on *kairos*. He realized that the introduction of new ideas took time to be assimilated and accommodated. "The ground of liberty is to be gained by inches," he says to Rev. Charles Clay (January 27, 1790), "[and] we must be contented to secure what we can get, from time to time, and eternally press forward for what is yet to get. It takes time to persuade men to do even what is for their own good." Likewise, "There is a snail paced gait for the advance of new ideas on the general mind, under which we must acquiesce," he writes to diplomat and politician Joel Barlow (December 10, 1807). "A forty years' experience of popular assemblies has taught me that you must give them time for every step you take. If too hard pushed, they balk, and the machine retrogrades." Years later, he writes to philosopher John Wilson (August 17, 1813):

> It is very difficult to persuade the great body of mankind to give up what they have once learned, and are now masters of, for something to be learned anew. Time alone insensibly wears down old habits, and produces small changes at long intervals, and to this process we must all accommodate ourselves, and be content to follow those who will not follow us.

To French economist and government official Pierre Samuel Du Pont de Nemours (January 18, 1802), he writes, "The habits of the governed determine in a great degree what it practicable."

The greatest obstacle was the Missouri issue, which seemed to demand resolution to the issue of slavery. At stake was the unity of the youthful nation. Jefferson famously summarizes his frustration in a letter to politician John Holmes (April 22, 1820): "The cessation of that kind of property [slavery], for so it is misnamed, is a bagatelle which would not cost me a second thought, if . . . a general emancipation and ex-patriation could be effected, and gradually and with due sacrifices, I think it might be. We have the wolf by the ears: and we can neither hold him, nor safely let him go. Justice is in one scale, and self-preservation in the other." The sentiment betrayed is that pushing the issue of emancipation at this time would result in perhaps permanent rupture of the nation, on which Jefferson was loath to gamble.

Jefferson knew that the time was *not* right (Greek, *ou kairos*) for the abolition of the institution of slavery, and so he resigned himself to the notion that his remaining years would be best spent pursuing something that could be seen to completion—namely, the creation of the University of Virginia. Though *kairos* was not right, *chronos* was on his side. Jefferson biographer Dumas Malone concludes: "There was no need for such an optimist to be in a hurry. He was confident that time was fighting for his ideas, and that human progress was certain, if only tyranny and artificial obstructions were removed."[63]

There is an additional reason that Jefferson prorogued the issue of slavery. After his stint as governor, he had come to be in the service of his country, not his state, and such an issue, Jefferson like most others believed,[64] each state was to resolve for itself. To Baptist minister and abolitionist Rev. David Barrow (May 1, 1815), Jefferson says, "Had I continued in the councils of my own state, [slavery] should never have been out of sight." He expatiates in the manner of *ou kairos* in a passage in the letter too pregnant with meaning for paraphrase:

> Unhappily [slavery] is a case for which both parties require long and difficult preparation. The mind of the master is to be apprised by reflection, and strengthened by the energies of conscience, against the obstacles of self interest, to an acquiescence in the rights of others; that of the slave is to be prepared by instruction and habit for self-government and for the honest pursuits of industry and social duty. Both of these courses of preparation require time, and the former must precede the latter. Some prog-

ress is sensibly made in it; yet not so much as I had hoped and expected. But it will yield in time to temperate & steady pursuit, to the enlargement of the human mind, and its advancement in science. We are not in a world ungoverned by the laws and power of a superior agent. Our efforts are in his hand, and directed by it; and he will give them their effect in his own time. Where the disease is most deeply sealed, there it will be slowest in eradication.

The letter to Barrow illustrates diminution of Jefferson's optimism that blacks could be emancipated and expatriated in his lifetime. The reason is the number of obstacles encountered over the years—foremost among them being a need to attend to his ponderous, ever-growing debt during his retirement, public resistance to emancipation,[65] and recognition of the tremendous costs involved in emancipation and expatriation.[66] In 1805, he writes to William Burwell (January 18):

I have long since given up the expectation of any early provision for the extinguishment of slavery among us. There are many virtuous men who would make any sacrifices to effect it, many equally virtuous who per-suade themselves either that the thing is not wrong, or that it cannot be remedied, and very many with whom interest is morality [i.e., those who recognize its immorality, but think sympathy is equivalent to action]. The older we grow, the larger we are disposed to believe the last part to be.

Some twelve years later, Jefferson writes to Dr. Thomas Humphreys (February 8, 1817) concerning *kairos* (and *chronos*):

Personally I am ready and desirous to make any sacrifices which shall insure their gradual but complete retirement from the States, and effec-tually . . . establish them elsewhere in freedom and safety. But I haven't perceived the growth of this disposition in the rising generation, of which I once had . . . hopes. No symptoms inform me that it will take place in my day. I leave it to time.

Just months before his death, Jefferson writes to politician James Heaton (May 20, 1826) about slavery: "A good cause is often injured more by ill-timed efforts of its friends than by the arguments of its enemies. . . . The revolution in public opinion which this case requires, is not to be expected in a day, or perhaps in an age. But time, which outlives all things, will outlive this evil also."

In 1825, Jefferson writes to author and abolitionist Frances Wright (August 7), who appealed to Jefferson for any sort of assistance on the issue of blacks' emancipation and colonization. Jefferson, who was then eighty-two years of age, excuses himself because of his years. "The abolition of the evil is not impossible; it ought never therefore to be despaired of. Every plan should be adopted, every experiment tried, which may be something towards the ultimate object."

The issue in the letter to Wright is still *kairos*, but of a different sort. Consistent with his progressivism, there is a proper time for each generation to have its say and move matters forward and a proper time for the generation in power to yield to youth and vigor. "The concerns of each generation are their own care," he writes to William Short, Jefferson's secretary while in France and lifelong friend (August 10, 1816). To fellow founding father, physician, and educator Benjamin Rush (August 17, 1811), Jefferson writes, "There is a fulness [*sic*] of time when men should go, and not occupy too long the ground to which others have a right to advance." To Virginia politician and editor John Hambden Pleasants, Jefferson says some two years prior to his death (April 19, 1824): "I willingly acquiesce in the institutions of my country, perfect or imperfect; and think it a duty to leave their modifications to those who are to live under them, and are to participate of the good or evil they may produce. The present generation has the same right of self-government which the past one has exercised for itself." Slavery was no longer his concern, but that of the next generation. That does not mean that Jefferson ceased to care about emancipation as he matured, but rather that he, consistent with his notion that "the earth belongs in usufruct to the living,"[67] believed that each generation should do its part in advancing the interests of humankind and that it was morally fitting, when the time was right, for one generation to move aside for the next one.

Such passages cannot be glossed over by calling them rationalizations for inactivity, for they are too numerous and Jefferson was anything but lazy. One can only conclude that he thought the eradication of slavery to be impossible in his day and, thus, he turned his remaining time and energy to something more opportune: education.

In pretermitting the issue of slavery, Jefferson is customarily charged with inconsistency. Following Jefferson's dilemma expressed in his letter to John Holmes, James and Alan Golden, for instance, write: "Because Jefferson's fear of insurrection took precedence over what was morally right, his reasoning on slavery during this phase of his leadership role fell far short of the well-articulated philosophy of private and public virtue that was an essential part of his rhetoric of virtue."[68] What *kairos* shows, however, for Jefferson's moral-sense ethics is that sometimes the right thing to do done before the time is right for its doing is the wrong thing to do. As Aristotle said, "Having such [moral] feelings (*pathē*) at the right times, about the right things, toward the right people, for the right end, and in the right way . . . is endemic to virtue."[69] That said, it is Jefferson's moral sensitivity and not his moral insensitivity that caused him to prorogue the issue of slavery.

## THE MEASURE OF A MAN

Andrew Burstein, we have seen, states that Jefferson ought to be faulted for failing to prove and improve himself concerning slavery and for being a poor Epicurean—namely, for causing greater pain in aiming to avoid pain. Burstein is, in effect, castigating Jefferson on both deontological and utilitarian grounds. In failing to do more on abolition of the institution of slavery, Jefferson failed on Kant's deontological grounds to develop fully his natural faculties[70] and he failed on Mill's utilitarian grounds to consider the effects of his moral inactivity on the lives of other persons, black Americans being considered equally.

Burstein is wrong to castigate Jefferson. Jefferson, whose political views were shaped by a philosophical vision of the good life that was an admixture of ancient virtue ethics, the moral-sense theory of his day, and Enlightenment liberalism,[71] was kept from doing more on the issue of slavery, an ethically charged issue for Jefferson, for political and moral reasons. First, Southern agrarianism depended on slave labor. The invention of the cotton gin made slave labor profitable and showed that free markets and improvements in technology would not make slavery disappear, as Jefferson had hoped.[72] The Missouri controversy functioned to highlight the economic need of slaves for Southern agrarianism and the subsequent political dimension of slavery. In addition, there were changes in the Republican Party—the avowed assimilation of Federalists within the Republican party[73]—that shifted it toward Federalism and its centralist, big-government tendencies. There was restoration of the National Bank, protective tariffs to assist northern manufactures, expansion of the army and navy, and greater centralization of authority in Washington to involve itself in states' concerns.[74]

The issue was throughout his life *ou kairos*: He recognized, in spite of concerns of an insurrection, that freeing slaves at a time when proslavery sentiment was widespread could do more harm than good. Political divisiveness reigned and slavery was a politically divisive issue. The survival of the union was always foremost in Jefferson's mind—no more than at the time of the Missouri question. For example, he writes to John Holmes (April 22, 1820): "I had for a long time ceased to read newspapers, or pay any attention to public affairs, confident they were in good hands, and content to be a passenger in our bark to the shore from which I am not distant. But this momentous question, like a fire bell in the night, awakened and filled me with terror. I considered it at once as the knell of the Union." Jefferson knew that despite any actions he might undertake, he would not see the emancipation and expatriation of slaves in his day, for the time was not right. Instead, he took advantage of slaves' labor in retirement to try to pay massive debts and reduce the bedlam of his remaining years.

Jefferson certainly could have done more to move the issue of the eradication of slavery. He did not, I think, because he gauged that his efforts would have had to have been considerable and that the return for those exhausting efforts would have been minimal, if not retrograde. He, thus, turned toward things he could do. One must not forget that many of his deeds, especially earlier in his political career, were aimed at the aboli-

tion of slavery and that he consistently spoke of slavery as a moral abomination. One must not forget that Jefferson fully respected the right of all
citizens to speak out on political issues and bought into the notions that
political decisions ought to reflect the majority opinion of citizens. There
was no clear-cut majority opinion on slavery. North disagreed with South.
The unity of the fledgling nation was at stake.

Critics—like Burstein, who chide Jefferson for refusing to do more
to end slavery—often tend to overpass Jefferson's forty years of mostly
uninterrupted duty to his country to the neglect of his family and other personal affairs, and the numerous other issues with which he was involved
with an eye to social and political improvement. Annette Gordon-Reed,
we have seen, morally castigates Jefferson for his mounting personal debts
as if that by itself negates all the good he has accomplished. He wrote the
Declaration of Independence, wrote and pushed numerous bills throughout
his life, practiced law with honesty and integrity and even argued pro bono
six appeals in freedom suits for claimants of mixed descent,[75] published
defense of the American continent in his *Notes on the State of Virginia*
in light of French naturalist Comte de Buffon's speculative criticisms,
fought for government that was truly representative of the will of the
people, worked to preserve the laws of Virginia for posterity, was a patron
and practitioner of the sciences of his day, wrote and passed his bill for
religious freedom, and even designed an award-winning moldboard for
plowing, which he refused to patent so that everyone wishing to use it
could have free use of it. Those are just a few of copious examples of
Jefferson's immersion in the affairs of his fellow men and his kindness
and generosity. Hasty and wholesale condemnation of Jefferson on slavery
or any other issue, I maintain, is a better barometer of the ignorance and
hypocrisy of hostile critics, than of Jefferson. Who are we to challenge his
exemplary record of involvement and achievement?

Here I am merely enjoining what I have been enjoining all along:
Scholars are obliged both to consider all available evidence before forming
a conclusion and to proportion all conclusions to the evidence given on
behalf of it. It is unconscionable to state *Jefferson was racist* without full
reflection on and precise understanding of the meaning of *racism* and

without duly considering and weighing all available evidence—without measuring the whole man. That is a claim that requires incontrovertible evidence both of prejudging and of a refusal to change if confronted by evidence to the contrary. Such evidence, if it exists, has yet to be disclosed. What evidence we do have, I suspect, is not completely unambiguous, but it does, I have tried to show, lean considerably toward the view that Jefferson was nonracist.

The most important question—one that I have asked elsewhere and one that would allow, if answerable, a definitive answer to the question of Jefferson's racism—is this: Were Jefferson alive today, would he still be committed to black inferiority? Though the question is counterfactual, the answer, I am positive, would be that he would not, for only a true racist could stubbornly cling to a false hypothesis in light of numerous disconfirmatory instances in front of his nose. Jefferson gave every indication that he was the sort of person who embraced truth, whatever its countenance.[76]

## UPSHOT

Let us now return to the question: Did Jefferson have an intimate liaison with Sally Hemings?

The most compelling argument is the "tiresome" argument from character. Jefferson, like any upstanding person of his stature in his time, would not have risked exposing his family to ridicule and shame just to have an outlet for his libido. Moreover, Jefferson would not have been unfeeling toward and indifferent to his mulatto children, if he had had any. Jefferson took very seriously the staple of much of Greek and Roman ethical thought—especially of Platonism, Peripateticism, and Stoicism— that the mark of a morally upright person was that his thoughts and deeds, his private and public personae, were consonant. His incapacity or unwillingness to do more on the issue of slavery was evidence, critics say, of inconsistency and, by today's evaluative standards, is reprehensible. Yet he ought not to be evaluated by today's standards.

Nonetheless, by the evaluative standards of any day, Jefferson was a remarkable person because he had a strong sense of duty and a profound engagement with the world around him. Leaving aside the issue of slavery, he took up in retirement the issue of educational reform. He was, I have elsewhere stated,[77] a living Stoic progressor. Regard for truth, authenticity, virtue, knowledge, equanimity, and his fellow human beings were the stuff the man comprised. He was incapable of the type of hatred that typifies racists. That he slipped up at times—for example, the Walker affair, the soldier at Chickahomony, and his hasty assessment of blacks, among other things—does not much tarnish his luster. Measuring the man—the *whole* man—by the norms of his time, it is probable that he comes out far ahead of the overwhelming majority of other men, critics included.

What have we gained from this undertaking?

I have not shown, because I cannot show, uninvolvement with Hemings. I cannot show that Jefferson was not the father of one or even all of Hemings's children. As Gordon-Reed stated in her first book, "There is no proof one way or another."[78] In spite of the DNA evidence, since her first book, there is still nothing to decide the issue one way or another. *Ou kairos*. Still, I hope to have shown convincingly that the received scholarly view—that Jefferson did have a relationship with Hemings that resulted in one or more children—is prodigiously flawed and not sustainable. Yet, as Jefferson says in his autobiography apropos of chatty politicians taking up one empty argument after another to no substantive end, "To refute indeed [is] easy, but to silence impossible."[79]

The time is right, however, both to reexamine the alleged liaison along with all the relevant evidence, pro and con—that is, to unframe the legend in the making—and proportion our conclusions with the relevant evidence available. Doing that, I suspect that we shall find what James Madison asserted two days after his great friend's death, "[Jefferson] will live in the memory and gratitude of the wise & good, as a luminary of science, as a votary of liberty, as a model of patriotism, and as a benefactor of humankind."[80]

# ADDENDUM

*I*n chapter 3, I mention the 2001 "Report of the Scholars Commission" on the Jefferson-Hemings matter and the subsequent book, *The Jefferson-Hemings Controversy: Report of the Scholars Commission.* The commission—comprising thirteen prominent, independent, and unpaid scholars—was put together at the bidding of the Thomas Jefferson Heritage Society, just after the puzzleheaded report of the Thomas Jefferson Memorial Foundation (TJMF) was released. Its aim was to review all the available evidence concerning the avowed paternity of Thomas Jefferson in a disinterested manner. The scholars who participated were Lance Banning (History, University of Kentucky), James Ceasar (Government and Foreign Affairs, University of Virginia), Robert Ferrell (History, Indiana University), Charles Kesler (Government, Claremont McKenna College), Alf Mapp Jr. (History, Old Dominion University), Harvey Mansfield (Government, Harvard University), David Mayer (Law and History, Capital University), Forrest McDonald (History, University of Alabama), Paul Rahe (Western Heritage, Hillsdale College), Thomas Traut (Biochemistry and Biophysics, University of North Carolina), Robert Turner (Law, University of Virginia), Walter Williams (Economics, George Mason University), and Jean Yarbrough (Government, Bowdoin College).

The scholars individually approached the evidence, though there were "extensive communications by e-mail, letter, and telephone."[1] When the scholars' research was completed, they gathered together for "approximately fifteen hours of face-to-face meetings at a hotel near Dulles Airport." In the end, all but one scholar—the sole dissenting voice being Paul Rahe—thought it was likely that Jefferson did not father any of Hemings's children, and there was general agreement on several conclusions:[2]

- Sally Hemings was a minor figure in Jefferson's life;
- The 1998 DNA study apropos of paternity of Hemings's children is misleading;
- Problems with Madison Hemings's 1873 account make his statement that Jefferson is his father questionable;
- Fraser Neiman's Monte-Carlo argument is unimpressive;
- Sally Hemings and her children received treatment no more special than other members of Sally's mother's family and treatment less favorable than certain other slaves;
- The resemblance of some of Hemings's children to Jefferson is explicable by Thomas's brother Randolph or any of Randolph's sons being the father;
- James Callender's 1802 accusations are "highly unpersuasive";
- The oral history concerning Jefferson's paternity is unreliable; and
- Randolph Jefferson is a more likely candidate for paternity of Eston Hemings than Thomas Jefferson.

They guardedly summarize their research:

In the end, after roughly one year of examining the issues, we find the question of whether Thomas Jefferson fathered one or more children by his slave Sally Hemings to be one about which honorable people can and do disagree. However, it is our unanimous view that the allegation is by no means proven; and we find it regrettable that public confusion about the 1998 DNA testing and other evidence has misled many people into believing that the issue is closed. With the exception of one member, whose views are set forth both below and in the more detailed appended dissent, our individual conclusions range from serious skepticism about the charge to a conviction that it is almost certainly untrue.[3]

Readers familiar with this heated issue might be taken aback that I have said little of the 2001 "Report of the Scholars Commission," while much that I say in *Framing a Legend* is in the spirit of their findings. The reasons are chiefly three.

First, I did not read the scholars' report when I wrote this book, though

I knew of it and had access to the findings through the webpage of the Thomas Jefferson Historical Society. The reason is, as my title implies, that much of the focus of the book is a critical examination of revisionist history and, to a lesser extent, the perverse "science" that presumably indicts Jefferson. Thus, my chief aim is not to show that Jefferson did not father children by Hemings. Addressing the question of Jefferson's involvement with Hemings is an aim, though a secondary aim. My chief aim is to show that the arguments of prominent scholars and scientists are prodigiously flawed. Thus, the question redounds, Why have so many scholars been seduced by the leading literature of the day, given its substantial flaws?

Second, the "Report of the Scholars Commission" is an appeal to authorities on the issue of paternity, and, as the TJMF's 2000 report shows, appeals to authorities are far from foolproof. I illustrate with a sketch of a form of the argument from authority.

> Person *p* maintains claim *c* is true.
> Person *p* is an expert on issues related to claim *c*.
> So claim *c* is true.

Here we might reasonably object that it is not enough for Person *p* to assert the truth of claim *c*. There must be consensus among authorities, for too much is on the line. And so we ask for a stronger inductive argument.

> Person *p* maintains claim *c* is true.
> Person *p* is an expert on issues related to claim *c*.
> There is consensus among authorities on issues related to claim *c* that claim *c* is true.
> So claim *c* is true.

Insofar as authorities are concerned, it seems there is little else beyond consensus for which we can rationally ask. After all, the argument from authority is an inductive argument and inductive arguments are never watertight.

Here we might still reasonably object that trust in consensus among authorities—like the authors of the 1998 DNA study, the author of the 2000 TJMF report, and the majority of historians acquainted with Jefferson and Hemings—is what got us into this sad, gordian state of affairs in the first place. The experts have made a pig's ear of Jefferson's life, and his legacy is up in the air. Thus, we acknowledge a general consensus among historians on the issue of Jefferson's paternity, but, appealing to the evidence that historians have mulled over in arriving at the consensus, we are perplexed that such a consensus exists.

And now the "Report of the Scholars Commission" in 2001 arrives at a conclusion opposite that of the report of the TJMF in 2000. How do two groups of scholars, working independently of each other and with access to the same data, arrive at inconsistent conclusions? Many readers, I suspect, will take the inconsistency as evidence that the authorities are massively confused and, given that, decide that the testimony of experts here is unreliable. There can be no trust in authorities. In that regard, appeal to the Scholars Commission on the issue of paternity by me would have done little to settle the issue in the minds of readers other than to show that one group of experts believes $x$ and another believes $\sim x$.

Yet the issue is not insoluble and members of the Scholars Commission are not confused. We have merely assumed something too obvious to need stating: that the consensus among authorities in the argument from authority ought to be based on a disinterested, thorough, and exhaustive examination of all available, relevant evidence. Not all groups of scholars are disinterested, thorough, and exhaustive, and many, as I have shown in chapter 5, nowise think history is in any sense an etiological discipline. They prefer to "deconstruct" writings, instead of analyzing them. Thus, we need to flesh out the argument from authority by adding another premise that blocks deconstruction.

Person $p$ maintains claim $c$ is true.

Person $p$ is an expert on issues related to claim $c$.

There is consensus among authorities on issues related to claim $c$ that claim $c$ is true.

The consensus among authorities is based on a disinterested, thorough, and exhaustive scientific examination of all available, relevant evidence.

So claim $c$ is true.

In sum, it seems that the TJMF failed (as I elaborate upon in chapter 5) and the Scholars Commission succeeded in that only the latter arrived at consensus through disinterested, thorough, and exhaustive scientific examination of all available, relevant evidence.

Research into the Jefferson-Hemings matter, I admit, has skewed my perception of the merit of contemporary history, much of which is unabashedly deconstructive as well as relativistic and revisionistic, come what may. If history is merely a matter of deconstructing texts and thereby constructing narratives that create historical personages, then, as I have shown in chapter 5, it is a Frankensteinian discipline not to be taken seriously.

It is well known that Jefferson was suspicious of history. He claimed in a letter to newspaper editor and politician John Norvell (June 14, 1807) that history did nothing other than tell us what bad government is. The sentiment is not as negative as it might seem. In his "Bill for the More General Diffusion of Knowledge," Jefferson adds, "The most effectual means of preventing the perversion of power into tyranny are to illuminate, as far as practicable, the minds of the people at large, and more especially to give them knowledge of those facts, which history exhibits, that possessed thereby of the experience of other ages and countries, they may be enabled to know ambition under all its shapes, and prompt to exert their natural powers to defeat its purposes."[4] In that regard, history functioned indirectly to teach us moral lessons. Yet he also patronized liberal, Whiggish interpretations of history,[5] and for that he has been roundly criticized.

Yet I think criticism of Jefferson's Whiggishness is misguided. Jefferson was clear that one of the most important duties of political authorities was to preserve unaltered political documents.[6] He himself worked to preserve the laws of Virginia and other significant legal and political documents.[7] He also pined for the day when newspapers would use truth, not scandalous verbiage, as the motivation for reports.[8] Thus, Whiggishness for Jefferson entailed, among other things, regard for truth and truth itself would be a sufficient goad for historians to do aright history.

Jefferson too was suspicious of persons with authority because, as we recognize in the quote in his "Bill for the More General Diffusion of Knowledge," he recognized a tendency for persons with power to abuse that power. That, I suspect, is what has happened with members of the 1998 DNA study and members of the 2000 TJMF report. Numerous other individual historians, swept up in the commotion, have merely jumped aboard the Jefferson-did-it bandwagon.[9] That is not necessarily to say that the aims of all such participants are insidious, but merely that the means, which necessitate the debasement of Thomas Jefferson and a blight on his legacy for his descendants and for all citizens of the United States to bear, on scrimpy evidence, are at least questionable. And so, it seems, because the strictures of aboveboard science—and I do think history is a science—are pretermitted by some groups of scholars and scientists in their eagerness to promote conclusions that are wish-based, not evidence-based, many will be soured by anything historians—even historians with integrity—have to say.

Where does such skepticism leave us? That leads us to my third reason, perhaps my most important reason, for leaving aside the Scholars Commission report.

Jefferson was suspicious of persons with power, but he had an uncommon faith in the moral integrity of the average person—slaves not excluded—and the capacity of most persons, given a modicum of education, to be capable of figuring things out for themselves and directing their own affairs.[10] Excepting matters of high-level science and politics, people did not need panels of experts to decide for them how to think about important affairs. As Jefferson writes to his nephew Peter Carr (August 10, 1785), even on questions of the existence of deity or the existence of an afterlife, "Your own reason is the only oracle given to you by heaven, and you are answerable not for the rightness but the uprightness of the decision."

Jefferson always encouraged people to investigate and think through matters that have a bearing on their everyday affairs or on their equanimity.[11] He also condemned the integrity of any scholars who asserted a scientific conclusion of sufficient boldness on any topic whatsoever on scrimpy evidence—see, for example, his *Notes on the State of Virginia*.[12] In such a manner, scientific integrity was overstepped.

As discussion of Jefferson's paternity on blogs and reviews of books by nonscholars shows, the experts have failed the nonexperts, and the non-experts are intelligent enough to know when they have been buffaloed. Thus, following Jefferson's lead apropos of faith in the average citizen, generally educated, this undertaking is in large measure an appeal to *consensus gentium*—that is, to the good judgment of average citizens. The average citizen has reason sufficient to weigh rationally the evidence and to decide for himself the issue of Jefferson's paternity. No appeal to authorities is needed. Each person, willing to accept the notion that there are reasonable canons of rationality, is as sound a judge as any other person of similar bent.

These things said, I ask readers not to take me or any of the numerous experts to whom I have referred in this undertaking as "authorities." Instead I invite readers to read the "Report of the Scholars Commission," all works arguing for Jefferson's vindication, and even all works indicting Jefferson—especially the ones I have singled out for criticism—to garner all the relevant, available evidence and form their own judgment in keeping with canons of rationality. The result of such inquiry, I am certain, will lead readers to healthy doubt on the issue of Jefferson's paternity.

# A TRANSCRIPT OF CALLENDER'S 1802 ARTICLE

"The President *Again*,"
by James Thomson Callender,
in *The Recorder*; or,
*Lady's and Gentleman's Miscellany*,
Published September 1, 1802, in Richmond, Virginia

## "THE PRESIDENT *AGAIN*"

*I*t is well known that the man, whom it delighteth the people to honor, keeps, and for many years past has kept, as his concubine, one of his own slaves. Her name is Sally. The name of her eldest son is Tom. His features are said to bear a striking although sable resemblance to those of the president himself. The boy is ten or twelve years of age. His mother went to France in the same vessel with Mr. Jefferson and his two daughters. The delicacy of this arrangement must strike every person of common sensibility. What a sublime pattern for an American ambassador to place before the eyes of two young ladies!

If the reader does not feel himself disposed to pause we beg leave to proceed. Some years ago, this story had once or twice been hinted at in Rind's Federalist. At that time, we believed the surmise to be an absolute calumny. One reason for thinking so was this. A vast body of people wished to debar Mr. Jefferson from the presidency. The establishment of this single fact would have rendered his election impossible. We reasoned thus; that if the allegation had been true, it was sure to have been ascertained and advertised by his enemies, in every corner of the continent. The suppression of so decisive an enquiry serves to shew that the common sense of the federal party was overruled by divine providence. It was the predestination of the supreme being that they should be turned out; that they should be expelled from office the popularity of a character, which, at that instant, was lying fettered and gagged, consumed and extinguished at their feet!

We do not wish to give wanton offence to many very good kind of people. Concerning a certain sort of connections, we have already stated that "of boys and batchelors, we have said nothing, and we have nothing to say." They will be pleased, therefore, to stand out of the way. When the king of Prussia was upon the point of fighting the great and decisive battle of Lissa, he assembled his principal officers, and, under the penalty of his utmost contempt, exhorted them to bravery. In the midst of this address, an old veteran dissolved into tears. "My dear general," said Frederic, "I did not refer to you." Some of our acquaintances are, upon the same principle, requested to believe that we do not, in this allusion, refer to them. We have formerly stated that supereminent pretensions to chastity are always suspicious. This hint was sufficiently plain to shew that the Recorder does not desire to set up a manufacture of wry faces. The writer of this essay does not bear the stamp of a Scots presbyterian parson of the last century. But still, we all know that some things may be overlooked, which can hardly be excused, and which it is impracticable either to praise, or even to vindicate. Such is human nature, and such is human life. One of our correspondents very justly observes that "there is nobody, of whom something disagreeable may not be said."

By this wench Sally, our president has had several children. There is not an individual in the neighbourhood of Charlottesville who does not believe the story; and not a few who know it.

If Duane sees this account, he will not prate any more about the treaty between Mr. Adams and Toussaint. Behold the favorite, the first born of republicanism! the pinnacle of all that is good and great! in the open consummation of an act which tends to subvert the policy, the happiness, and even the existence of this country!

'Tis supposed that, at the time when Mr. Jefferson wrote so smartly concerning negroes, when he endeavoured so much to belittle the African race, he had no expectation that the chief magistrate of the United States was to be the ringleader in shewing that his opinion was erroneous; or, that he should chuse an African stock whereupon he was to engraft his own descendants.

Duane and Cheetham are not worth asking whether this is a lie or not? But censor Smith is requested to declare whether the statement is a federal misrepresentation? Mute! Mute! Mute! Yes very mute! Will all those republican printers of political biographical information be upon this point. Whether they stir, or not, they must feel themselves like a horse in a quicksand. They will plunge deeper and deeper, until no assistance can save them.

The writer of this piece has been arraigned as capable of selling himself to a British ambassador. The impeachment was made by a printer, who is in the confidence of Mr. Jefferson. The president had the utmost reason to believe that the charge was an utter fiction. This charge was met in a decisive stile. We, at once, selected and appealed to the testimony, or belief, of five persons, who were intimately acquainted with the situation of Callender, at the period of the pretended project of sale. These were Mr. Israel Israel, Dr. James Reynolds, Mr. John Beckley, Mr. John Smith, federal marshal of Pennsylvania, and Mr. Mathew Carey, bookseller, whose name has been heard of in every county and corner of the United States. This appeal harmonised with the feelings of innocence and defiance. If the friends of Mr. Jefferson are convinced of his innocence, they will make an appeal of the same sort. If they rest in silence, or if they content themselves with resting upon a general denial, they can not hope for credit. The allegation is of a nature too black to be suffered to remain in suspence. We should be glad to hear of its refutation. We give it to the world under the firmest belief that such a refutation never can be made. The African venus is said to officiate, as housekeeper at Monticello. When Mr. Jefferson has read this article, he will find leisure to estimate how much has been lost or gained by so many unprovoked attacks upon

J. T. CALLENDER[1]

# A TRANSCRIPT OF MADISON HEMINGS'S ACCOUNT

**INTERVIEW OF MADISON HEMINGS
BY SAMUEL WETMORE,
"LIFE AMONG THE LOWLY, NO. 1,"
*PIKE COUNTY (OHIO) REPUBLICAN*,
PUBLISHED MARCH 13, 1873**

*I* never knew of but one white man who bore the name of Hemings; he was an Englishman and my great grandfather. He was captain of an English trading vessel which sailed between England and Williamsburg, Va., then quite a port. My great-grandmother was a full-blooded African, and possibly a native of that country. She was the property of John Wales, a Welchman. Capt. Hemings happened to be in the port of Williamsburg at the time my grandmother was born, and acknowledging her fatherhood he tried to purchase her of Mr. Wales, who would not part with the child, though he was offered an extraordinarily large price for her. She was named Elizabeth Hemings. Being thwarted in the purchase, and determined to own his own flesh and blood he resolved to take the child by force or stealth, but the knowledge of his intention coming to John Wales' ears, through leaky fellow servants of the mother, she and the child were taken into the "great house" under their master's immediate care. I have been informed that it was not the extra value of that child over other slave children that induced Mr. Wales to refuse to sell it, for slave masters then, as in later days, had no compunctions of conscience which restrained them from parting mother and child of however tender age, but he was restrained by the fact that just about that time amalgamation began, and the child was so great a curiosity that its owner desired to raise it himself that he might see its outcome. Capt. Hemings soon afterwards sailed from Williamsburg, never to return. Such is the story that comes down to me.

Elizabeth Hemings grew to womanhood in the family of John Wales, whose wife dying she (Elizabeth) was taken by the widower Wales as his concubine, by whom she had six children—three sons and three daughters, viz: Robert, James, Peter, Critty, Sally and Thena. These children went by the name of Hemings.

Williamsburg was the capital of Virginia, and of course it was an aristocratic place, where the "bloods" of the Colony and the new State most did congregate. Thomas Jefferson, the author of the Declaration of Independence, was educated at William and Mary College, which had its seat at Williamsburg. He afterwards studied law with Geo. Wythe, and practiced law at the bar of the general court of the Colony. He was afterwards elected a member of the provincial legislature from Albemarle county. Thos. Jefferson was a visitor at the "great house" of John Wales, who had children about his own age. He formed the acquaintance of his daughter Martha (I believe that was her name, though I am not positively sure,) and intimacy sprang up between them which ripened into love, and they were married. They afterwards went to live at his country seat Monticello, and in course of time had born to them a daughter whom they named Martha. About the time she was born my mother, the second daughter of John Wales and Elizabeth Hemings was born. On the death of John Wales, my grandmother, his concubine, and her children by him fell to Martha, Thomas Jefferson's wife, and consequently became the property of Thomas Jefferson, who in the course of time became famous, and was appointed minister to France during our revolutionary troubles, or soon after independence was gained. About the time of the appointment and before he was ready to leave the country his wife died, and as soon after her interment as he could attend to and arrange his domestic affairs in accordance with the changed circumstances of his family in consequence of this misfortune (I think not more than three weeks thereafter) he left for France, taking his eldest daughter with him. He had sons born to him, but they died in early infancy, so he then had but two children—Martha and Maria. The latter was left home, but afterwards was ordered to follow him to France. She was three years or so younger than Martha. My mother accompanied her as a body servant. When Mr. Jefferson went to France Martha was just budding into womanhood. Their stay (my mother's and Maria's) was about eighteen months. But during that time my mother became Mr. Jefferson's concubine, and when he was called back home she was enciente by him. He desired to bring my mother back to Virginia with him but she demurred. She was just beginning to understand the French language well, and in France she was free, while if she returned to Virginia she would be re-enslaved. So she refused to return with him. To induce her to do so he promised her extraordinary privileges, and made a solemn pledge that her children should be freed at the age of twenty-one years. In consequence of his promise, on which she implicitly relied, she returned with him to Virginia. Soon after their arrival, she gave birth to a child, of whom Thomas Jefferson was the father. It lived but a short time. She gave birth to four others, and Jefferson was the father of all of them. Their names were Beverly, Harriet, Madison (myself), and Eston—three sons and one daughter. We all became free agreeably to the treaty entered into by our parents before we were born. We all married and have raised families.

Beverly left Monticello and went to Washington as a white man. He married a white woman in Maryland, and their only child, a daughter, was not known by the white folks to have any colored blood coursing in her veins. Beverly's wife's family were people in good circumstances.

Harriet married a white man in good standing in Washington City, whose name I could give, but will not, for prudential reasons. She raised a family of children, and so far as I know they were never suspected of being tainted with African blood in the community where she lived or lives. I have not heard from her for ten years, and do not know whether she is dead or alive. She thought it to her interest, on going to Washington, to assume the role of a white woman, and by her dress and conduct as such I am not aware that her identity as Harriet Hemings of Monticello has ever been discovered.

Eston married a colored woman in Virginia, and moved from there to Ohio, and lived in Chillicothe several years. In the fall of 1852 he removed to Wisconsin, where he died a year or two afterwards. He left three children.

As to myself, I was named Madison by the wife of James Madison, who was afterwards President of the United States. Mrs. Madison happened to be at Monticello at the time of my birth, and begged the privilege of naming me, promising my mother a fine present for the honor. She consented, and Mrs. Madison dubbed me by the name I now acknowledge, but like many promises of white folks to the slaves she never gave my mother anything. I was born at my father's seat of Monticello, in Albemarle county, Va., near Charlottesville, on the 18th day of January, 1805. My very earliest recollections are of my grandmother Elizabeth Hemings. That was when I was about three years old. She was sick and upon her death bed. I was eating a piece of bread and asked if she would have some. She replied: "No, granny don't want bread any more." She shortly afterwards breathed her last. I have only a faint recollection of her.

Of my father, Thomas Jefferson, I knew more of his domestic than his public life during his life time. It is only since his death that I have learned much of the latter, except that he was considered as a foremost man in the land, and held many important trusts, including that of President. I learned to read by inducing the white children to teach me the letters and something more; what else I know of books I have picked up here and there till now I can read and write. I was almost 21 1/2 years of age when my father died on the 4th of July, 1826.

About his own home he was the quietest of men. He was hardly ever known to get angry, though sometimes he was irritated when matters went wrong, but even then he hardly ever allowed himself to be made unhappy any great length of time. Unlike Washington he had but little taste or care for agricultural pursuits. He left matters pertaining to his plantations mostly with his stewards and overseers. He always had mechanics at work for him, such as carpenters, blacksmiths, shoemakers, coopers, &c. It was his mechanics he seemed mostly to direct, and in their operations he took great interest. Almost every day of his later years he might have been seen among them. He occupied much of the time in his office engaged in correspondence and reading and writing. His general temperament was smooth and even; he was very undemonstrative. He was uniformly kind to all about him. He was not in the habit of showing partiality or fatherly affection to us children. We were the only children of his by a slave woman. He was affectionate toward his white grandchildren, of whom he had fourteen, twelve of whom lived to manhood and womanhood. His daughter Martha married Thomas Mann Randolph by whom she had thirteen children. Two died in infancy. The names of the living were Ann, Thomas Jefferson, Ellen, Cornelia, Virginia, Mary, James, Benj. Franklin, Lewis Madison, Septemia and Geo. Wythe. Thos. Jefferson Randolph was Chairman of the Democratic National Convention in Baltimore last spring which nominated Horace Greeley for the Presidency, and Geo. Wythe Randolph was Jeff. Davis' first Secretary of War in the late "unpleasantness."

Maria married John Epps, and raised one son—Francis.

My father generally enjoyed excellent health. I never knew him to have but one spell of sickness, and that was caused by a visit to the Warm Springs in 1818. Till within three weeks of his death he was hale and hearty, and at the age of 83 years walked erect and with a stately tread. I am now 68, and I well remember that he was a much smarter man physically, even at that age, than I am.

When I was fourteen years old I was put to the carpenter trade under the charge of John Hemings, the youngest son of my grandmother. His father's name was Nelson, who was an Englishman. She had seven children by white men and seven by colored men—fourteen in all. My brothers, sister Harriet and myself, were used alike. We were permitted to stay about the "great house," and only required to do such light work as going on errands. Harriet learned to spin and to weave in a little factory on the home plantation. We were free from the dread of having to be slaves all our lives long, and were measurably happy. We were always permitted to be with our mother, who was well used. It was her duty, all her life which I can remember, up to the time of father's death, to take care of his chamber and wardrobe, look after us children and do such light work as sewing, and Provision was made in the will of our father that we should be free when we arrived at the age of 21 years. We had all passed that period when he died but Eston, and he was given the remainder of his time shortly after. He and I rented a house and took mother to live with us, till her death, which event occurred in 1835.

In 1834 I married Mary McCoy. Her grandmother was a slave, and lived with her master, Stephen Hughes, near Charlottesville, as his wife. She was manumitted by him, which made their children free born. Mary McCoy's mother was his daughter. I was about 28 and she 22 years of age when we married. We lived and labored together in Virginia till 1836, when we voluntarily left and came to Ohio. We settled in Pebble township, Pike County. We lived there four or five years and during my stay in the county I worked at my trade on and off for about four years. Joseph Sewell was my first employer. I built for him what is now known as Rizzleport No. 2 in Waverly. I afterwards worked for George Wolf Senior. and I did the carpenter work for the brick building now owned by John J. Kellison in which the Pike County Republican is printed. I worked for and with Micajab Hinson. I found him to be a very clever man. I also reconstructed the building on the corner of Market and Water Streets from a store to a hotel for the late Judge Jacob Row.

When we came from Virginia we brought one daughter (Sarah) with us, leaving the dust of a son in the soil near Monticello. We have born to us in this State nine children. Two are dead. The names of the living, besides Sarah, are Harriet, Mary Ann, Catharine, Jane, William Beverly, James Madison, Ellen Wales. Thomas Eston died in the Andersonville prison pen, and Julia died at home. William, James and Ellen are unmarried and live at home in Huntington township, Ross County. All the others are married and raising families. My post office address is Pee Pee, Pike County Ohio.

# LAST WILL AND TESTAMENT OF THOMAS JEFFERSON

*T*homas Jefferson of Monticello in Albemarle, being of sound mind and in my ordinary state of health, make my last will and testament in manner and form as follows.

I give to my grandson Francis Eppes, son of my dear deceased daughter Mary Eppes, in fee simple, all that part of my lands at Poplar Forest lying West of the following lines, to wit, Beginning at Radford's upper corner near the double branches of Bear creek and the public road, & running thence in a straight line to the fork of my private road, near the barn, thence along that private road (as it was changed in 1817) to it's crossing of the main branch of North Tomahawk creek, and, from that crossing, in a direct line over the main ridge which divides the North and South Tomahawk, to the South Tomahawk, at the confluence of two branches where the old road to the Waterlick crossed it, and from that confluence up the Northernmost branch (which separates McDaniel's and Perry's fields) to it's source, & thence by the shortest line to my Western boundary. and having, in a former correspondence with my deceased son in law John W. Eppes contemplated laying off for him with remainder to my grandson Francis, a certain portion in the Southern part of my lands in Bedford and Campbell, which I afterwards found to be generally more indifferent than I had supposed, & therefore determined to change it's location for the better; now to remove all doubt, if any could arise on a purpose merely voluntary & unexecuted, I hereby declare that what I have herein given to my sd grandson Francis is instead of and not additional to what I have formerly contemplated.

I subject all my other property to the payment of my debts in the first place.

Considering the insolvent state of affairs of my friend & son in law Thomas Mann Randolph, and that what will remain of my property will be the only resource against the want in which his family would otherwise be left, it must be his wish, as it is my duty, to guard that resource against all liability for his debts, engagements or purposes whatsoever, and to preclude the rights, powers and authorities over it which might result to him by operation of law, and which might, independantly of his will, bring it within the power of his creditors, I do hereby devise and bequeath all the residue of my property real and personal, in possession or in action, whether held in my own right, or in that of my dear deceased wife, according to the powers vested in me by deed of settlement for that purpose, to my grandson Thomas J. Randolph, & my friends Nicholas P. Trist, and Alexander Garrett & their heirs during the life of my sd son in law Thomas M. Randolph, to be held & administered by them, in trust, for the sole and separate use and behoof of my dear daughter Martha Randolph and her heirs. and, aware of the nice and difficult distinctions of the law in these cases, I will further explain by saying that I understand and intend the effect of these limitation to be, that the legal estate and actual occupation shall be vested in my said trustees, and held by them in base fee, determinable on the death of my sd son in law, and the remainder during the same time be vested in my sd daughter and her heirs, and of course disposable by her last will, and that at the death of my sd son in law, the particular estate of sd trustees shall be determined and the remainder, in legal estate, possession and use use become vested in my sd daughter and her heirs, in absolute property for ever.

In consequence of the variety and indescribableness of the articles of property within the house at Monticello, and the difficulty of inventorying and appraising them separately and specifically, and its inutility, I dispense with having them inventoried and appraised; and it is my will that my executors be not held to give any security for the administration of my estate. I appoint my grandson Thomas Jefferson Randolph my sole executor during his life, and after his death, I constitute executors my friends Nicholas P. Trist and Alexander Garrett joining to them my daughter Martha Randolph after the death of my sd son in law Thomas M. Randolph.

Lastly I revoke all former wills by me heretofore made; and in Witness that this is my will, I have written the whole with my own hand on two pages, and have subscribed my name to each of them this 16th day of March one Thousand eight hundred and twenty six. Th: Jefferson

I Thomas Jefferson of Monticello in Albemarle make and add the following Codicil to my will, controuling the same so far as it's provisions go.

I recommend to my daughter, Martha Randolph, the maintenance and care of my well-beloved sister Anne Scott Marks, and trust confidently that from affection to her, as well as for my sake, she will never let her want a comfort.

I have made no specific provision for the comfortable maintenance of my son in law Thomas M. Randolph, because of the difficulty and uncertainty of devising terms which shall vest any beneficial interest in him which the law will not transfer to the benefit of his creditors to the destitution of my daughter and her family and disablement of her to supply him: whereas property placed under the executive right of my daughter and her independant will, as if she were a femme sole, considering the relations in which she stands both to him and his children, will be a certain resource against want for all.

I give to my friend James Madison of Montpellier my gold-mounted walking staff of animal horn, as a token of the cordial and affectionate friendship which for nearly now an half century, has united us in the same principles and pursuits of what we have deemed for the greatest good of our country.

I give to the University of Virginia my library, except such particular books only, and of the same edition, as it may already possess, when this legacy shall take effect. The rest of my said library remaining after those given to the University shall have been taken out, I give to my two grandsons in law Nicholas P. Trist and Joseph Coolidge.

To my grandson Thomas Jefferson Randolph I give my silver watch in preference of the golden one, because of it's superior excellence. my papers of business going of course to him, as my executor, all others of a literary or other character I give to him as of his own property.

I give a gold watch to each of my grand children who shall not have already received one from me, to be purchased and delivered by my executor, to my grandsons at the age of 21. and grand-daughters at that of sixteen.

I give to my good, affectionate, and faithful servant Burwell his freedom, and the sum of three hundred Dollars to buy necessaries to commence his trade of painter and glazier, or to use otherwise as he pleases. I give also to my good servants John Hemings and Joe Fosset their freedom at the end of one year after my death: and to each of them respectively all the tools of their respective shops or callings: and it is my will that a comfortable log house be built for each of the three servants so emancipated on some part of my lands convenient to them with respect to the residence of their wives, and to Charlottesville and the University, where they will be mostly employed, and reasonably convenient also to the interest of the proprietor of the lands; of which houses I give the use of one, with a curtilage of an acre to each, during his life or personal occupation thereof.

I give also to John Hemings the services of his two apprentices, Madison and Eston Hemings, until their respective ages of twenty one years, at which period respectively, I give them their freedom. and I humbly and earnestly request of the legislature of Virginia a confirmation of the bequest of freedom to these servants, with permission to remain in this state where their families and connections are, as an additional instance of the favor, of which I have recieved so many other manifestations, in the course of my life, and for which I now give them my last, solemn, and dutiful thanks.

In testimony that this is a Codicil to my will of yesterday's date, and that it is to modify so far the provisions of that will, I have written it all with my own hand, in two pages, to each of which I subscribe my name this 17th day of March one thousand eight hundred and twenty six. Th: Jefferson

[The following text is included only in the court copy of the will.]

At a court held for Albemarle County the 7th of August 1826.

This instrument of writing purporting to be the last will and testament of Thomas Jefferson Deceased was produced into court and the hand writing of the testator proved by the oath of Valentine W. Southall and ordered to be recorded.

Teste: Alexander Garrett CC

# NOTES

## FOREWORD

1. Newell G. Bringhurst, *Fawn McKay Brodie: A Biographer's Life* (Norman: University of Oklahoma Press, 1999), p. 212.

2. Karyn Traut, "Thomas Jefferson: Brother's Keeper—A Playwright's Progress," *The Jefferson-Hemings Controversy: Report of the Scholars Commission*, ed. Robert F. Turner (Durham, NC: Carolina Academic Press, 2011), p. 331.

3. Bringhurst, *Fawn McKay Brodie*, p. 215.

4. Garry Wills, "Uncle Thomas's Cabin," *New York Review of Books*, April 18, 1974, p. 27.

5. Michael Kammen, "Jefferson: Farmer, Architect, Rebel, Statesman & Etc.," *Washington Post*, July 7, 1974, p. D1.

6. Turner, *Jefferson-Hemings Controversy*, p. 69.

7. Joseph J. Ellis, "Jefferson: Post-DNA," *William and Mary Quarterly* 57 (January 2000); also available online through PBS *Frontline* at http://www.pbs.org/wgbh/pages/frontline/shows/jefferson/enigma/ellis.html (accessed January 17, 2013).

8. See, for example, Turner, *Jefferson-Hemings Controversy*, p. 218.


## PREFACE

1. R. B. Bernstein, *Thomas Jefferson* (New York: Oxford University Press, 2003), pp. 195–96.


## CHAPTER 1: MINING JEFFERSON'S ORE

1. Fawn Brodie, *Thomas Jefferson: An Intimate History* (New York: W. W. Norton, 1974), p. 25.

2. Ibid., pp. 15–16.

3. Ibid., p. 16. On the veridicality of Israel Jefferson's testimony, see Cynthia H. Burton, *Jefferson Vindicated* (Keswick, VA: self-published, 2005), p. 91.

4. Brodie, *Thomas Jefferson*, pp. 47–48.

5. Ibid., pp. 49–50.

6. Ibid., p. 49.

7. Ibid., pp. 51–52.

8. Ibid., p. 52.

9. Ibid., p. 53.

10. Ibid., pp. 53–54.

11. Ibid., pp. 54–55.

12. Ibid., pp. 61–63.

13. Ibid., p. 470.

14. Ibid.

15. Ibid., p. 28.

16. Ibid., pp. 28–29.

17. Ibid., pp. 90–91.

18. For example, see TJ to Peter Carr, August 19, 1785; TJ to Benjamin Rush, April 21, 1803; TJ to James Fishback, September 27, 1809; TJ to Isaac Engelbrecht, February 25, 1824. All letters are taken from *The Writings of Thomas Jefferson*, eds. Andrew Adgate Lipscombe and Albert Ellery Bergh (Washington, DC: Thomas Jefferson Memorial Association, 1903–1904).

19. Brodie, *Thomas Jefferson*, pp. 73–74.

20. Walker was defeated by James Monroe for a seat in the US Senate in 1790, so there is political motivation for leakage of the rumor. For more on Jefferson and Walker, see Dumas Malone, *Jefferson the Virginian* (Boston: Little, Brown, 1948), pp. 447–48.

21. Brodie, *Thomas Jefferson*, p. 76.

22. See Malone, *Jefferson the Virginian*, p. 155.

23. Brodie, *Thomas Jefferson*, pp. 77–79.

24. M. Andrew Holowchak, "Jefferson as 'Philologist,'" in *Dutiful Correspondent: Philosophical Essays on Thomas Jefferson* (Lanham, MD: Rowman & Littlefield, 2012), pp. 3–25.

25. Brodie, *Thomas Jefferson*, pp. 80–85. There is some reason to regard the story as bogus. See Burton, *Jefferson Vindicated*, p. 21.

26. Brodie, *Thomas Jefferson*, pp. 29–30.

27. For example, Maria Cosway to TJ, October 30, 1786; and February 15, 1787.

28. Brodie, *Thomas Jefferson*, p. 32.

29. Mary-Jo Kline, "Review," *New England Quarterly* 47, no. 4 (1974): 623–25.

30. Brodie, *Thomas Jefferson*, pp. 24–25.

31. Virginius Dabney, *The Jefferson Scandals* (New York: Dodd, Mead, 1980), p. 45.

32. There is also the testimony, published in the same paper months later, of former slave Israel Jefferson.

33. Burton, *Thomas Jefferson Vindicated*, p. 7; and Eyler Robert Coates Sr., "Research Report on the Jefferson-Hemings Controversy: A Critical Analysis," in *The Jefferson-Hemings Myth: An American Tragedy* (Charlottesville: Thomas Jefferson Heritage Society, 2001), p. 105.

34. Dabney, *Jefferson Scandals*, p. 103.

35. Brodie, *Thomas Jefferson*, p. 474.

36. Dabney, *Jefferson Scandals*, p. 123.

37. Brodie, *Thomas Jefferson*, p. 441.

38. See M. Andrew Holowchak, "Jefferson's Moral Agrarianism: Poetic Fiction or Moral Vision?" *Agriculture and Human Values* 28 (2001): 497–506.

39. Brodie, *Thomas Jefferson*, p. 474.

40. Coates, "Research Report on the Jefferson-Hemings Controversy," p. 105.

41. Ibid., pp. 234 and 239.

42. Brodie, *Thomas Jefferson*, pp. 234 and 239.

43. Burton, *Jefferson Vindicated*, pp. 20–22.

44. Brodie, *Thomas Jefferson*, p. 234.

45. Dabney, *Jefferson Scandals*, p. 40.

46. Brodie, *Thomas Jefferson*, p. 243.

47. Ibid., p. 473.

48. James Thomson Callender, *Richmond Recorder*, September 1, 1802, quoted in Burton, *Jefferson Vindicated*, p. 15.

49. Burton, *Jefferson Vindicated*, p. 15.

50. Callender prophesied, "The name of SALLY will walk down to posterity alongside of Mr. Jefferson's own name. The name of Agrippina is as distinctly remembered as that of Nero." James Thomson Callender, "The President *Again*," *Richmond Recorder*, September 27, 1802. See William G. Hyland Jr., "A Civil Action: Sally Hemings v. Thomas Jefferson," *American Journal of Trial Advocacy* 31, no. 1 (2007): 2–5.

51. Brodie, *Thomas Jefferson*, pp. 248 and 352–53.

52. Ibid., pp. 291–92.

53. Dabney, *Jefferson Scandals*, p. 81.

54. Brodie, *Thomas Jefferson*, p. 250.

55. Gilbert Chinard, *Thomas Jefferson: The Apostle of Americanism* (1929; repr., Ann Arbor, MI: University of Michigan Press, 1962), pp. 17 and 299.

56. Burton, *Jefferson Vindicated*, pp. 26–28 and 40–45.

57. William G. Hyland Jr., *In Defense of Thomas Jefferson: The Sally Hemings Sex Scandal* (New York: St. Martin's Press, 2009), pp. 59–72.

58. Dumas Malone, *The Sage of Monticello* (Charlottesville: University of Virginia Press, 1971), p. 447.

59. M. Andrew Holowchak, *Freud: From Individual Psychology to Group Psychology* (Lanham, MD: Jason Aronson Press, 2012); *Freud and Utopia: From Cosmological Narcissism to the "Soft Dictatorship" of Reason* (Lanham, MD: Lexington Books, 2011); "When Freud (Almost) Met Chaplin," *Perspectives on Science* 20, no. 1 (2012): 44–74; "Freud on Philosophy and Philosophers: Patching the Gaps in the Universe with Nightcaps and Dressing-Gown Tatters," *International Forum for Psychoanalysis* (March 2011): 1–12; "The Problem of Unassailability: Freud, Analogy, and the Adequacy of Constructions in Analysis," *Psychoanalytic Psychology* (forthcoming); "The 'Soft Dictatorship' of Reason: Freud on Science, Religion, and Utopia," *Philo* 13, no. 1 (2010); and "Technology and Freudian Discontent: Freud's 'Muffled Meliorism' and the Problem of Human Annihilation," *Sophia* 49, no. 1 (2010).

60. See Michael Lavin, "On Behalf of Free Association," in *Radical Claims in Freudian Psychoanalysis: Point/Counterpoint* (Lanham, MD: Jason Aronson Press, 2011), pp. 153–66.

61. Malone, *Jefferson the Virginian*, p. 161.

62. Plato, *Republic*, trans. G. M. A. Grube (Indianapolis: Hackett Publishing, 1992), p. 575a.

63. See Cicero, *Tusculan Disputations*, trans. J. E. King (Cambridge: Harvard University Press, 1945), V.94.

64. See Holowchak, "Jefferson's Liberal 'Eudaimonism'" and "Jefferson and Science," in *Dutiful Correspondent*, pp. 51–68 and 131–56.

65. For example, TJ to Gen. Thomas Nelson, February 21, 1781; TJ to Dr. James Curie, January 18, 1786; TJ to Martha Jefferson Randolph, January 26, 1793; TJ to Samuel Smith, August 22, 1798; TJ to Judge John Tyler, June 28, 1804; TJ to James Sullivan, May 21, 1805; TJ to William Duane, March 22, 1806; and TJ to George Logan, June 20, 1816, in *The Writings of Thomas Jefferson*, ed. Paul Leicester Ford (New York: Putnam, 1892). (Recall that unless otherwise indicated, all letters are culled from this source.)

66. For example, TJ to John Randolph, August 25, 1775; TJ to Richard Henry Lee, June 17, 1779; TJ to George Washington, May 28, 1781; TJ to James Monroe, May 20, 1782; TJ to William Short, December 14, 1789; TJ to James Madison, June 9, 1793; TJ to James Sullivan, February 9, 1797; TJ to Martha Jefferson Randolph, November 23, 1807; TJ to Richard M. Johnson, March 10, 1808; and TJ to P. S. Du Pont de Nemours, March 2, 1809.

67. See M. Andrew Holowchak, "Carrying One's Goods from City to City: Seneca on Friendship, Self-Sufficiency, and the Disdain of Fortune," *Ancient Philosophy* 26, no.1 (2006): 93–110.

68. John Chester Miller, *The Wolf by the Ears* (New York: Macmillan, 1977), p. 207.

69. Clifford Egan, "How Not to Write a Biography: A Critical Look at Fawn Brodie's *Thomas Jefferson*," *Social Science Journal* 14 (April 1977): 129–30.

70. Holman Hamilton, "Review," *Journal of Southern History* 41, no. 1 (1975): 107–109.

71. Garry Wills, "Uncle Tom's Cabin," *New York Times Review of Books* 21, no. 6, April 18, 1974.

72. Hyland, *In Defense of Thomas Jefferson*, p. 146.

73. Merrill D. Peterson, *Thomas Jefferson and the New Nation: A Biography* (New York: Oxford, 1970), p. 707.

74. Dumas Malone and Steven H. Hochman, "A Note on Evidence: The Personal History of Madison Hemings," *Journal of Southern History* 41, no. 4 (1975): 523–28.

75. Brodie, *Thomas Jefferson*, pp. 229–30.

76. Ibid., p. 245.

77. TJ to James Madison, September 6, 1789.

78. Holowchak, "Reason and the Moral Sense," in *Dutiful Correspondent*, pp. 159–76.

79. Brodie, *Thomas Jefferson*, p. 371.

80. E. S. Gaustad, "Religion," in *Thomas Jefferson: A Reference Biography*, ed. Merrill D. Peterson (New York: Charles Scribner's Sons, 1986), p. 283.

81. Brodie, *Thomas Jefferson*, p. 372.

82. Bruce Mazlish, "Review," *Journal of American History* 61, no. 4 (1975): 1090–91.

83. Brodie, *Thomas Jefferson*, p. 277.

84. Ibid., p. 263.

85. Ibid., p. 294.

86. Ibid., pp. 295 and 365.

87. Maria Jefferson Eppes to TJ, January 11, 1803.

88. Brodie, *Thomas Jefferson*, p. 365.

89. Ibid., p. 296.

90. Ibid., p. 264.

91. Ibid., p. 297.

92. Ibid., p. 294.

93. Ibid., p. 222.

94. Ibid., p. 25.

95. Jefferson states that he did not have the wherewithal to complete his autobiography: "To write history requires a whole life of observation, of inquiry, of labor and correction. Its materials are not to be found among the ruins of a decayed memory." TJ to Josephus B. Stuart, May 10, 1817.

96. Brodie, *Thomas Jefferson*, pp. 279 and 445.

97. Ibid., p. 25.

98. Ibid., p. 298.

99. Ibid., p. 291.

100. Ibid., p. 293.

101. See also ibid., p. 296.

102. Sigmund Freud, *Dora: An Analysis of a Case of Hysteria* (New York: Simon & Schuster, 1997), p. 69.

103. In Burton, *Jefferson Vindicated*, p. 18.

104. Brodie, *Thomas Jefferson*, p. 299.

105. Ibid., p. 300.

106. Ibid., p. 470.

107. Ibid., pp. 291–92.

108. Ibid., p. 381.

109. Bacon, in response to an interview by Rev. Hamilton W. Pierson, said, "She was not his [Jefferson's] daughter; she was ____'s daughter." Rev. Hamilton W. Pierson, *Jefferson at Monticello: The Private Life of Thomas Jefferson* (New York, 1862), p. 110.

110. Brodie, *Thomas Jefferson*, p. 435.

111. Jennifer Jensen Wallach, "The Vindication of Fawn Brodie," *Massachusetts Review* 43, no. 2 (2002): 278.

112. Ibid., p. 280.

113. Ibid., p. 281.

114. Hyland, *In Defense of Thomas Jefferson*, p. 167.

115. Wallach, "Vindication of Fawn Brodie," p. 281.

116. Holowchak, *Freud and Utopia*, pp. 124–26.

117. Wallach, "Vindication of Fawn Brodie," p. 282.

118. Ibid.

119. Ibid., p. 285.

120. Ibid., p. 285–86.

121. Ibid., p. 294n38.

122. Ibid., p. 286.

123. David N. Mayer, "The Thomas Jefferson-Sally Hemings Myth and the Politicalization of American History," http://www.ashbrook.org/articles/mayer-hemings.html (accessed June 21, 2011).

124. Quoted in Wallach, "Vindication of Fawn Brodie," p. 287.

125. Ibid., pp. 290–93.

126. Plato, *Meno*, trans. G. M. A. Grube (Indianapolis, IN: Hackett Publishing, 2002), pp. 97e–98a.

# CHAPTER 2: CONTROLLING THE DISCOURSE

1. E. M. Halliday, *Understanding Thomas Jefferson* (New York: HarperCollins Publishers, 2001), p. 260.

2. Annette Gordon-Reed, *Thomas Jefferson and Sally Hemings: An American Controversy* (Charlottesville: University of Virginia Press, 1997), pp. 3–4.

3. Cataloged meticulously by Burton. Cynthia H. Burton, *Jefferson Vindicated: Fallacies, Omissions, and Contradictions in the Hemings Genealogical Search* (Keswick, VA: self-published manuscript), pp. 113–44.

4. Gordon-Reed, *Thomas Jefferson and Sally Hemings*, p. xiv.

5. Ibid., p. xix.

6. See also Gordon-Reed, *Thomas Jefferson and Sally Hemings*, pp. xv, 2–5, and 46–48.

7. Excepting steel pennies, which were created when there was a shortage of copper during World War II.

8. Gordon-Reed, *Thomas Jefferson and Sally Hemings*, p. xviii.

9. Annette Gordon-Reed, *The Hemingses of Monticello* (New York: W. W. Norton, 2008), p. 402.

10. Ibid., p. 316.

11. Ibid., p. 298.

12. William G. Hyland Jr., *In Defense of Thomas Jefferson: The Sally Hemings Sex Scandal* (New York: St. Martin's Press, 2009), pp. 40–41.

13. William Howard Adams, *The Paris Years of Thomas Jefferson* (New Haven, CT: Yale University Press, 2000), p. 222.

14. Virginius Dabney, *The Jefferson Scandals* (New York: Dodd, Mead, 1980), pp. 46–48.

15. Eyler Robert Coates Sr., "Research Report on the Jefferson-Hemings Controversy: A Critical Analysis," in *The Jefferson-Hemings Myth: An American Tragedy* (Charlottesville: Thomas Jefferson Heritage Society, 2001), pp. 75–116.

16. Richard E. Dixon, "The Case against Thomas Jefferson: A Trial Analysis of the Evidence on Paternity," in *Jefferson-Hemings Myth*, pp. 125–62.

17. See M. Andrew Holowchak, *Critical Reasoning and Science: Looking at Science with an Investigative Eye* (Lanham, MD: University Press of America, 2007), pp. 120–21.

18. Eric Foner, "The Master and the Mistress," *New York Times*, October 3, 2008, http://www.nytimes.com/2008/10/05/books/review/Foner-t.html (accessed May 31, 2011).

19. Gordon-Reed, *Hemingses of Monticello*, p. 563.

20. "Why Jefferson Scholars Were the Last to Know," *New York Times*, November 3, 1998.

21. Gordon-Reed, *Thomas Jefferson and Sally Hemings*, p. xii.

22. "Interview: Annette Gordon-Reed," PBS, http://www.pbs.org/wgbh/pages/frontline/shows/jefferson/interviews/reed.html (accessed May 31, 2011).

23. Annette Gordon-Reed, "Engaging Jefferson: Blacks and the Founding Father," *William and Mary Quarterly* 57, no. 1 (2000): 174.

24. Burton, *Jefferson Vindicated*, pp. 113–44.

25. Ibid., pp. 115–19.

26. David N. Mayer, "The Thomas Jefferson-Sally Hemings Myth and the Polit-icalization of American History," http://www.ashbrook.org/articles/mayer-hemings.html (accessed June 21, 2011).

27. Editor Samuel Wetmore too had much to gain as well. See Dabney, *Jefferson Scandals*, pp. 48–49.

28. Dumas Malone, *Jefferson & His Time*, vol. 4, *Jefferson the President, First Term, 1801–1805* (Charlottesville: University of Virginia Press, 1970), p. 498n11.

29. Race seems to color all her scholarship. In an essay on Jefferson and Madison, she finds a place for a comment on Jefferson's racism. Annette Gordon-Reed, "The Resonance of Minds: Thomas Jefferson and James Madison," *The Cambridge Companion to Thomas Jefferson*, ed. Frank Shuffleton (Cambridge: Cambridge University Press, 2009), p. 187.

30. Foner, "Master and the Mistress."

31. Mayer, "Thomas Jefferson-Sally Hemings Myth."

32. "The Hemingses of Monticello, by Annette Gordon-Reed," goodreads, http://www.goodreads.com/book/show/3364462-the-hemingses-of-monticello (accessed June 7, 2012).

33. Jefferson would have approved of such an appeal to popular sentiment, given his belief in the good judgment of the people, suitably educated, though I do not pretend that the reviews are representative of the majority of reviewers.

34. Gordon-Reed, *Thomas Jefferson and Sally Hemings*, p. xvii.

35. Ibid., p. 226.

36. Ibid., p. 224.

37. "Hemingses of Monticello, by Annette Gordon-Reed."

38. Gordon-Reed, *Thomas Jefferson and Sally Hemings*, p. 224.

39. Jeffersonian scholar Peter J. Onuf writes: "By themselves the DNA tests cannot prove TJ's paternity, as Dr. Foster has taken pains to emphasize: they demonstrate a match between Eston Hemings's descendants and a line of Jefferson descendants traceable to TJ's uncle. Another Jefferson male could have been responsible for this match." That conceded, he adds: "The probability of such an alternative scenario is very low, however, as the documentary research of stage members at the Thomas Jefferson Memorial foundation has demonstrated. The case for TJ's paternity was already very strong before the DNA tests were undertaken." As irrefragable evidence for that claim, he merely refers to Gordon-Reed's first book, in which, we have seen, she is agnostic on the issue of paternity. Peter J. Onuf, *Jefferson's Empire: The Language of American Nationhood* (Charlottesville: University of Virginia Press, 2000), pp. 225–26.

40. For example, James L. Golden and Alan L. Golden, *Thomas Jefferson and the Rhetoric of Virtue* (Lanham, MD: Rowman & Littlefield Publishers, 2002), p. 441; and R. B. Bernstein, *Thomas Jefferson* (Oxford: Oxford University Press, 2003), pp. 195–96.

41. Gordon-Reed, *Hemingses of Monticello*, p. 25. Author and critic Conor Cruise O'Brien claims that Hemings's importance, irrespective of a liaison, is that she was a slave, his wife's half sister, and his personal servant. She was certainly not his personal servant and it is unclear whether she was the half sister of his wife. Conor Cruise O'Brien, *The Long Affair: Thomas Jefferson and the French Revolution, 1785–1800* (Chicago: University of Chicago Press, 1996), p. 298.

42. Gordon-Reed, *Hemingses of Monticello*, p. 325.

43. Gordon-Reed, *Thomas Jefferson and Sally Hemings*, p. 234.

44. See M. Andrew Holowchak, "Jefferson's Liberal 'Eudaimonism,'" in *Dutiful Correspondent: Philosophical Essays on Thomas Jefferson* (Lanham, MD: Rowman & Littlefield, 2012), pp. 51–68.

45. So known for his generosity was Jefferson that he received a letter from an unknown New Yorker, who was "verry [*sic*] much in want of a little money." The man said, "I have heard that you are very good to the nedy [*sic*]." Dumas Malone, *Jefferson and His Time*, vol. 3, *The Ordeal of Liberty* (Boston: Little, Brown, 1962), p. 176.

46. Gordon-Reed, *Thomas Jefferson and Sally Hemings*, pp. 132–33. As Jeffersonian scholar Gilbert Chinard notes, hospitality to travelers, due to difficulties with travel, was a "sacred right" that was "most scrupulously observed" in Jefferson's day. Gilbert Chinard, *Thomas Jefferson: The Apostle of Americanism* (Ann Arbor, MI: University of Michigan Press, [1929] 1962), p. 7. Additionally, Gordon-Reed makes it seem as if Jefferson's ponderous debt was endemic to Jefferson. She fails to place Jefferson in the early eighteenth-century-Virginia climate, where debt was the norm, not the exception. See, for instance, Jefferson's letter to daughter Maria Jefferson Eppes, January 7, 1798, and Dumas Malone, *The Sage of Monticello* (Charlottesville: University of Virginia Press, 1981), pp. 301–15 and 447–78.

47. Gordon-Reed, *Thomas Jefferson and Sally Hemings*, p. 133. Note that her inclusion of the emotive word *awful* in her question suggests an appeal to pity and hints at the real motive behind her quest: racism in Jefferson and in the scholarship on Jefferson. Awfulness is not the issue; evidence is.

48. "To keep a Virginia estate together," Jefferson writes to President James Monroe, "requires in the owner both skill and attention. Skill I never had, and attention I could not have; and really, when I reflect on all circumstances, my wonder is that I should have been so long as sixty years in reaching the result to which I am now reduced." TJ to James Monroe, March 8, 1826.

49. Gordon-Reed, *Thomas Jefferson and Sally Hemings*, p. 133.

50. Ibid.

51. That is the reason why logicians assert that from an impossible state of affairs, a contradiction, anything follows deductively—formally, $(A \ \& \sim A) \rightarrow P$ is a tautology.

52. Gordon-Reed, *Hemingses of Monticello*, p. 654.

53. Gordon-Reed, *Thomas Jefferson and Sally Hemings*, p. xiv.

54. Gordon-Reed, "Engaging Jefferson," p. 180.

55. Gordon-Reed, *Thomas Jefferson and Sally Hemings*, p. 121.

56. Gordon-Reed, *Hemingses of Monticello*, p. 312.

57. Ibid., p. 315.

58. Ibid., p. 319.

59. Ibid., p. 322.

60. She never answers the question of rape, but settles on a lengthy discussion on the possibility of rape as indicative of the evil of slavery. She then discusses the need to be led by particulars—facts—and not generalizations from historical tendencies. Ibid., p. 361.

61. Ibid., p. 329.

62. Gordon-Reed, "Resonance of Minds," p. 187.

63. Thomas Jefferson, "Query XIV," in *Thomas Jefferson: Writings*, ed. Merrill D. Peterson (New York: Library of America Press, 1984), p. 265.

64. Ibid.

65. See John C. Miller, "Slavery," *Thomas Jefferson: A Reference Biography*, ed. Merrill D. Peterson (New York: Charles Scribner's Sons, 1986), p. 424.

66. Gordon-Reed, *Thomas Jefferson and Sally Hemings*, pp. 126–27.

67. Andrew Burstein, *The Inner Jefferson: Portrait of a Grieving Optimist* (Charlottesville: University of Virginia Press, 1996), p. 116; Douglas L. Wilson, "Jefferson and the Republic of Letters," *Jeffersonian Legacies*, ed. Peter S. Onuf (Charlottesville: University of Virginia Press, 1993), p. 69; and Peter S. Onuf, "The Scholar's Jefferson," *William and Mary Quarterly* 50, no. 4 (1993): 690.

# CHAPTER 3: RATIONALIZATIONS AND SECRETS

1. Andrew Burstein, *The Inner Jefferson: Portrait of a Grieving Optimist* (Charlottesville: University of Virginia Press, 1995), p. xii.

2. Ibid., pp. xii–xiii.

3. Ibid., p. 290.

4. Ibid., pp. 191–92.

5. See Sigmund Freud, "The Acquisition and Control of Fire," *The Standard Edition of the Complete Works of Sigmund Freud*, ed. James Strachey (New York: W. W. Norton, 1964), pp. 185–96.

6. Burstein, *Inner Jefferson*, p. 231.

7. Andrew Burstein in a PBS interview, http://www.pbs.org/jefferson/archives/interviews/Burstein.htm (accessed April 7, 2011).

8. Rick Shankman, "The Unknown Jefferson: An Interview with Andrew Burstein," *History News Network*, George Mason University, July 25, 2005, http://hnn.us/articles/13102.html (accessed April 4, 2011).

9. Annette Gordon-Reed, *Thomas Jefferson and Sally Hemings: An American Controversy* (Charlottesville: University of Virginia Press, 1997), p. 141.

10. Andrew Burstein, "Jefferson's Rationalizations," *William and Mary Quarterly* 57, no. 1 (2000): 196. This point is made also by Gordon-Reed.

11. M. Andrew Holowchak, "Jefferson on African Americans," in *Dutiful Correspondent: Philosophical Essays on Thomas Jefferson* (Lanham, MD: Rowman & Littlefield, 2012), pp. 203–28.

12. TJ to Don Valentine de Foronda, October 4, 1809, in *The Writings of Thomas Jefferson*, ed. Paul Leicester Ford (New York: Putnam, 1892).

13. For example, August 1, 1816; January 11, 1817; August 15, 1820; and June 1, 1822.

14. For example, September 2, 1813; December 25, 1813; May 3, 1816; April 19, 1817; May 26, 1817.

15. Andrew Burstein, *Jefferson's Secrets* (New York: Basic Books, 2005), pp. 4–5.

16. Ibid., p. 114.

17. Ibid., p. 115.

18. Burstein, *Inner Jefferson*, p. 231.

19. Burstein, *Jefferson's Secrets*, p. 115.

20. Cynthia H. Burton, *Jefferson Vindicated: Fallacies, Omissions, and Contradictions in the Hemings Genealogical Search* (Keswick, VA: self-published), p. 109.

21. Burstein, *Jefferson's Secrets*, p. 115.

22. Burton, *Jefferson Vindicated*, pp. 52–60.

23. Ibid., p. 56.

24. For more on plausible Jeffersons other than Thomas Jefferson, see Burton, *Jefferson Vindicated*, pp. 52–73.

25. See M. Andrew Holowchak, *Critical Reasoning and Science: Looking at Science with an Investigative Eye* (Lanham, MD: University Press of America, 2007), pp. 101–102.

26. Burstein, *Jefferson's Secrets*, pp. 115–16.

27. For example, Burton, *Jefferson Vindicated*, pp. 113–44; and Robert F. Turner, ed., *The Jefferson-Hemings Controversy: Report of the Scholars Commission* (Durham, NC: Carolina Academic Press, 2011).

28. William G. Hyland Jr., *In Defense of Thomas Jefferson: The Sally Hemings Sex Scandal* (New York: St. Martin's Press, 2009), p. 166.

29. Burstein, *Jefferson's Secrets*, pp. 118–23.

30. Ibid., p. 120.

31. Ibid., p. 151.

32. Ibid., pp. 152–53.

33. Ibid., p. 153.

34. Ibid., p. 155.

35. Cynthia Burton, *Jefferson Vindicated*, pp. 20–22.

36. Ibid., pp. 130–31.

37. Ibid., pp. 125–28.

38. Burstein, *Jefferson's Secrets*, p. 155.

39. Ibid., p. 180.

40. Ibid., pp. 178–79.

41. Ibid., p. 158.

42. Bernard Bailyn, "Thomas Jefferson," *Faces of Revolution: Personalities and Themes in the Struggle for American Independence* (New York: 1992), pp. 22–41.

43. See also TJ to Edmund Randolph, September 17, 1792; TJ to William Hamilton, April 22, 1800; TJ to Don Valentine de Foronda, October 4, 1809; TJ to Albert Gallatin, April 24, 1811; and TJ to Francis Wayles Eppes, May 21, 1816.

44. For example, Adrienne Koch, *The Philosophy of Thomas Jefferson* (New York: Columbia University Press, 1943), pp. 40–43; and Jean M. Yarbrough, "The Moral Sense, Character Formation, and Virtue," in *Reason and Republicanism: Thomas Jefferson's Legacy of Liberty*, eds. Gary L. McDowell and Sharon L. Noble (Lanham, MD: Rowman & Littlefield, 1997), pp. 280–82.

45. Holowchak, "Reason and the Moral Sense," in *Dutiful Correspondent*, pp. 159–76.

46. Burstein, *Jefferson's Secrets*, p. 164.

47. Ibid.

48. Ibid.

49. Aristotle, *Politics*, trans. C. D. C. Reeve (Indianapolis, IN: Hackett Publishing, Inc., 1998), I.13.

50. See M. Andrew Holowchak, *Happiness and Greek Ethical Thought* (London: Continuum, 2004), p. 223.

51. Aristotle, *Politics*, 1277b24–5.

52. Plato, *Phaedrus*, trans. Alexander Nehamas and Paul Woodruff (Indianapolis, IN: Hackett Publishing, 1995), 231a–233a. For more on Greek homoeroticism, see Holowchak, *Happiness and Greek Ethical Thought*, pp. 222–23.

53. Plato, *Symposium*, trans. Alexander Nehamas and Paul Woodruff (Indianapolis, IN: Hackett Publishing, 1989), 180d–185c.

54. Burstein, *Jefferson's Secrets*, p. 164.

55. Karl Lehmann, *Thomas Jefferson: American Humanist* (1965; repr., Charlottesville: University of Virginia Press, 1994), p. 84.

56. Burstein, *Jefferson's Secrets*, p. 166.

57. See Holowchak, "Happiness and Pleasure: Epicurean Hedonism," in *Happiness and Greek Ethical Thought*, pp. 64–89.

58. I have argued elsewhere, however, that Jefferson paid mouth honor to Epicurus's ethics and was much more influenced by the Greek and Roman Stoics: M. Andrew Holowchak, "The Reluctant Politician: Thomas Jefferson's Debt to Epicurus," *Eighteenth-Century Studies* 45, no. 2 (2012): 277–97; Holowchak, "The March of Morality: Making

Sense of Jefferson's Moral Sense," in *Th. Jefferson & Philosophy: Essays on the Philosophical Cast of Jefferson's Writings* (Lanham, MD: Lexington Books, 2013), chap. 8; and Holowchak, *Dutiful Correspondent*, pp. 17–22.

59. Burstein, *Jefferson's Secrets*, pp. 167–68.

60. Ibid., p. 158.

61. Burstein, "Jefferson's Rationalizations," pp. 186–87.

62. Burstein, *Inner Jefferson*, p. 187.

63. Ibid., p. 157.

64. S. A. A. D. Tissot, "A Treatise on the Diseases Incident to Literary and Sedentary Persons," trans. James Kirkpatrick (London: A. Donaldson, 1772). Originally titled *De la santé des gens de lettres* (1768).

65. M. Andrew Holowchak, *Critical Reasoning & Philosophy: A Concise Guide for Reading, Evaluating, and Writing Philosophy*, 2nd ed. (Lanham, MD: Rowman & Littlefield, 2011), pp. 61–63.

66. Burstein, *Jefferson's Secrets*, p. 187.

67. Hyland, *In Defense of Thomas Jefferson*, pp. 152–53.

68. Silvio Bedini, "Man of Science," in *Thomas Jefferson: A Reference Biography*, ed. Merrill D. Peterson (New York: Charles Scribner's Sons, 1986), p. 274.

69. Burstein, *Jefferson's Secrets*, p. 183.

70. Burstein, *Inner Jefferson*, p. 182.

71. Lehmann, *Thomas Jefferson*, p. 5.


# CHAPTER 4: THE "TIRESOME" ARGUMENT FROM CHARACTER

1. TJ to James Maury, April 25, 1812, in *The Writings of Thomas Jefferson*, ed. Paul Leicester Ford (New York: Putnam, 1892).

2. Fawn Brodie, *Thomas Jefferson: An Intimate History* (New York: W. W. Norton, 1974), p. 414.

3. Ibid., pp. 414–15.

4. Though Brodie sometimes refers to Erik Erikson, her explanations of Jefferson's behavior are plainly Freudian.

5. See also TJ to Don Valentine de Foronda, October 4, 1809.

6. Joseph Ellis, *American Sphinx: The Character of Thomas Jefferson* (New York: Alfred A. Knopf, 1997), p. 306.

7. See M. Andrew Holowchak, "The Reluctant Politician: Thomas Jefferson's Debt to Epicurus," *Eighteenth-Century Studies* 45, no. 2 (2012): 277–97.

8. See M. Andrew Holowchak, "The (Stoic) Sage of Monticello," *Clio* (forthcoming).

9. Adrienne Koch, *The Philosophy of Thomas Jefferson* (New York: Columbia University Press, 1943), pp. 40–43.

10. Strangely, he disavows Stoicism, due to its overdemanding ideals. TJ to John Adams, April 8, 1816. See also M. Andrew Holowchak, *Dutiful Correspondent: Philosophical Essays on Thomas Jefferson* (Lanham, MD: Rowman & Littlefield, 2012), pp. 17–22.

11. TJ to Martha Jefferson, April 7, 1787; TJ to Peter Carr, August 10, 1787; TJ to Martha Jefferson Randolph, February 5, 1801; and TJ to Ellen Wayles Randolph, November 27, 1801.

12. See also "Bill for the More General Diffusion of Knowledge," in *Thomas Jefferson: Writings*, ed. Merrill D. Peterson (New York: Library of America Press, 1984); TJ to John Jay, June 17, 1789; TJ to Wilson Cary Nicholas, March 26, 1805; TJ to Caesar Rodney, February 10, 1810; TJ to P. S. Du Pont de Nemours, April 24, 1816.

13. Politician Edward Coles also reports that Jefferson expressly denied having a relationship with Sally Hemings. There are also other "implied denials," collected by Burton. See Cynthia H. Burton, *Jefferson Vindicated* (Keswick, VA: self-published, 2005), pp. 30–37.

14. Jennifer Jensen Wallach, "The Vindication of Fawn Brodie," *Massachusetts Review* 43, no. 2 (2002): 287–90.

15. Annette Gordon-Reed, *Thomas Jefferson and Sally Hemings: An American Controversy* (Charlottesville: University of Virginia Press, 1997), p. 121.

16. Ibid.

17. Henry Randall, *The Life of Thomas Jefferson*, vol. 1 (New York: Derby & Jackson, 1858), p. 13. Strongmen today are able to flip several times a tire that weighs one thousand pounds, but we are asked to believe Jefferson's father could do the rough equivalent of flipping two such tires at the same time. I can claim some authority here, as I coached the 2009 and 2010 World's Strongest Man, Žydrūnas Savickas.

18. Fawn Brodie, *Thomas Jefferson: An Intimate History* (New York: W. W. Norton, 1974), p. 34.

19. James A. Bear Jr., "Memoirs of Edmund Bacon," *Jefferson at Monticello* (Charlottesville, VA: 1967), p. 71.

20. Silvio A. Bedini, *Jefferson and Science* (Thomas Jefferson Foundation: Monticello Monograph Series, 2002), p. 72.

21. Dumas Malone, *Thomas Jefferson: A Brief Biography* (1933; repr., Thomas Jefferson Memorial Foundation, 1986), p. 12.

22. Gilbert Chinard, *Thomas Jefferson: The Apostle of Americanism* (1929; repr., Ann Arbor: University of Michigan Press, 1962), pp. 6–7.

23. Robert M. Johnstone Jr., "The Presidency," *Thomas Jefferson: A Reference Biography*, ed. Merrill D. Peterson (New York: Charles Scribner's Sons, 1986), p. 353.

24. Gordon-Reed, *Thomas Jefferson and Sally Hemings*, p. 247.

25. Annette Gordon-Reed, *The Hemingses of Monticello: An American Family* (New York: W. W. Norton, 2008), p. 96.

26. Gordon-Reed, *Thomas Jefferson and Sally Hemings*, p. 234.

27. TJ to Maria Cosway, February 15, 1787.

28. Gordon-Reed, *Thomas Jefferson and Sally Hemings*, p. 123.

29. M. Andrew Holowchak, "Reason and the Moral Sense," in *Dutiful Correspondent: Philosophical Essays on Thomas Jefferson* (Lanham, MD: Rowman & Littlefield, 2012), pp. 159–76.

30. Annette Gordon-Reed, "Engaging Jefferson: Blacks and the Founding Father," *William and Mary Quarterly* 57, no. 1 (2000): 177.

31. Andrew Burstein, *The Inner Jefferson: Portrait of a Grieving Optimist* (Charlottesville: University of Virginia Press, 1995), p. 290.

32. Andrew Burstein in a PBS interview, http://www.pbs.org/jefferson/archives/interviews/Burstein.htm (accessed April 7, 2011).

33. That is, only for Eston Hemings. Like her mother, Sally might have had multiple lovers.

34. Rick Shankman, "The Unknown Jefferson: An Interview with Andrew Burstein," *History News Network*, George Mason University, July 25, 2005, http://hnn.us/articles/13102.html (accessed April 4, 2011).

35. Andrew Burstein, "The Problem of Jefferson Biography," *Virginia Quarterly Review* (1994), pp. 403–20, http://www.vqronline.org/articles/1994/summer/burstein-problem-jefferson-biography/ (accessed June 7, 2011).

36. Dumas Malone, *Jefferson the President: First Term, 1801–1805* (Charlottesville: University of Virginia Press, 1970), p. 214.

37. This idiom's meaning generally now has the sense of "without basis in fact."

38. Merrill D. Peterson, *Thomas Jefferson and the New Nation: A Biography* (New York: Oxford, 1970), p. 707.

39. John C. Miller, "Slavery," *Thomas Jefferson: A Reference Biography*, ed. Merrill D. Peterson (New York: Charles Scribner's Sons, 1986), p. 429.

40. Conor Cruise O'Brien, *The Long Affair: Thomas Jefferson and the French Revolution, 1785–1800* (Chicago: University of Chicago Press, 1996), p. 22.

41. For difficulties, see · Cynthia H. Burton, *Jefferson Vindicated: Fallacies, Omissions, and Contradictions in the Hemings Genealogical Search* (Keswick, VA: self-published, 2005), pp. 134–36.

42. See Holowchak, "Reason and the Moral Sense."

43. TJ to Joseph Priestley, April 9, 1803; TJ to Benjamin Rush, April 21, 1803; TJ to John Adams, October 12, 1813; TJ to Charles Thomson, January 9, 1816; and TJ to William Short, August 4, 1820.

44. Charles Flinn Arrowood, *Thomas Jefferson and Education in a Republic* (New York: McGraw-Hill Book Company, 1930), pp. 15–16.

45. Ibid., p. 16.

46. TJ to Dugald Stewart, April 26, 1824.

47. TJ to Thomas Jefferson Randolph, December 29, 1811.

48. Merrill D. Peterson, ed., *Thomas Jefferson: Writings* (New York: Library of America, 1984), pp. 4–5.

49. Lester J. Cappon, *The Adams-Jefferson Letters: The Complete Correspondence between Thomas Jefferson & Abigail & John Adams* (Chapel Hill: University of North Carolina Press, 1987), p. 557.

50. Brodie, *Thomas Jefferson*, pp. 22–23.

51. He recorded data from the first croaking of frogs, the singing of whip-poor-wills, and the fruition of vegetables to the wrangling of political debates, the dimensions of buildings, and the time it took to pass from one place to the next. Edward T. Martin, *Thomas Jefferson: Scientist* (New York: Henry Schuman, 1952), p. 18.

52. James A. Bear Jr., "Monticello," *Thomas Jefferson: A Reference Biography*, ed. Merrill D. Peterson (New York: Charles Scribner's Sons, 1986), p. 439.

53. Brodie, *Thomas Jefferson*, pp. 340–41.

54. Ibid., p. 341.

55. Henry Adams, *History of the United States during the Administrations of Jefferson and Madison*, vol. 1 (Upper Saddle River, NJ: Prentice-Hall, 1963), p. 75.

56. Virginius Dabney, *The Jefferson Scandals* (New York: Dodd, Mead, 1980), pp. 95–96.

57. Ibid., p. 95.

58. Ibid., p. 107.

59. Brodie, *Thomas Jefferson*, p. 474.

60. Ellen Randolph Coolidge to Joseph Coolidge, October 24, 1858, in Peter Onuf, *The Mind of Thomas Jefferson* (Charlottesville: University of Virginia Press, 2007), p. 61.

61. Martin, *Thomas Jefferson: Scientist*, p. 20.

62. From Cruise O'Brien, *Long Affair*, p. 36.

63. Thomas Jefferson, "Query XIV," *Notes on the State of Virginia*, in Peterson, *Thomas Jefferson: Writings*, p. 267.

64. The sole exception is his amassing debt.

65. William G. Hyland Jr. et al., "Civil Action: Sally Hemings v. Thomas Jefferson," *American Journal of Trial Advocacy* 31, no. 1:17:44–45.

66. Dumas Malone, *Jefferson and His Time*, vol. 1, *Jefferson the Virginian* (Boston: Little, Brown, 1948), p. 143.

67. Martin, *Thomas Jefferson: Scientist*, pp. 6–7.

68. Karl Lehmann, *Thomas Jefferson: American Humanist* (1965; repr., Charlottesville: University of Virginia Press, 1994), p. 10.

69.  Jefferson answers the charge of atheism in a letter to Benjamin Waterhouse (July 19, 1822), who had asked in a prior letter for permission to publish one of Jefferson's letters on religion to countermand the charge of atheism. To address the charge of atheism would thrust Jefferson's head into a "hornet's nest." He writes to Levi Lincoln (January 1, 1802): "Don Quixote undertook to redress the bodily ills of this world, but the redressment of mental vagaries would be an enterprise more than Quixotic. I should as soon undertake to bring the crazy skulls of Bedlam to sound understanding, as inculcate reason into that of an Athanasian. I am old and tranquility is now my *summum bonum*. Keep me therefore from the fire and faggots of Calvin and his victim Servetus."

70.  See M. Andrew Holowchak, *Greek Ethics and Happiness* (London: Continuum Books, 2004).

71.  For example, TJ to Thomas Law, June 13, 1814; and TJ to Francis Eppes, May 21, 1816.

# CHAPTER 5: HIGH PRIESTS OF
# THE MORAL TEMPLE

1.  Eugene A. Foster et al., "Jefferson Fathered Slave's Last Child," *Nature* 396, no. 5 (November 1998): 27.

2.  Ibid., pp. 27–28.

3.  Herbert Barger, "The Jefferson-Hemings DNA Study," in *The Jefferson-Hemings Myth: An American Travesty* (Charlottesville: Thomas Jefferson Heritage Society, 2001), p. 31.

4.  Ibid., pp. 27–29.

5.  Eyler Robert Coates Sr., "Research Report on the Jefferson-Hemings Controversy: A Critical Analysis," in *Jefferson-Hemings Myth*, pp. 96–97.

6.  "Mission Statement," Monticello.org, http://www.monticello.org/site/about/mission-statement (accessed July 27, 2012).

7.  Lance Banning, "Thomas Jefferson and Sally Hemings: Case Closed?" *Claremont Review of Books* (Summer 2001): 9–10.

8.  White McKenzie Wallenborn, "A Committee Insider's Viewpoint," in *The Jefferson-Hemings Myth: An American Travesty* (Charlottesville: Thomas Jefferson Heritage Society, 2001), pp. 57–63.

9.  White McKenzie Wallenborn, "Minority Report of the Monticello Research Committee on Thomas Jefferson and Sally Hemings," March 23, 2000, Monticello.org, http://www.monticello.org/site/plantation-and-slavery/minority-report-monticello-research-committee-thomas-jefferson-and-sally (accessed June 26, 2012).

10.  Fraser D. Neiman, "Coincidence or Causal Connection? The Relationship

between Thomas Jefferson's Visits to Monticello and Sally Hemings' Conceptions," *William and Mary Quarterly* 57, no. 1 (2000): 199–206.

11. Neiman, "Coincidence or Causal Connection?"

12. From the Latin *quod erat demonstratum*, which asserts that precisely what was promised to be proven has been proven.

13. Cynthia H. Burton, *Jefferson Vindicated* (Keswick, VA: self-published, 2005); William G. Hyland Jr., *In Defense of Thomas Jefferson: The Sally Hemings Sex Scandal* (New York: St. Martin's Press, 2009), p. 51.

14. William G. Hyland Jr. et al., "A Civil Action: Sally Hemings v. Thomas Jefferson," *American Journal of Trial Advocacy* 31, no. 1 (2007): 17–21.

15. Hyland, *In Defense of Thomas Jefferson*, p. 193.

16. Steven T. Corneliussen, "Sally Hemings, Thomas Jefferson, and the Authority of Science," http://www.tjscience.org/HemingsTJscience.htm (accessed June 17, 2011).

17. See M. Andrew Holowchak, *Critical Reasoning and Science: Looking at Science with an Investigative Eye* (Lanham, MD: University Press of America, 2007), pp. 68–69.

18. Corneliussen, "Sally Hemings, Thomas Jefferson, and the Authority of Science."

19. Neiman, "Coincidence or Causal Connection?" p. 210.

20. David Murray, "Present at the Conception," in *The Jefferson-Hemings Myth: An American Travesty* (Charlottesville: Thomas Jefferson Heritage Society, 2001), p. 119.

21. Neiman, "Coincidence or Causal Connection?"

22. For example, R. B. Bernstein, *Thomas Jefferson* (Oxford: Oxford University Press, 2003), p. 196; and Jan Lewis, "Introduction," *William and Mary Quarterly* 57, no. 1 (2000): 121–24.

23. Lewis, "Introduction," p. 122.

24. James L. Golden and Alan L. Golden, *Thomas Jefferson and the Rhetoric of Virtue* (Lanham, MD: Rowman & Littlefield, 2002), pp. 446–49.

25. See Wallenborn, "Minority Report of the Monticello Research Committee on Thomas Jefferson and Sally Hemings."

26. Hyland, *In Defense of Thomas Jefferson*, pp. 126–27.

27. Golden and Golden, *Thomas Jefferson and the Rhetoric of Virtue*, pp. 449–50.

28. Douglas L. Wilson, "Thomas Jefferson and the Character Issue," *Atlantic Monthly*, November 1992, p. 62.

29. Jeffrey L. Pasley, "Politics and the Misadventures of Thomas Jefferson's Modern Reputation: A Review Essay," *Journal of Southern History* 72, no. 4 (2006): 888–91 and 893.

30. Ibid.

31. Ibid., pp. 888–92.

32. David N. Mayer, "The Thomas Jefferson-Sally Hemings Myth and the Politicalization of American History," http://www.ashbrook.org/articles/mayer-hemings.html (accessed June 21, 2011).

33. Murray, "Present at the Conception," pp. 123–24.

34. See also TJ to Dr. James Curie, January 18, 1786; TJ to Alexander White, September 10, 1797; TJ to Dr. Benjamin Rush, September 23, 1800; TJ to Judge John Tyler, June 28, 1804; TJ to James Sullivan, May 21, 1805; TJ to DeWitt Clinton, May 24, 1807; TJ to Thomas Law, January 15, 1811; and TJ to George Logan, June 20, 1816, in *The Writings of Thomas Jefferson*, ed. Paul Leicester Ford (New York: Putnam, 1892).

35. Brooke Allen, "Jefferson the Skeptic," *Hudson Review* 59, no. 2 (2006): 212–13.

36. Thomas Jefferson, *Jefferson's Literary Commonplace Book*, ed. Douglas L. Wilson (Princeton: Princeton University Press, 1989), pp. 52–53.

37. A word, difficult to translate, that has the sense of craftsperson, artist, or technician—someone in possession of a particular skill, delineable by rules pertaining to the proper execution of that skill.

38. Plato, *Phaedrus*, trans. Alexander Nehemas and Paul Woodruff (Indianapolis: Hackett Publishing, 1995).

39. Mayer, "Thomas Jefferson-Sally Hemings Myth and the Politicalization of American History."

40. Pasley, "Politics and the Misadventures of Thomas Jefferson's Modern Reputation," p. 896.

41. Annette Gordon-Reed, *Thomas Jefferson and Sally Hemings: An American Controversy* (Charlottesville: University of Virginia Press, 1997), p. 233.

42. Annette Gordon-Reed, *The Hemingses of Monticello* (New York: W. W. Norton, 2008), p. 291.

43. Ibid., p. 292.

44. Ibid.

45. Ibid., p. 338.

46. David E. Schrader, "Thomas Jefferson's Lives: Learning from History," *Sons of the American Revolution Magazine* 107, no. 1 (2012), pp. 21–22.

47. Here I am greatly indebted to Herbert Barger.

48. Stephen Conrad, "Putting Rights Talk in Its Place: The Summary View Revisited," in *Jeffersonian Legacies*, ed. Peter Onuf (Charlottesville: University of Virginia Press, 1993), p. 28n65.

49. TJ to Pierre Samuel Du Pont de Nemours, April 24, 1816.

50. For example, TJ to Elbridge Gerry, January 26, 1799; TJ to Joseph Priestly, January 27, 1800; TJ to John Adams, June 15, 1813; TJ to Benjamin Waterhouse, March 3, 1818; TJ to Judge Spencer Roane, September 6, 1819; TJ to John Adams, August 15, 1820; TJ to Marquis de Lafayette, December 26, 1820; TJ to Judge Spenser Roane, March 9, 1821.

# CHAPTER 6: A "CONVENIENT DEFECT OF VISION"

1. M. Andrew Holowchak, "Jefferson on African Americans," in *Dutiful Correspondent: Philosophical Essays on Thomas Jefferson* (Lanham, MD: Rowman & Littlefield, 2012), pp. 203–28.

2. Robert McColley, *Slavery and Jeffersonian Virginia* (Urbana: University of Illinois Press, 1964), p. 124.

3. Winthrop D. Jordan, *White over Black: American Attitudes toward the Negro, 1550–1812* (Baltimore: Penguin Books, 1969), pp. 429–31 and 453.

4. William Cohen, "Thomas Jefferson and the Problem of Slavery," *Journal of American History* 56, no. 3 (1968): 506–25.

5. John C. Miller, *The Wolf by the Ears: Thomas Jefferson and Slavery* (Charlottesville: University of Virginia Press, 1977), pp. 96–97.

6. Garrett Ward Sheldon, *The Political Philosophy of Thomas Jefferson* (Baltimore: Johns Hopkins University Press, 1991), p. 139.

7. Paul Finkelman, "Thomas Jefferson and Antislavery: The Myth Goes On," *Virginia Magazine of History and Biography* 102, no. 2 (1994): 203–208.

8. Conor Cruise O'Brien, *The Long Affair: Thomas Jefferson and the French Revolution, 1785–1800* (Chicago: University of Chicago Press, 1996), pp. 316–18.

9. Howard Temperly, "Jefferson and Slavery: A Study in Moral Philosophy," *Reason and Republicanism: Thomas Jefferson's Legacy of Liberty*, ed. Gary L. McDowell and Sharon L. Noble (Lanham, MD: Rowman & Littlefield, 1997), pp. 86, 89–90, and 97–98.

10. Nicholas Magnis, "Thomas Jefferson and Slavery: An Analysis of His Racist Thinking as Revealed by His Writings and Political Behavior," *Journal of Black Studies* 29, no. 4 (1999): 491–509.

11. Andrew Burstein, *Jefferson's Secrets* (New York: Basic Books, 2005), p. 120.

12. Annette Gordon-Reed, *Thomas Jefferson and Sally Hemings: An American Controversy* (Charlottesville: University of Virginia Press, 1997), p. 3.

13. Cynthia A. Kierner, "Sex, Science, and Sensibility at Jefferson's Monticello," *Reviews in American History* 33, no. 3 (2005): 337.

14. Thomas Jefferson, *Notes on the State of Virginia*, in *Thomas Jefferson: Writings*, ed. Merrill D. Peterson (New York: Library of America, 1984), pp. 269–70.

15. Jefferson's use of *prejudices* here is incautious and betrays some sense of what we call today "experimenter's bias."

16. Peterson, *Thomas Jefferson: Writings*, pp. 264–66.

17. Jefferson, "Query XIV," in ibid., p. 264.

18. See M. Andrew Holowchak, *Dutiful Correspondent: Philosophical Essays on Thomas Jefferson* (Lanham, MD: Rowman & Littlefield, 2012), pp. 93–130.

19. Jefferson, "Query XIV," pp. 266–67.

20. Jefferson, "Query VI," p. 187.

21. Jefferson, "Query XIV," p. 267.

22. Mapp writes, "moral stature . . . Jefferson considered the most important measure of human worth." Alf Mapp Jr., *Thomas Jefferson: America's Paradoxical Patriot* (Lanham, MD: Rowman & Littlefield, 1987), p. 172.

23. Jefferson, "Query XIV," pp. 268–69.

24. See also TJ to Maria Cosway, October 12, 1786; and TJ to James Fishback, June 5, 1809 in *The Writings of Thomas Jefferson*, ed. Paul Leicester Ford (New York: Putnam, 1892).

25. Golden and Golden list eights steps that Jefferson followed to ensure the reliability, meaningfulness, and persuasiveness of his accumulated data in the *Notes on the State of Virginia*. Buying into the hypothesis that Jefferson fathered children by his slave Sally Hemings, they then, in the final chapter of the book, in an addendum, argue that Jefferson was uncharacteristically lax apropos of steps on the issue of blacks. James Golden and Alan Golden, *Thomas Jefferson and the Rhetoric of Virtue* (Lanham, MD: Rowman & Littlefield, 2002), pp. 325–26, 417–58, and 465–68.

26. Later in the same year, Jefferson admits to diplomat and politician Joel Barlow that black scientist Benjamin Banneker has a "very common stature," and he admits to having written a "soft answer" in his letter to abolitionist Henri Grégoire. TJ to Joel Barlow, October 8, 1809.

27. See, for example, TJ to David Barrow, May 1, 1815.

28. Mapp, *Thomas Jefferson*, p. 171.

29. See also John Howe, "Republicanism," in *Thomas Jefferson: A Reference Biography*, ed. Merrill D. Peterson (New York: Charles Scribner's Sons, 1986), p. 75.

30. Seneca, *On Leisure*, trans. John W. Basore (Cambridge: Harvard University Press, 2001), V.3.

31. Douglas L. Wilson, "Thomas Jefferson and the Character Issue," *Atlantic Monthly*, November 1992, p. 62.

32. For example, Epictetus, *Handbook*, trans. Nicholas P. White (Indianapolis: Hackett, 1983), §45.

33. Leonard W. Levy, *Jefferson and Civil Liberties: The Darker Side* (Cambridge: Harvard University Press, 1963), p. xi.

34. Virginius Dabney, *The Thomas Jefferson Scandals: A Rebuttal* (New York: Dodd, Mead, 1981), p. 102.

35. David N. Mayer, "The Thomas Jefferson-Sally Hemings Myth and the Politicization of American History: Individual Views of David N. Mayer Concurring with the Majority Report of the Scholars Commission on the Jefferson-Hemings Matter," April 9, 2001, pp. 20–23, http://www.ashbrook.ort/articles/mayer-himings.html (accessed June 11, 2011).

36. Andrew Burstein in a PBS interview, http://www.pbs.org/jefferson/archives/interviews/Burstein.htm (accessed June 11, 2011).

37. TJ to Peter Carr, August 17, 1785; TJ to Maria Cosway, October 12, 1786, and TJ to James Fishback, September 27, 1809; and TJ to Thomas Law, June 13, 1814.

38. Gilbert Chinard, *The Literary Bible of Thomas Jefferson: His Commonplace Book of Philosophers and Poets* (1928; repr., New York: Greenwood Press, 1969), pp. 6 and 16; Adrianne Koch, *The Philosophy of Thomas Jefferson* (Gloucester, MA: Peter Smith, 1957), pp. 8 and 40; Jean M. Yarbrough, "The Moral Sense, Character Formation, and Virtue," *Reason and Republicanism: Thomas Jefferson's Legacy of Liberty*, ed. Gary L. McDowell and Sharon L. Noble (Lanham, MD: Rowman & Littlefield, 1997), pp. 281–82.

39. Lord Kames, *Essays on the Principles of Morality and Natural Religion: Corrected and Improved, in a Third Edition*, ed. Mary Catherine Moran (Indianapolis: Liberty Fund, 2005), pp. 76 and 92.

40. For example, TJ to Joseph Priestley, April 9, 1803. For more, see Holowchak, "Jefferson and Jesus," in *Dutiful Correspondent*, pp. 93–110.

41. See Holowchak, *Dutiful Correspondent*, p. 171.

42. Kames, *Essays on the Principles of Morality and Natural Religion*, pp. 64–65.

43. Holowchak, *Dutiful Correspondent*, p. 160.

44. For example, TJ to Marquis de Chastellux, June 7, 1785, and "Second Inaugural Address," May 5, 1805, in Peterson, *Thomas Jefferson: Writings*, p. 520.

45. Jefferson, "Query XIV," p. 264.

46. Ibid.

47. Ibid., p. 288.

48. Ibid., pp. 213–14.

49. TJ to Henry St. George Tucker, August 28, 1797.

50. Jefferson, "Query XVIII," in Peterson, *Thomas Jefferson: Writings*, p. 289.

51. It is not astonishing that Jefferson turns to the issue of the number and condition of the militia in the next query—"Query IX."

52. Burstein, *Jefferson's Secrets*, pp. 125 and 136–39.

53. TJ to Charles Willson Peale, August 20, 1811.

54. For example, TJ to St. John de Crevècoeur, January 15, 1787; TJ to Marquis de Lafayette, April 11, 1787; TJ to James Madison, June 9, 1793; TJ to John Taylor, December 19, 1794; and TJ to John Hollins, February 19, 1809.

55. Jefferson, "Query XIV," p. 273. See also TJ to Ralph Izzard, 1788; and TJ to J. W. Eppes, 1787.

56. From Dumas Malone, *Jefferson the President: First Term, 1801–8105* (Boston: Little, Brown, 1970), p. 354.

57. It also has the senses of "due measure," "proportion," and "fitness."

58. My translation. Hippocrates, *Precepts*, trans. W. H. S. Jones (Cambridge: Harvard University Press, 1868), pp. 313–14.

59. Sophocles, *Aiax*, trans. Hugh Lloyd-Jones (Cambridge: Harvard University Press, 1994), p. 1168.

60. Plato, *Republic*, trans. Paul Shorey (1930; repr., Cambridge: Harvard University Press, 1994), 374c.

61. Pausanias, *Guide to Greece*, trans. W. H. S. Jones (Cambridge: Harvard University Press, 1918), V.xiv.9.

62. Karl Lehmann, *Thomas Jefferson: American Humanist* (1965; repr., Charlottesville: University of Virginia Press, 1994), pp. 11–14.

63. Dumas Malone, *Jefferson and His Time*, vol. 1, *Jefferson the Virginian* (Boston: Little, Brown, 1948), p. xiv.

64. Dumas Malone, *The Sage of Monticello* (Charlottesville: University of Virginia Press, 1981), pp. 318–19.

65. For example, Jefferson, "Autobiography," in Peterson, *Thomas Jefferson: Writings*, p. 44.

66. TJ to Rev. Jared Sparks, February 4, 1824.

67. TJ to James Madison, September 6, 1789. See also TJ to John Wayles Eppes, June 24, 1813; TJ to John Taylor, May 28, 1816; TJ to Samuel Kercheval, July 12, 1816; and TJ to John Cartwright, June 5, 1824.

68. Golden and Golden, *Thomas Jefferson and the Rhetoric of Virtue*, p. 427.

69. My translation. Aristotle, *Nicomachean Ethics*, trans. H. Rackham (Cambridge: Harvard University Press, 1990), 1106b21-2.

70. Immanuel Kant, *Grounding for the Metaphysics of Morals*, trans. James W. Ellington (1981; repr., Indianapolis, IN: Hackett, 1993), §423.

71. Holowchak, *Dutiful Correspondent*, pp. 159–60.

72. John Taylor, *Arator*, ed. M. E. Bradford (Indianapolis: Liberty Classics, 1977), p. 115.

73. See, for example, TJ to Henry Dearborn, October 31, 1822; TJ to Samuel Smith, August 2, 1823; and TJ to Robert Garnett, February 14, 1824.

74. John C. Miller, *The Wolf by the Ears: Thomas Jefferson and Slavery* (New York: Free Press, 1977), pp. 210–26.

75. This suggested emotional involvement, according to Merkel. William G. Merkel, "A Founding Father on Trial: Jefferson's Rights Talk and the Problem of Slavery during the Revolutionary Period," *Rutgers Law Review* 595 (2011–2012): 608.

76. For example, TJ to Dr. Maese, January 15, 1809; TJ to Capt. Isaac Hillard, October 9, 1810; and TJ to James Madison, March 23, 1815.

77. Holowchak, *Dutiful Correspondent*, pp. 17–22.

78. Gordon-Reed, *Thomas Jefferson and Sally Hemings*, p. 226.

79. Jefferson, "Autobiograph," in Peterson, *Thomas Jefferson: Writings*, p. 52.

80. James Madison to Nicholas P. Trist, July 6, 1826, in Golden and Golden, *Thomas Jefferson and the Rhetoric of Virtue*, p. 459.

# ADDENDUM

1. Robert F. Turner, ed., *The Jefferson-Hemings Controversy: Report of the Scholars Commission* (Durham, NC: Carolina Academic Press, 2011), pp. xiii and 5–6.

2. Ibid., pp. 7–17.

3. Ibid., p. 18.

4. Thomas Jefferson, "Bill for the More General Diffusion of Knowledge," in *Thomas Jefferson: Writings*, ed. Merrill D. Peterson (New York: Library of America, 1984), p. 365.

5. For example, TJ to Col. William Duane, August 12, 1819; and TJ to John Adams, November 25, 1816, in *The Writings of Thomas Jefferson*, ed. Paul Leicester Ford (New York: Putnam, 1892).

6. TJ to Ebenezer Hazard, February 18, 1791; TJ to William Wirt, August 14, 1814; TJ to John Adams, August 10, 1815; and TJ to Hugh Taylor, October 4, 1823.

7. TJ to George Wythe, January 16, 1796; TJ to William Waller Hening, January 14, 1807, and December 1, 1809; and TJ to Hugh P. Taylor, October 4, 1823.

8. For example, TJ to John Norvell, June 14, 1807; and TJ to Judge William Johnson, June 12, 1823.

9. See M. Andrew Holowchak, "The Historical Pillorying of Thomas Jefferson: The 'Seismic Effect' of a DNA Study Gone Wrong," http://www.tjheritage.org/newscom-files/TheHistoricalPilloryingofThomasJefferson.pdf (accessed January 6, 2013).

10. See M. Andrew Holowchak, "The 'Great Experiment,'" in *Dutiful Correspondent: Philosophical Essays on Thomas Jefferson* (Lanham, MD: Rowman & Littlefield, 2012), pp. 29–49.

11. For example, Jefferson, "Bill for the More General Diffusion of Knowledge," p. 365.

12. Peterson, *Thomas Jefferson: Writings*, pp. 269–70.

# APPENDIX A: A TRANSCRIPT OF CALLENDER'S 1802 ARTICLE

1. To see the original transcript, please visit the Jefferson archives at PBS, http://www.pbs.org/jefferson/archives/documents/frame_ih195822.htm (accessed January 28, 2013).

# INDEX

**291**